THE DOBERMAN PINSCHER

Brains and Beauty

ROD HUMPHRIES AND JOANNA WALKER

Wiley Publishing, Inc.

Howell Book House

Published by Wiley Publishing, Inc., New York, NY

For general information on our other products and services or to obtain technical support please contact our Customer Care Department within the U.S. at 800-762-2974, outside the U.S. at 317-572-3993 or fax 317-572-4002.

Wiley also publishes its books in a variety of electronic formats. Some content that appears in print may not be available in electronic books.

Library of Congress Cataloging-in-Publication Data:

    Humphries, Rod.
    The Doberman pinscher : brains and beauty / Rod Humphries & Joanna Walker.
        p. cm.
      Includes bibliographical references (p.).
      ISBN: 978-1-62045-730-6
      1. Doberman pinscher. I. Walker, Joanna. II. Title.
      SF429.D6H86 1999
      636.73'6—dc21   99-16705   CIP

Manufactured in the United States of America.

10 9 8 7 6 5 4 3

Dedication

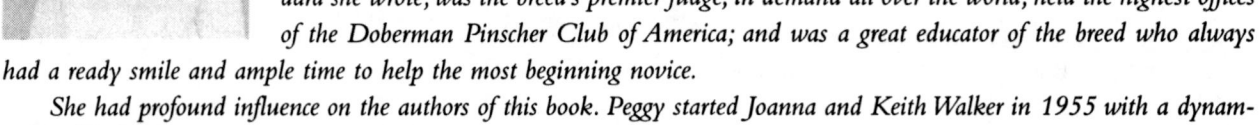

To Peggy Adamson, affectionately known as Mrs. Doberman. The most influential man in the world of Dobermans, Francis Fleitmann, handed the breed torch to Peggy in the 1940s, and she carried it with great distinction until she was taken before her time after a vehicular accident in 1996. She was 88 years young.

Peggy, of Damasyn kennel fame, devoted her life to Dobermans. She owned and bred many of the immortals of the Doberman breed; sculptured the breed for many years through the standard she wrote; was the breed's premier judge, in demand all over the world; held the highest offices of the Doberman Pinscher Club of America; and was a great educator of the breed who always had a ready smile and ample time to help the most beginning novice.

She had profound influence on the authors of this book. Peggy started Joanna and Keith Walker in 1955 with a dynamic bitch, Ch. Damasyn the Waltzing Brook, CD, and helped them learn the sport of showing dogs. She was later a passionate supporter of Joanna's work in Pilot Dogs and never missed an opportunity to tell Joanna how proud she was of her training so many great ambassadors for the breed.

Peggy had a friendship with Rod Humphries that started with correspondence in the 1960s—and despite Peggy scolding Rod for not dating his correspondence (which drove the meticulous Peggy crazy), it blossomed into visits to each other's homes in Australia and the United States, and many hours of jaw sessions. Peggy took a keen interest in Rod's breeding program in both countries.

Peggy had a devoted following worldwide, and she will not be forgotten. It is with great pride, pleasure and a real tinge of sadness that we dedicate this book to Peggy Adamson, the historical Matriarch of our breed.

Acknowledgments

To all those who have gone before; especially the breeders who established and perpetuated this unique and wonderful breed and the chroniclers who told the world all about it.

To the late Peggy Adamson, who passed so much of her knowledge of Doberman history to the authors, which is now part of this chronicle.

To Frank Grover, historian/breeder/judge and a founder of the Doberman Pinscher Educational Foundation, who has also provided historical information over the years that has found its way into this book.

To Frances (Fran) Guthrie Knueppel, Best-in-Show winning artist who had her first Doberman thrust upon her by her son-in-law, Rod Humphries, and her daughter, Lynne, in 1976. She has been a devotee and owner ever since. We are honored that she could do sketches for this book.

To Barbara Kolk, a librarian at the AKC Library in New York, who cheerfully chased information to fill gaps in historical data.

To Ann Lanier, former publisher of the *Doberman Quarterly* and now of the Doberman Pinscher Educational Foundation, who also has an insatiable appetite for Doberman history and who shared much of the Foundation's and her own library with the authors.

From client No. 22 (Rod Humphries) to Dr. Tucker Robinson, DVM, and chief veterinary technician Leslie Walenta at Rose-Rich Veterinary Clinic in Richmond, Texas, who have not only been Doberman lovers and owners and provided care to many generations of Bikila Dobermans in the past quarter century, but have also provided technical information for this book and other projects.

To artist and Doberman owner Kevin Roeckl, who has done so much to promote the proper image of the Doberman and who also provided photos for this book.

To photographer Mary Knueppel and the Bikila Dobermans for being so patient in the grooming photos.

To all the Doberman fancy, who provided most of the photographs for this book.

To Howell editor Beth Adelman, whose compassion and patience, when mixed with her total professionalism, make her a writer's dream.

To the spouses, Keith Walker and Lynne Humphries, who also displayed incredible patience to go along with their great support.

And finally, Rod Humphries wants to acknowledge three remarkable women in his life: his wife Lynne, his mother Mavis and his sister Gae. All faced the surgeon's knife and fought and beat cancer during the writing of this book, yet never once did they seek sympathy. They just kept saying, "You'd better get on with that book, Rod." God bless 'em!

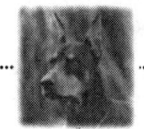

Contents

Introduction

"We may affirm absolutely that nothing great in the world has been accomplished without Passion."
—Georg Wilhelm Friedrich Hegel (1770–1831)

The eminent German philosopher knew about passion. He did not know the Doberman Pinscher, nor could he have known of Herr Karl Frederich Louis Dobermann, the man after which the breed is named, because Hegel died just a few years before Herr Doberman was born. But he would have recognized the passion in the heart of Herr Dobermann as he set about planting the seeds of a new breed of dog in the last part of the 19th century. Some have claimed that Herr Dobermann was a man who drank too much beer and charged too much for his dogs; that Otto Goeller (himself the owner of a liqueur factory), the man who formalized the breed and drew up the first standards, was more of a Doberman puppy mill than a true breeder. But despite these claims of shortcomings, these men, above all, had a passion for dogs, and in this case a black-and-rust animal that would become one of the most popular breeds in the world.

The first one hundred years of the Doberman Pinscher have seen a parade of people passionate about the breed. In the United States, people such as Theo Jager, George Earle, Hermie Fleitmann, Howard Mohr, Glenn Staines and later Peggy Adamson and others, by sheer devotion moved the breed to new levels of quality and popularity. But for every icon there are multitudes of lesser-knowns whose deep love and support of the breed have been equally incalculable. More than anything, they have helped to battle misguided public opinion that Dobermans somehow house the devil in black coat, cropped ears, and docked tail.

The authors had their fires lit in vastly different ways. Joanna Walker was captivated by a Doberman standing in the light at the top of the stairs in an American movie thriller shown in her bomb-ravaged England in 1945. There had been minor imports into England prior to World War II, but the real popularity was still a few years away. Joanna just had to have one, and her American serviceman husband, Keith, gave her a Doberman pup as a wedding gift. Later Peggy Adamson would enter her life with the first show girl, Mitzi—Ch. Damasyn the Waltzing Brook, CD.

Rod Humphries first spied a Doberman in the then-Non-Sporting Group when he was exhibiting a Samoyed in the same group at a show in Australia in the early 1960s. Wow! The emerging new breed had only arrived in Australia 10 years before, but its growth had been retarded by the original importer who kept all the bitches so that nobody else could breed. Rod researched the breed for a couple of years, consuming all he could from the United States, and purchased his first male pup in Australia in 1966. The pup was a full brother-sister breeding, which is probably why Rod promotes inbreeding and line breeding today. He had this ambition, a dream, to own a large English-style manor with mazes of hedges and gardens, and Dobermans as far as the eye could see. He moved to America instead and has fulfilled that dream, but rather than gardens and hedges, there are pecan trees and live oaks on a property in Texas. . . but still Dobermans as far as the eye can see. (Just nine, really.)

The fire sparked by these first Dobermans truly engulfed Joanna and Rod. You know it is passion when so much of your world revolves around your dogs. They become part of the family, and you even buy a home or plan a new house with the Doberman very much in mind. Your weekends are no longer spent at the beach or the golf course, but traveling to dog shows and performance trials, sometimes hundreds of miles away. You don't care how much time and money you lose when you breed, because you only want to produce better dogs. You fight the blood and the bacteria, shed tears over the stillborn, and know that everything that can go wrong, does—and yet you still come back for more, year after year after year.

We want every Doberman owner to share that passion. Unfortunately, so many pups are purchased on a whim and then discarded. This book will be read by many first-timers, so we implore the reader to feel the passion before buying a Doberman puppy. It has to be a fire in the belly; a decision that not only comes from the head but, more importantly, from the heart.

Joanna and Rod know that if you have the passion, a Doberman pup will return it tenfold. And who knows, it may carry you on a wave to the top of the show or performance rings, and later into the world of breeding.

Truly, nothing great in this world, including in Dobermans, can be accomplished without passion.

Foreword

The Doberman Pinscher may just be the Dog for all Reasons. He—or she—manages to fill whatever role is called for: fierce defender, loving companion, police dog, guide dog, therapy dog—the list goes on. He will even try, on occasion, to curl that beautiful body small enough to be a lap dog.

Although there hasn't, as yet, been a Dobie in my household, I have had the pleasure of knowing several well. Each has been special, yet no two alike. A close friend has had a succession of Dobermans—all red females: Cinnamon, then Pebbles, followed by Pooh Bear, and now Asia. Each new girl came in with an impossible place to fill so, wisely, each simply carved out a different unfillable place of her own. Sable was another special Dobie friend. She lived in Hawaii along with three smaller dogs and conducted herself accordingly—as just a *taller* small dog.

The intimidating image of the fierce Doberman—the villain dog from hell, as depicted in movies and on television—is the picture many people have who don't know the breed. If trained for that, then of course the Doberman will become the ferocious animal on night guard duty or at the side of a security guard, but you can bet he will be the *best* at what he does. As I mentioned, he will excel at whatever the job calls for.

It was Lyric, a fine young Dobie guide-dog-in-training, who introduced me to Joanna Walker. For anyone who wishes to know more about this magnificent breed, you've come to the right place. Joanna Walker and Rod Humphries know, love and understand this complex creature perhaps better than anyone.

Read on.

BETTY WHITE

Betty White with Joanna Walker and Lyric. (Prentice Howe)

(Joanna Walker)

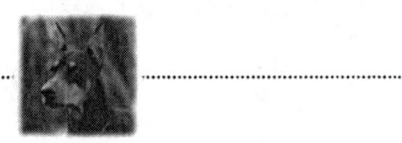

Is the Doberman Right for You?

One of the time-worn statements you'll find when you read almost any literature on the Doberman Pinscher is "The Doberman is not for everyone." We planned to avoid the phrase here, just because it is so well-used, but it is the quickest way to bring into focus the fact that the Doberman is not a generic dog that just happens to have a different look—albeit a pretty appealing one.

Doberman fanciers love to describe the overall appearance of the breed as The Look of Eagles. This elegance is a major reason for the visual appeal of the Doberman in the show ring, in the obedience ring, or in any of the sports that Dobermans and other canines love to play. There is no such thing as an ugly Doberman Pinscher—some are just more beautiful than others.

The square, chiseled appearance, with athleticism oozing from every well-defined muscle, gives the impression that the Doberman might be the Michael Jordan of any canine league. In fact, people who are sports nuts invariably fall in love with the Doberman because physically and aesthetically it is the canine equivalent of the athletes they see on the small screen any night of the week.

And if your momma wouldn't let you grow up to be a cowboy and have a horse, then maybe you see the Doberman as the nearest canine to the equine. Many do, and it is quite amazing the number of people

Doberman fanciers call that elegant appearance The Look of Eagles. This is Ch. Wingates Leading Edge, CDX, CGC, TDI, ROM. (Ellice)

But while this magnificently muscled animal with a majestic gallop and a statuesque appearance may be overwhelmingly appealing, especially because it is a "wash and wear" kind of dog with that easy coat, the question is: Are you ready to live with a Doberman Pinscher?

DEVOTED AND DEMANDING

This animal is not an ornament. It is as complex a being as any on this planet with, we might add, an inherent ability to guard and protect. It is demanding—oh how it can be demanding! It is so devoted that it wants to be with you at all times: in the car, on the couch and in the bed. It wants to back up and sit on the couch next to you, or just on your lap. The head will always be pushing into your hand for a pat, invariably when you are about to sip a steaming cup of coffee. The dog just wants to be with you and be touched by you. For some this is a blessing in a pet; for others, it could well be a nuisance.

This can be an extremely energetic breed, quite rambunctious, especially when with a playmate. These dogs know how to play rough. They jump and twirl in a circle and hit with their rump. Their reckless abandon in the open field, and quite often in the house, illustrates a fearless attitude toward injury. And a mighty disregard for the table lamp.

who can't get a horse for whatever reason, but end up owning a Doberman. It's also quite common for people with horses to have Dobermans.

When a Doberman runs at you in fun, turn backwards to protect your knees, making sure that your legs bend the right way. Then, if the dog runs into you, or believes that you are as indestructible as the dog thinks itself to be, at least you won't be in the hospital with a seriously hyperextended knee—or worse.

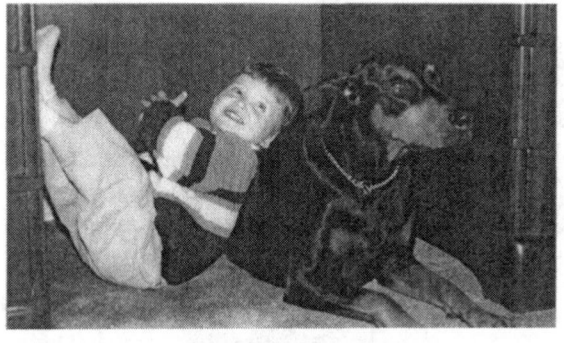

Dobermans just want to be with you. Gregory and Bonnie both love to nap under the desk. (Joanna Walker)

scientists say, a dog has the intelligence level of a five- or six-year-old child, then the Doberman is *magna cum laude* in the canine kindergarten class. This breed is mentally quick, just as capable of learning obedience exercises at a record pace as it is of opening the kennel door, or any other door if it is humanly, or caninely, possible.

INTELLIGENCE TO SPARE AND ENERGY TO BURN

The Doberman needs exercise to burn energy. It is not sufficient to lock your dog in a small yard and expect it to run on its own. An energetic Doberman deprived of an outlet for that energy and left to its own devices can be a very destructive animal, indeed—sometimes to its own detriment. Bored Dobermans have a penchant for eating things that are not good for them: blankets, balls, sticks and many other objects that can cause obstructions. One could write a book on the foreign objects swallowed and surgically removed from within the Doberman; they are legendary.

Otto Goeller, the first authority on the breed, promoted the Doberman as "the dog with the human brain." We wouldn't go that far, as we'd like to think that we have an edge when it comes to gray matter over our pet dogs. But if, as the

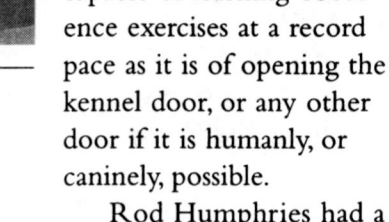

Rod Humphries had a female Doberman shipped to him for breeding several years ago. To keep her quiet and away from the other animals, he placed her in a Great Dane–size crate in a cottage on his property. She would be safe there, he thought. Later that day, however, Rod noticed that his stud dog had been missing for a short while. He found that the male dog had opened the cottage door with his teeth, somehow flicked or mouthed open the very sophisticated lock on his lady's crate, and was sheepishly grinning ear to ear while breeding with her in the crate! Love, and Dobermans, will always find a way.

This breed requires exercise for body and brain. Oh yes, some can be turned into couch potatoes, but don't count on it; the couch might just become a big chew toy. Dobermans demand to be doing something, especially with their owners. Training classes, dog shows, field trials, long walks in the neighborhood or runs in the field or

Your Doberman's energy can be channeled in all kinds of creative ways. Roeckle's Black Jake knows how to make himself useful. (Kevin Roeckle)

forest are just some of the things an owner needs to do to have a healthy and happy Doberman.

The Doberman just wants to be doing something with you, even if it is sitting in the car on a trip to the supermarket. If you work or have children who need to be taxied to Little League or soccer games, leaving you no time to spend with the canine member of the family, then the Doberman is not for you. Staying locked in the yard, or an area of the house or lying in a crate all day is not good for any breed, especially not a Doberman.

THE DOBERMAN DISPOSITION

And what of the Doberman disposition? The bond between Doberman and family is incredibly strong, and the dog's willingness to protect that family is legendary. But as an owner, are you ready for a natural guard dog that will protect its family, barking at windows and doors, sometimes when you think it's unnecessary?

As we'll explain in more detail in the next chapter, American breeders have purposely toned down the original temperament of the breed, but good breeders still want to retain boldness as a prime characteristic in their dogs. Boldness means being fearless, outgoing, and up for anything, anytime, anywhere. There are Dobermans that are not bold; dogs that are shy and use avoidance maneuvers when faced with unfamiliar circumstances. Conversely, there are dogs that are over-aggressive. These dogs are in the minority, however, and should be avoided at all costs.

The American Doberman is not the untouchable, one-man dog of the past, but there are still strong protection drives that most breeders in this country are happy to maintain—up to a point. Many will argue that there is no fathomable reason to get into bite training with their dogs, nor to breed dogs generation after generation that will do hard protection work. After years of trying to make the Doberman a general-purpose family dog, they think it is counterproductive, and that dogs with generations of animals behind them who are selected for sharpness, prey drives, hardness and fighting spirit could lead to problems.

We are of the opinion that most Dobermans from American lines still have an inherent suspicion of things that are "not right," of strangers who may be acting inconsistently or threats to family or property. Dogs from good American breeding programs will act positively, they will patrol perimeter fences and bark and threaten when necessary.

The Germans and their disciples say this is not enough, however, and that a Doberman must prove it can protect and be able to back it up with a bite, if necessary. The American breeders, on the other hand, say all dogs know how to bite because it is part of their hereditary disposition. The question is whether a breeding program should be based on dogs that are trained for generations to do so with gusto. There is absolutely no doubt that in America, where public suspicion of the Doberman is still deep-seated, the mere presence of a Doberman is sufficient in 99 percent of cases to deter any problem.

There have been a number of times when our dogs stepped between us and danger in life-threatening situations. Joanna Walker well remembers the time her dog, Ch. Marks-Tey Shawn, CD, handled two intruders who entered her Illinois home. Rod Humphries also recalls an intruder entering his home in Australia, forcing his way through a back door that led to a room where one of his Dobermans was sleeping. The dog flew at him and grabbed the would-be thief on the rear as he was scrambling over the fence. She had a piece of his pants in her mouth as evidence of a job well done. Neither of these dogs was trained in protection or bite work—they were just Dobermans from a sound American breeding program. (Humphries' dog happened to be an all-breed

The instinct to protect home and family comes naturally to Dobermans. (Joanna Walker)

Best-in-Show winner who had trotted quietly around the conformation ring earlier in the day.)

In a nonthreatening episode at his home in Texas, three friends unwittingly entered Rod's property late one night and were intercepted by three Dobermans. The dogs froze them with growling and barking until Rod extricated them. The dogs had met these people before, but these were unusual circumstances and the dogs were not taking anything for granted. Conversely, regular workers who come and go on the property are checked and then greeted heartily by the dogs, making a rub behind the ear or a stroke down the back a necessary entry toll. Rarely today do American Dobermans hit first and ask questions later—a very welcome trait indeed.

Dobermans on the whole have strong prey instincts, which means they are stimulated to chase and bring prey to ground. No one should be shocked at such a statement; most breeds have strong natural prey instincts. They are dogs, after all. The difference, though, is that many dogs do not run at such high speed and have as much single-minded determination as the Doberman. Dogs that chase tennis balls and sticks and fly through the air to pull down Frisbees are, for the most part, exhibiting their prey instincts. That said, Dobermans and cats do get along, especially if the dog is raised from a pup to accept a cat. Joanna Walker's family has always had cats, particularly Siamese, who have lived in peaceful co-existence with their Dobermans.

Rod Humphries had a dog of American breeding in Australia who illustrated both protection and prey instincts in one memorable incident. A deadly poisonous snake, ready to strike, confronted Rod and his dogs in the Australian bush. His male Doberman immediately took charge, grabbing the snake and smashing

Cats and dogs? Why not! They get along especially well if they are raised together. (Joanna Walker)

it incessantly on a rock until he had crushed the head. The dog's instinct to keep the fangs away from his body during a five-minute bashing was quite extraordinary.

But the Doberman can also have a soft side. The Walkers' Ch. Mesmerol Bari of Marks-Tey, CD, ROM, rescued a baby squirrel that had fallen out of a nest and took it to his owners. The squirrel became his good buddy, living with the Walkers until he was 11 years old.

This is Ch. Mesmerol Bari of Marks-Tey, CD, ROM, with his pal Charlie, whom he rescued as a baby. They stayed friends for 11 years. (Joanna Walker)

Boss von Donautal, owned by Julianne and Rick Ferado, was a qualified wilderness search-and-rescue dog—he had an outstanding record and many titles.

We mention the prey instincts of the Doberman because the dog loves to chase, and sometimes it might be the neighbor's kid who runs screaming to mommy that the dog was trying to eat him. Most of the time this is in fun, a harmless escapade, but some highly stimulated dogs will nip or bite when they finally reach the person they have been chasing. And although the dog may have meant no harm, the neighbor doesn't want to know about prey instincts.

Some Dobermans, like many breeds of dog, will stalk a person in play. This can also be misinterpreted by protective parents. Dogs and kids are trainable, but a prospective owner must know from the start that the prey instincts of Dobermans and countless other breeds have severely jolted unwitting owners. Too many people who buy a dog, including a Doberman, expect it to act and behave with human logic and instincts. Dogs most definitely do not. And prospective dog owners, no matter the breed, have to accept the fact that they are dealing with animals that are descended from the wolf and are just a few genes removed from the wild.

The Doberman is a dog that requires intelligent handling. It is a very proud animal that is likely to react negatively to any person who does not show it reasonable respect. Rough handling will be met with stubbornness or confrontation. This is a super-intelligent and loving protector, an athlete extraordinaire who needs training and an outlet for its physical energy. This is a super dog, a super breed, but, as we said in the beginning, it is not for everyone.

CHAPTER 2

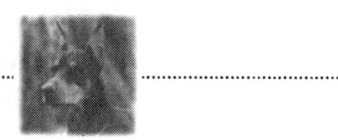

Herr Dobermann Builds a Breed

Der *Dobermannpinscher* was a product of the New Age of Purebred Dogs in the 19th century, particularly in the last quarter of the 1800s when there was a tremendous interest in and focus on officially formalizing an incredibly large number of breeds. Those were the pioneering days of the international canine cult, which today produces a staggering number of dog shows and all kinds of trials and exhibitions every week across the planet.

If one studies the history of dog breeds, it is amazing how many of them were formalized in this period of relative social peace and prosperity in the last quarter of the 19th century. Many breeds had been around for centuries, yet it was only then that formalization suddenly became popular. Explorers and military conquerors had long ago discovered and taken home exotic dog breeds from faraway countries. Now, in this fast-shrinking world, the breeds were quickly becoming internationally known. The aristocrats and the wealthy had long been enamored with purebred dogs. Now, apparently, that interest was percolating down to the growing middle class.

There was a social status that came with owning purebreds and, of course, money to be gained from breeding and selling the slew of newly formalized purebred dogs. The advent of dog shows also brought

9

bragging rights to the owners of different breeds. In the late 1800s, breed after breed began to crystallize with the formation of breed clubs and the beginning of regional and then national stud books. Many of the breeds had been around for centuries, but it wasn't until the late 1800s that breed enthusiasts joined together in clubs and began writing official standards.

There was a whole new awareness of purebred dogs, no doubt spurred by dog shows and the magazines and pamphlets that featured dogs. There was consolidation of breeds that had been around for centuries and tinkering with others. In fact, many hybrid dogs were bred to become purebred strains, including the Doberman.

Germany, fresh from unification and a new prosperity, was a pioneer with Britain in this amazing international canine surge. Germany gave the world some of its most popular breeds, including the Rottweiler; the Deutche Dogge (known elsewhere as the Great Dane); the German Shepherd Dog; the Standard, Giant and Miniature Schnauzers; the Dachshund; the Boxer; the Weimaraner; the German Shorthaired Pointer; the German Wirehaired Pointer; the Miniature Pinscher; the Affenpinscher; the German Pinscher and, of course, the Dobermannpinscher. All were formalized in the later part of the 1800s.

THE ROOTS OF THE DOBERMAN

The Doberman had its roots in and around Apolda, a thriving textile and industrial city of some 20,000 people in the province of Thueringia, in eastern Germany. (The photo at the start of this chapter is a picture of Apolda in the 1870s.) There is great irony about the history of the Doberman. Along with the Jack Russell Terrier, the Cavalier King Charles Spaniel, the Gordon Setter, and, more obliquely, the Saint Bernard and the Keeshond, the Doberman is one of the few breeds named after a single person.

One would expect that when a breed is named after its founder, there would be a detailed recorded history. No such luck! Yes, we know the names of some of his early dogs, and even what they looked like, but the real origins of the breed named after Karl Frederick Louis Dobermann (1834–94) from Apolda have never been uncovered and most certainly passed with him. In fact, it is doubtful that Herr Dobermann ever wrote anything down for posterity because he obviously never had a grand plan—he was haphazard in his breeding, and never could have foreseen what history would do for his dogs. In fact, it wasn't until after his death that the breed was officially given his name.

Some historians have stated that dogs resembling the early Doberman were around before Herr Dobermann became a dog breeder. This type of dog, which evolved in and around Apolda, was known in areas far beyond as "Thueringiapinschers." Locally in Apolda these same dogs were sometimes known as "Schnupps" or "Bellings," or police and soldier dogs. They were later sometimes loosely referred to as "Dobermann's pinschers."

For much of his life, Herr Dobermann was an employee of the city of Apolda, being something of a jack-of-all-trades. He spent time working as a skinner at the municipal slaughterhouse, where it

Karl Friedrich Louis Dobermann (left), circa 1870, with Herr Rable and Herr Bottger, believed to be fellow watchmen. All three were said to be passionate about both dogs and beer.

experimental breedings. Herr Dobermann also was employed at one time as an official of the tax office, which required him to perform the thankless task of personally collecting taxes. And he spent some time as a night police officer, accompanied by very ferocious dogs.

Herr Dobermann bought a home in Apolda in 1880—a move that allowed him room to increase his breeding activities. He befriended two other watchmen, Herr Rable and Herr Bottger, who were also interested in dog breeding. Theodore F. Jager, the first significant Doberman importer and breeder in the United States, wrote in his 1910 book *The Police Dog* that these three friends "loved, next to dogs, good health-giving beer, and the three to invest all their earnings in this 'liquid bread' as they considered it, was a rule of their lives which they never broke."

The three men were all regulars at the annual dog market in Apolda, which offered dogs in all shapes and sizes falling into such diverse categories as Luxury Dogs, House Dogs, Butcher Dogs, Pinschers and Hounds. Aggressive and fearless police-soldier dogs in particular appealed to Herr Dobermann and his friends. Apparently, he would see a tough, aggressive black-and-tan dog on the street and remark to friends, "That's my dog," or more likely, "That's my kind of dog."

has been said that he helped slaughter and skin stray dogs and other animals. There appears little doubt that some of the stray dogs were used in

Early Dobermans in Germany were trained to be touched only by their master. This is a policeman and his Doberman in the early 1900s.

INTO THE MIX

In historical references one will find any number of combinations of breeds espoused as the origin of the Doberman. They include the German breeds of the Rottweiler, the Great Dane (Deutsche Dogge), the old bob-tailed German Shepherd (not the modern breed), the original black-and-tan German Pinscher, the Weimeraner and the German Shorthaired pointer, plus the French herding and guard dog, the Beauceron and two English breeds, the Greyhound and the Manchester Terrier.

In 1933, the German Dobermann Club tried to put the issue to rest by interviewing old-timers like Goswin Tischer, a contemporary of Herr Dobermann, and Dobermann's youngest son, Robert. The club concluded that the old German Pinscher had been the main ingredient in the Doberman mix.

But before the decade was over, Philipp Gruenig, a breeder-judge who was the greatest historian on early Dobermans, wrote in his definitive book *The Dobermann Pinscher*: "In the blood synthesis which became the Dobermann Breed the German Pinscher contributed exceedingly little more than his name. . ." Gruenig said he would "only hint that in his (the Dobermann's) veins flowed the blood of the Rottweiler, Shepherd, Pinscher and Beauceron." Gruenig recorded crosses to the Manchester Terrier and English Greyhound shortly before and after the turn of the century.

If one looks at the history of the region with the Roman occupation for two centuries—which entrenched the mastiff herding and guard dogs, the forebear of the Rottweiler—and Napoleon's occupying forces in the early 1800's which entrenched the Beauceron of neighboring France, it is highly likely that these two breeds, both with black-and-rust markings like the Doberman, were indeed the major players. It is certainly conceivable that they could have been inter-mixed to produce the butcher dogs of Germany in the 19th century.

Research by Rod Humphries provides compelling evidence that the Beauceron, or Berger de Beauce, whose recorded history dates to 1578, could be *the* major player. Unlike the black Rottweiler, the Beauceron originally came in multiple colors (with identical rust markings) which are close to the modern American Doberman: black, reddish black, gray (blue), tawny (fawn) or light brown to reddish orange (red) and harlequin. The French standard eliminated all but the black and rust and the harlequin in the late 1960's. The standard today "tolerates" some white hairs on the chest, just as in

The French guard and shepherd, the Beauceron, bears an undeniable resemblance to the Doberman and certainly influenced the development of the breed in the 1890s. (Ron & Debbie Skinner)

Selective cross-breeding to the Rottweiler helped shape the Doberman as we know it today. (Muriel Freeman)

the American Doberman standard. The head is more Doberman that the mastiff type of the Rottweiler. Black is genetically the dominant color in the Beauceron and the early viciousness of the Doberman might also be traced to the then one-master French guard dog. The Beauceron today has behavioral traits very characteristic of the Doberman.

An article published in a German dog magazine a few years after Herr Dobermann's death reported that in the late 1860s he bought two dogs from Christian Dietsch, said by some historians to be a butcher from Schoeten, near Apolda, and by others to be the owner of a gravel pit in Apolda. Maybe Dietsch owned both, but certainly he was interested in dog breeding. Dietsch had bred his blue-gray bitch of Pinscher origin to a butcher's black dog. The offspring proved to be

The sleek, elegant figure of the Greyhound was injected into the mix, with spectacular effect. (Elizabeth Campbell)

good guard dogs, and Herr Dobermann crossed those with a black-and-tan German Pinscher.

Another of Herr Dobermann's sons, Louis Dobermann, who was a master of woven goods in Apolda, years later said that in early 1870 his father owned a black male with red markings and a heavy gray undercoat called Schnupp. Remember, dogs of that particular kind were commonly referred to as "Schnupps." It could well be that Herr Dobermann's Schnupp was the result of Dietsch's breeding or from Dobermann's crosses with a German Pinscher. Whatever Schnupp's origin, according to Dobermann's son he was "a dog of great intelligence as is seldom found. He was

clever and fearless and knew how to bite. My father could not have chosen a better one." Some historians conclude that Schnupp was actually castrated and that he was unlike the early Dobermans in appearance.

Herr Dobermann also had a bitch called Bisart, definitely of the early breed type—a black dog with red markings and less gray undercoat than Schnupp. (Herr Dobermann had originally called her Bismarck, but he was warned that he could get into trouble with authorities if he used the name of the Iron Chancellor, Prince Otto v Bismarck.)

Bisart, in turn, produced a black bitch with a natural bobtail that Herr Dobermann called Pinko. Dobermann retained Pinko for breeding, as he and others were interested in trying to produce bobtailed dogs so that they would not have to dock the dogs' tails. Tail docking had been introduced in Roman times because it was believed that docking at 40 days prevented rabies. Otto Goeller owned some bobtailed dogs when he first wrote the standard of the breed in 1899, and he was still trying to genetically lock in the trait at that time. Goeller finally admitted failure in the early part of the century when it was obvious that the crosses with the Manchester Terrier and the English Greyhound had genetically overridden the natural bobtail.

THE BREED GETS A NAME

While Herr Dobermann has his name on the breed, two breeders from his hometown of Apolda, Otto Goeller (1852–1922) of v Thueringin Kennel (named after the region) and Goswin Tischler

While the breed is named after Dobermann, establishing the breed was Otto Goeller's work. He is seen here in the early 1900s with two dogs from his Thueringen Kennel.

Graf Belling v Groenland, born in 1898, was one of the famous Five-Star Litter.

(1859–1939) of v Groenland Kennel (named after the street on which he lived) were the architects and promoters who truly put the breed on the map. Goeller, who owned a liqueur factory, was persuaded to get into the breeding business by a friend, Oskar Vorwerk, a merchant and poultry breeder from Hamburg who himself had developed a new breed of poultry. Goeller's residence was overrun with dogs and he produced hundreds and hundreds over the years. He apparently named

the breed after Dobermann; formed the first breed club in Germany, the German National Doberman Pinscher Club; and issued the first written standard, all in August 1899. It was a busy month!

Goeller was also the first to write with authority on the breed, issuing a number of pamphlets at the turn of the century. His dogs were eventually world renowned, with some coming to the United States. But if Goeller was the front man, Tischler is the one who made the first major splash as a breeder in 1898, the year before the first standard was written, with an historic litter known internationally simply as the Five-Star Litter: Belling, Greif, Krone, Lottchen and Tilly II, all v Groenland. Belling (or Graf Belling, as his name was sometimes recorded) was originally owned by Goeller.

The first significant, well-bred dog imported into the United States was a son of Greif v Groenland. His name was Bertel v Hohenstein, and he was born in 1905 and imported two years later. Bertel became the first pillar of the breed in the United States.

Goeller produced his own superstar in 1904, Hellegraf v Thueringin, a red male that historian Gruenig called in his book "one of the mightiest stud dogs of any age or breed. . . . Let the name be written in letters of fire." Hellegraf was taller than many of the dogs of his time, and passed the height on to his offspring. His stock was, of course, in demand for the emerging breed in the United States, and two animals with concentrated Hellegraf breeding—Annagret II v Thueringen and a stud dog, Claudius v Thueringen—were sent together to the United States in 1908.

Hellegraf v Thueringin, born in 1904, was one of the great dogs of his day. Several of his offspring made their way to the United States before World War I.

Prinz Modern v Ilm Athen, born in 1909, was sent to neutral Holland to escape the ravages of World War I. He was one of the great stud dogs of his day.

Another major breeder of those early times was Gustav Krumbholz of the Ilm-Athen kennel in Wickerstedt, near Apolda. It was through Krumbholz's kennel that the first major cross with the Manchester Terrier was injected into the Doberman breed. In 1901, Krumbholz used one of the prominent v Groenland Five-Stars, Greif, on a

black bitch named Lady v Ilm-Athen who, in 1899, was one of the earliest entries in the German stud books. Lady was undeniably part Manchester Terrier. The result was a black male named Prinz Modern v Ilm-Athen, who became one of the greatest stud dogs in the early history of the breed and whose closely linebred descendents found their way to the United States in the first decade of the 1900s.

EXPERIMENTS AND REFINEMENTS

All the early Dobermans had coarse hair and a longer coat with very light straw markings. In fact, at the turn of the century the Doberman and the Rottweiler looked very much alike, and some

These early dogs from Otto Goeller's kennel look more like Beaucerons than they do modern Doberman Pinschers. The process of experimentation and refinement went on for a long time before the type we recognize today was established.

experts observed that it was hard to distinguish a coarse Doberman from a fine Rottweiler. The Doberman was a squat, unattractive animal with a thick coat and a heavy undercoat. It had heavy jowls, an extremely broad skull, light eyes and light straw markings. Lady, however, had the short, close hair and deep, rich tan markings that personified the Manchester Terrier.

The injection of blood from an English terrier did not necessarily please all the German breeders. They didn't like the smaller size, and for many it was a heavy price to pay when they lost much of the aggression and ferocity of the German Doberman.

The stud books of today are meticulously kept, and offspring can be registered only if they're born to a registered purebred sire and dam. But at the time breeds were being formalized, there were several different Doberman stud books and the records were loose, to say the least. In 1908, a black bitch simply named Stella, listed as being whelped in Ried in the Hessia area of Germany, appeared in the stud books. There were conflicting facts about her heritage, but historian Gruenig wrote that he personally thoroughly investigated her background while she was still alive and found that she was undoubtedly the product of a black English Greyhound sire and a black Doberman dam. Gruenig said that villagers around Mannheim and Ludwigshafen worked in the industrial plants and had money to breed dogs. They were quite adept at experimentation, and Stella was just one of those experiments. "The injection of this greyhound blood into our Dobermann breed can be approved to the extent that it reconstituted the breed's sharpness, which suffered a severe setback from the admixture with the blood of the gentle Manchester Terrier," wrote Gruenig.

Stella gave the Doberman world two very prominent offspring: the black bitch Sybille v Langen, sired by a dog named Lord v Ried born in 1909; and the red dog Roland vd Haide, born in 1910 from a repeat breeding. Sybille had a typical Greyhound look, and her head was characteristic of that breed with a decided lack of underjaw. There are many modern Dobermans in the United States with the same head type, lacking underjaw or having a "shark mouth," as we authors often refer to it. Sybille, however, did a lot of good things for the breed, but Gruenig said her brother Roland was "preeminently qualified to ruin the entire breed and forthwith proceeded to exercise his talents. Lack of taste, ignorance and other unfathomed motives of our judges permitted this grotesque caricature of a Doberman to win officially recorded high honors. His devastating hereditary influence was soon forcibly active and observable. His progeny was mostly narrow but deep chested monstrosities, unbelievably coarse with wide open, round eyes. For the real Dobermann fancier and expert they were anathema." Gruenig called this the "Roland curse." "He was so uncommonly coarse that it required a decade and a half to repair the damage he had done."

The Greyhound experiment did not stop with Stella. There were quite a few other crosses, and it was reported that brindle-coated Dobermans appeared in the early part of the century. In fact,

THE WAR YEARS

What follows are excerpts from Philipp Gruenig's book *The Dobermann Pinscher:*

Most of the German breeders were at the front and inescapable necessity compelled their remaining dependents to have their highly prized and dearly loved household pets put to a merciful death as the only alternative to starvation and suffering along with their owners. How deeply this cut into the heart of a true dog lover can be testified to by me. On the second day of mobilization, the day on which I was ordered to the front, no less than 18 half-grown pups from my kennel fell victim to strychnine. It had to be; to safeguard them from the more horrible fate of death from slow starvation. In a moment of weakness, induced by the hope of saving them, I retained two of my best dogs, Walhall v Jaegerhof (a litter sister to Edelblut) and Ebbo v Adalheim (a son of Marko v Luetzellinden).

They died miserably of malnutrition in 1916. Untold thousands suffered the same pain I did, for wives and children barely escaped the same fate of starvation. . . .

It is not to be wondered at that the neutral foreigner took advantage of and profited by this state of affairs, especially when a dog was pressed upon him by the German breeder and fancier as a means of saving its life as the natural expression of his deep love for it. . . . [T]he high tide of the Dobermann in Holland dates from about this period and continues until the more or less consolidation of the breed in Germany is effected in 1922. That in the years during and immediately following the war much of our best breeding stock was sold or traded at prices that be better left unmentioned is a bald fact. To be quite honest about it, only the rising flood of inflation put an end to this ignoble barter.

Goeller was still interested as late as 1912 in putting more colors, including brindles and possibly even harlequins, into the official standard. Gruenig wrote that in 1902 there was even an experimental cross with a Gordon Setter, which has black and rust markings similar to the Doberman. The idea was to improve the color of the Doberman coat, especially in the rust areas. The long hair of the setter was apparently recessive to the short hair of the Doberman, but as many as 10 generations later, longer hair and thick undercoat still appeared when the recessive genes found a mate and were flushed to the surface.

It was, after all, the New Age of Purebred Dogs, and the search for better animals was in full stride.

WAR COMES TO GERMANY

The chilling reality of war and its devastating effect on ordinary people and their animals was never better chronicled than by Gruenig, an historian, dog breeder, judge and German soldier, when he discussed World War I in his book, published in the United States in 1939.

Gruenig wrote with obvious pain about how dogs, including Dobermans, were trapped and used for food by desperate people. He said that many German breeders sent their dogs to neutral countries, hoping they would be spared.

AN AMAZING REBIRTH

But amazingly, by 1920, a mere two years after the end of the war, the German breeders had rebounded with great vigor. Systematic breeding programs were again producing dogs the rest of the world was clamoring for. Much of the demand came from soldiers of occupying forces, especially the Americans, who brought the German Dobermans home, playing a major part in popularizing the breed here.

The quality of the 119 Dobermans at the Munich Sieger show in 1921 was considered excellent. But few were prepared for the tremendous leap in quality and numbers seen just a year later at the Berlin Sieger show. There were 223 entries, of which authority William Sidney Schmidt remarked: "The breed had reached almost perfection. It was at its pinnacle, carrying through on the same level during a number of years to follow."

(Kristina Johnsen)

CHAPTER 3

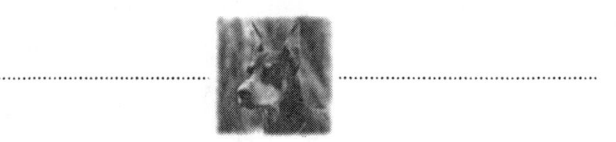

America Charts Its Own Course

T here is no doubt that a handful of immigrating Germans at the turn of the century brought Dobermans into the United States, or purchased them through contacts back home after they were established in America. It appears that the first Doberman arrived in the United States in 1898, a year before the first official standard of the breed was drawn up by Otto Goeller. A young man in his early 20s, E.R. Saalman, has been credited with bringing in the first Doberman—probably not a very good one. Saalman settled in Rochester, New York—the same area of the country where the first important and recorded history of the breed began in 1908. Saalman bred and owned Dobermans for 50 years, and the Doberman Pinscher Club of America awarded him with a scroll and a special DPCA Medal for his contributions to the breed at the National Specialty Show in Miami in 1957. Saalman, who had moved to Florida, died a month later at the age of 83.

TWO GENTLEMEN OF ROCHESTER

The important beginning and consolidation of the breed in the United States came primarily through two men of German heritage who also settled in Rochester: Theodore F. Jager and, surprisingly, Wilhelm

Dobermann, whom Jager said was "the last of his family and name hailing from Apolda." Jager was granted the first kennel name for the breed in the United States, "Doberman," by the American Kennel Club in 1908, and a year later it was listed under the joint names of Jager and W. Dobermann. (Today it would be against the rules to name a kennel after a specific breed.)

Jager and Dobermann obviously had strong contacts in Germany, and imported the cornerstones of the breed into this country. They had a string of firsts: the first major imports, a dog and two bitches that arrived in the fall of 1907; the first registered kennel in 1908; the first Doberman registered with the American Kennel Club, a black-and-rust male named Doberman Intelectus, AKC No. 122650 in 1908; the first American champion, the imported Hertha v Hohenstein in 1912; and the first male and first American-bred champion, Doberman Dix, also in 1912. They also produced the first blue-coated dogs in the United States.

The first two dogs of Jager and Dobermann came from the Hohenstein kennel in Bleicherode, Germany, which was an offshoot of Goeller's Thueringen kennel in Apolda. Hohenstein was the kennel of Albert Ammon, who purchased his foundation bitch from Goeller in 1899. The first major imports, a pair of blacks imported together, were a good linebred male named Bertel v Hohenstein (who was born in September 1905 and imported shortly after his second birthday) and Hertha v Hohenstein (born in April of 1907 and imported as a puppy). Bertel was a son of Greif v Groenland, from the Five-Star Litter. Bertel's grandmother was sired by Greif's brother, Graf Belling v Groenland,

Grief v Groenland, born in 1898, was behind the first major import to the United States.

giving America good linebred stock on which to build.

In those early days, stud books were much looser and many dogs changed names when they changed owners. It was not unusual for a dog to have three or four different names. So when Jager and Dobermann purchased Bertel and Hertha v Hohenstein, they changed their official names in the United States to Bertel Doberman and Hertha Doberman. They also imported other prominent dogs from Germany that were registered in the United States as Doberman Lump, Gerta

Doberman, Duchess Chica de Doberman and Duchess Elsie de Doberman. The original German names of these dogs are lost.

Jager and Dobermann wasted no time in breeding their new pair. Hertha was only 14 months old when she produced her historic first litter by Bertel on June 20, 1908, producing Intelectus, the first Doberman registered with the AKC. In fact, Intelectus was the only registration in that inaugural year. Hertha was bred twice more to Bertel and to a number of other studs, but her best producing stock came from her kennel partner. These two dogs were the most successful imported Dobermans in the early establishment of the breed in this country.

There is absolutely no doubt that Jager and Dobermann were on the cutting edge of the new breed with an obvious pipeline to the best dogs in Germany. The most impressive show Doberman in Germany at that time was a black male, Prinz Carlo Viktoria, who, at about 24½ inches at the withers (the top of the shoulder), was the epitome of the then-accepted standard. He was the German Sieger (National Specialty winner) in 1907 and 1908 and, obviously, his stock was coveted in America. Hertha, the bitch that Jager and Dobermann imported, was a half-sister to Prinz Carlo's dam. Now they wanted to shore up on the blood of the striking young German Sieger, so they imported no less than four dogs to achieve their goal.

Gerta Doberman, a red granddaughter of Graf Belling v Groenland, was bred to Prinz Carlo in Germany and had that litter on Christmas Eve of 1908. She was bred to him again at her next heat and was shipped in whelp to the United States. One of her daughters from the first breeding, Duchess Elsie de Doberman, came along with her. Gerta had her second litter by Prinz Carlo in New York on July 2, 1909. At about the same time, a son and a daughter of Prinz Carlo—Weddo v Eichtal and Duchess Chica de Doberman—were also shipped to Jager and Dobermann.

Most of the American Doberman fancy was concentrated in the Northeast, and a number of breeders in addition to Jager and Dobermann imported dogs from top German kennels that were all closely tied genetically. So much of the breeding at the beginning of any new breed has to be incestuous, and the Americans apparently were not timid in going after the best with inbreeding. Knowledgeable breeders of today still use judicious inbreeding and linebreeding, but in the beginning much of it was out of necessity because there was such a small number of dogs to breed to.

WHEN GERMAN STOCK RULED

Judging by imports to the United States in the early days of the breed, all Doberman fanciers were well aware of the great German dogs and their hereditary powers, and went after their stock with a passion. In Chapter 2 we mentioned Prinz Modern v Ilm-Athen, undeniably the grandson of a Manchester Terrier. Prinz was born in Germany in 1901, yet within a short time his blood was prominent in the United States. It came here primarily through the bitch Flora v Konigshof, who was born in 1908 and was imported in whelp in 1910 by Mr. and Mrs. Herman Meyer of

Philadelphia. The Meyers apparently bred under two kennel prefixes, Fern Felsen and Geholz. Flora was the result of breeding a Prinz son (Rolf v Konigshof) to a Prinze granddaughter (Norma v Groenland). Flora arrived in whelp to a great-grandson of Prinz, Vito vd Wumme. In the pedigree of that German-bred litter whelped in America, the great Prinz appeared three times in four generations.

The big red dog that Gruenig said should have his name written in letters of fire, Goeller's mighty Hellegraf v Thueringen, was obviously a must for the savvy breeders in America. Max Donath of New Jersey secured two major coups and most certainly had fellow Northeast fanciers licking their lips when he imported two of Goeller's v Thueringen animals with plenty of Hellegraf blood in their pedigrees in 1908. These were the stud Claudius v Thueringen, and the bitch Annagret II v Thueringen. Annagret was the result of a mother-son inbreeding. (Hellegraf was bred to Carmen v Thueringen; their son, Hellegraf v Thueringen II, was bred back to his mother to produce Annagret.) Claudius was a grandson of Hellegraf's sire, Landgraf Sighart v Thueringen, and was also a grandson of the German Sieger Graf Wedigo v Thueringen. That tied in nicely for Donath's breeding program, because Graf Wedigo was a full brother of Carmen, the dam of Annagret.

Those breeders with animals related to Tischler's Five-Star litter through the Hohenstein and Prinz imports also had to be pleased. Claudius's dam was Irmgart v Thueringen, who

This is Graf Wedigo v Thueringen, born in 1901. We'd hardly recognize him as a Doberman today.

was sired by Greif, and Graf Wedigo was a son of Graf Belling v Groenland.

Jager, Dobermann, the Meyers, Donath and another prominent kennel (St. Marychell, owned by Mr. and Mrs. A. Vucassovitch near Boston) were the key people who mixed and matched the imported and home-grown stock in a strong grassroots period for the breed leading up to and during World War I (1914–18). Jager and Dobermann dominated with 26 of the 28 AKC registrations in 1909—the second year the breed was eligible for registration. The numbers of registered dogs were not staggering registrations in the early days—far from it. There were 27 in 1910, 24 in 1911, 35 in 1912, 23 in 1913, and

29 in the first year of the war. But it was a grassroots consolidation.

Some historians have said the Americans did not get the very best stock from the German breeders at that time, but they did get dogs from Germany's best kennels and best sires. The breed was still very much in its infancy, and the German dogs were also going through drastic changes in basic breed type. About 20 males and a dozen bitches were imported before World War I. This wasn't a huge base from which to work, but the American breeders did a remarkable job with such a small gene pool. When the real boom of imports flooded America in the 1920s, the dogs of the "old type" provided a good foundation on which to use the newly imported, new-type German dogs. Eventually they had to give way, genetically and in the show ring, to the dogs of the new era, but not before they established a firm foothold for the Doberman in the United States.

A QUESTION OF TEMPERAMENT

Many of the German imports, both before and after World War I, had very sharp temperaments. The early Dobermans produced in Germany

---

THE NUMBERS DON'T LIE

The Doberman breed in the United States hardly skipped a beat during the war years. Registrations with the AKC went over the 1,000 mark for the first time in 1934, and after war broke out in Europe in 1939, Doberman registrations in America surprisingly kept rising steadily. There were 1,414 registrations in 1939; 1,506 in 1940; 1,637 in 1941; and 1,701 in 1942, a figure that placed the Doberman at No. 12 in the entire canine world that year. There was a slight downturn to 1,530 in 1943 and to 1,329 in 1944, but in the last year of the war (1945) there was a huge leap in registrations to 3,154.

There was also a sudden boom in the first two years of peacetime, as registrations jumped to as high as 5,078 in 1947. Things did cool off a little in the 1950s and early 1960s, when the registrations hovered between 3,000 and 4,000, but then it took off again in 1965. This led to an incredible boom that reached an absolutely amazing 81,964 registrations in 1978.

Boom is invariably followed by bust. Market saturation and unstable dogs produced by unscrupulous breeders hurt the reputation of the Doberman. Registration numbers began a freefall, and by the end of the 1980s the breed had dropped from second place to 20th, with a more realistic 21,782 registered. In the last decade of the century, the numbers evened out to about 17,000 a year. In 1998, registrations dipped again to 15,637, making the Doberman Pinscher the 22nd most popular breed.

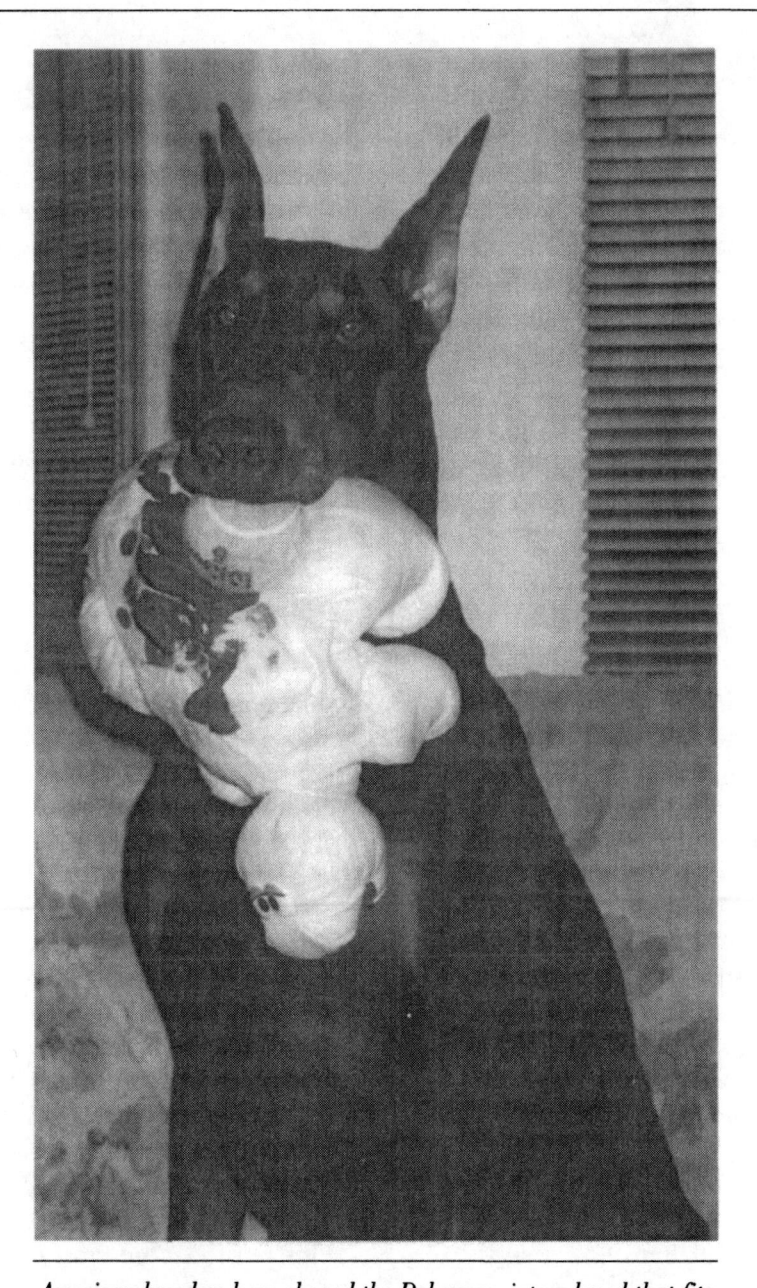

American breeders have shaped the Doberman into a breed that fits the American lifestyle.

beginning 100 years ago were extremely sharp, aggressive dogs, touchable by only one master. German fanciers thought this was just fine.

However, American breeders and fanciers have been working since the 1920s to shape the basic demeanor of the breed to fit the culture, laws and lifestyles of the United States. In 1935, the Americans completely separated themselves from the official German standards of the breed and produced their own Doberman Pinscher.

While the checkered history of the Doberman cannot be easily swept from the minds of the general public in the United States, there is grand irony in that Europeans—especially the Germans, in whose country the breed originated—and the many disciples of German dogs in this country have vehemently denounced the breed in America today for allegedly being too soft and no longer able to act as a working dog, a fearless protector. In Germany, where the national Doberman club and breeders are forever encouraging "sharpness," "fighting spirit," "prey drives" and "hardness" in the activity of Schutzhund (a sport that tests protection work as well as tracking and obedience), protection and bite work is required for official registrations.

German breed enthusiasts snicker at the modern American Doberman as a mere shell of the original concept of the breed. Europeans and those promoting European dogs in the United States say that people in this country have compromised the breed by producing mild animals fraught with weak temperaments whose main attribute is that it can look pretty and stare at bait in the conformation show ring.

The Americans are being assailed on one side of the Atlantic for breeding animals that are too soft, and on the other for breeding ticking time bombs that may eventually turn on their masters. To complete this interesting circle, the majority of American Doberman fanciers are not shy about criticizing the European dogs, particularly those from Germany, as being too sharp, too hard and having too strong a prey drive and fighting spirit. American Doberman fanciers say that the image of the breed in this country cannot afford to have even the slightest impression of overly aggressive dogs, and that bite work in Schutzhund is just asking for trouble in this highly litigious country.

The truth is that no sweeping descriptions, no stereotypes, can be truly applied to the animals on either side of the Atlantic. More important is that Americans, 100 years removed from when the first Dobermans were developed in Germany, live in a vastly different place and time with enormous changes in the law of the land and guidelines of behavior.

The history, including the debate, is important not only to the prospective Doberman owner who is reading this book to get an insight into the breed in America today, but also to the established breeder, fancier and owner, who should be fully aware of the actual and philosophical differences that exist in the breed.

AMERICAN AND GERMAN DOGS—A WORLD OF DIFFERENCE

The early Dobermans in Germany were smaller, rougher-coated animals of no particular beauty.

They were temperamentally sharp, one-man dogs who could strike fear into the hearts of any interloper. The aggressive, fearless nature of the early Dobermans was the prime factor in promoting and selling them as protection animals. These dogs were capable of doing many things, including hunting and service work, but a fierce protection drive was the primary attraction. The dogs were trained from birth to be handled only by one master and/or the immediate family, and any dog that allowed itself to be touched by outsiders was not considered a good Doberman.

Schutzhund competition has become one of the dividing issues in the Doberman fancy today. (Gay Glazbrook)

The Doberman Pinscher Club of America (DPCA), formed in 1921, adopted the German standard for the breed that was written in 1920. But when the Germans issued an updated version in 1925 that included stronger language on sharpness of temperament, the Americans balked. Even though they were 10 years away from writing their first true American standard, the DPCA stuck with the 1920 version.

The 1920 standard said that a Doberman should be "pleasant in manner and character.

Faithful, fearless, attentive and a reliable watchdog. Sure defender of his master, distrustful toward strangers, possessing conspicuous power of comprehension and great capability of training. In consequence of his characteristics, physical beauty and attractive size, an ideal house dog and escort."

However, the 1925 German standard said that the Doberman should be "Loyal, fearless, courageous and an extremely watchful dog who possesses very much natural sharpness and high intelligence. Despite his fiery temperament he is very obedient and easily trained. He has a most excellent sense of smell, is of great endurance and the ideal of a house dog, companion and protector."

There was obvious concern in the area of public relations for the new breed in America. The German dog was rowdy and aggressive and often had to be muzzled in public. This was definitely a one-man dog, untouchable by anyone other than its master. The belligerence was already becoming unacceptable in the United States.

The fork in the road for the Doberman came in August 1935, when the DPCA introduced its own standard for the first time, completely re-writing the old German standard, particularly in the area of temperament. The American standard still included the word "aggressive" but added as a fault "shyness and bad temper." It also eliminated the German description "distrustful of strangers." The 1935 American standard said of the Doberman's temperament: "Energetic, watchful, determined and alert; loyal and obedient, fearless and aggressive."

A FATEFUL WESTMINSTER WIN

In 1939 the top German dog, Ferry v Raufelsen, was brought to America for one reason: to win Best in Show at this country's most prestigious dog show, the Westminster Kennel Club Show in New York. Ferry, who had been a Sieger (national champion) at the German show in 1938, fulfilled the goal of his importer, the wealthy Geraldine Hartley Dodge, by beating more than 3,000 dogs to win Best in Show.

But there was a price in the area of public relations. The dog reportedly bit one man at the hotel where he was being housed, and the three judges in the Breed, Group and Best in Show at Westminster wouldn't lay a hand on him. It was also very noticeable to ringside observers that his handler, McClure Hailey, was very adept at keeping his hands away from the dog. He was merely doing what many other handlers did with German imports in the show ring in those days to avoid being bitten. Ferry was the terror of Dodge's Giralda Farm in New Jersey and was reportedly

Ferry v Raufelsen was the first Doberman to win Westminster, but his temperament was a public relations nightmare.

beaten to death by a terrified kennel helper at his new home years later.

In the first review of the standard after Ferry's victory, the DPCA in 1942 completely dropped the word "aggressive" as part of the Doberman's temperament, and "viciousness" was added to "shyness" as a major fault. Four years later, Howard Mohr of the White Gate kennels in Philadelphia, one of the pioneers of the breed, thoroughly condemned the German breeders for the bad reputation the temperament of their dogs had garnered. Writing in *Popular Dogs* magazine, Mohr said, "There is an old adage which says: 'Give a dog an ill name and hang him.' It has been 'hung' on the Doberman. The reason for this bad name is not far to seek—the German breeder is entirely to blame. From its inception the breed has been trained for guard and police work. The German theory was to make the dog a one-man dog, distrustful of everyone but his master; to take food from no one but his master, and to guard his master's possessions with his life. This sort of training through many dog generations has, of course, left its imprint, and the senseless savaging of their dogs by the Germans has hurt the breed in the various lands of its adoption."

In the next standard review two years later, the DPCA in 1948 made a landmark decision by declaring that a dog who was vicious or shy should be disqualified from the show ring. It was a daring move by the DPCA—no breed had ever taken such a step. It was not an easy sell to the American Kennel Club, but it was finally accepted and became an historic moment in the breed.

The American breeders were very determined in their drive to improve the temperament of the breed and to increase its public acceptance. Frank Grover, a highly respected breeder-judge who is also a historian and a lifetime member of the national German club, the Dobermann Verein, wrote that it was "a quiet process but a determined one. Handsome males of extraordinary beauty were not considered as sires because of poor behavior reported from breeder to breeder. After many years and generations of labor and hard decisions, American Dobermans became one of the most stable and best mannered of the larger breeds."

A SPLIT DEVELOPS

Did the American breeders go too far in softening the temperament of the Doberman? In the softening process did the Americans lose the protection drives and guarding ability of the breed? The Germans and breeders from other European countries, and their disciples in the United States, say most emphatically that Dobermans have lost their character.

The American breeders and fanciers strongly deny that they have compromised the character of the breed. They argue just as strongly that the inherent qualities of the guard dog Doberman remain fixed in the breed, but they choose not to overly exploit them and promote them in such sports as Schutzhund, where bite work and hardness are applauded. America is not Germany, they say. Different culture, different laws, different lifestyle. Also, the litigious nature of the United States, the fact that some insurance companies will not provide homeowner's insurance to people owning a Doberman and the multitude of vicious dog laws (many of them breed-specific that continue to point a finger at the Doberman many years after they have ceased to be a muzzled public menace) have influenced breeding decisions.

The legacy of the split is still plainly evident today. The American Doberman versus the German Doberman produces a passionate debate that reaches deep into the actual, cultural and philosophical differences between the two countries.

Doberman breeding in Germany is very controlled, disciplined and functional. It is the German way. German breeders, while they obviously do not want the untouchable sharp dogs of yesteryear, do passionately want to maintain a strong semblance of the original concept of the dog produced by Herr Dobermann. They absolutely require protection drives, bite work with courage and hardness and a willingness to work as an integral part of the breeding requirements. Under the rules of the German Dobermann Verein, no dog can be bred for registered offspring unless it passes the Zuchttauglichkeitsprufung (ZTP), which has three aspects: conformation, temperament testing and protection work. Then the breeding dogs are required to have a working certificate with a minimum of Schutzhund I, which includes obedience, tracking and protection bite work.

Americans have always cherished their individuality and independence and have never been ones to be so controlled—certainly not in such a thing as dog breeding. So American breeders are bound only to prove that the sire and dam of a litter are registered and are, in fact, the true parents for that litter to be registered. There are no other requirements—much to the chagrin of European Doberman breeders and fanciers and their disciples in America.

Americans also have very pointed questions about the dogs from the German system. Are there no pet dogs in Germany where average families receive castoffs from the master breeding program, they ask.

American breeders say the working spirit of the Doberman is still evident today in the tough jobs these dogs are called upon to do. (Bev Mueller)

The Germans and their American disciples reply that by heavily testing all breeding stock for temperament and protection drives, they have a real handle on the future of the offspring. Undesirable character traits put a dog out for life. They just cannot be bred, ever, for registered offspring. The Germans bristle at any suggestion that the German Doberman is an attack dog. It is a controlled protection dog, they say.

ARGUMENTS ACROSS THE ATLANTIC

The arguments about the German Doberman versus the American Doberman reached a flash point in the mid-1980s. The argument reached a crescendo when there was a strong move to introduce the German activity of Schutzhund, with its protection work, into the mainstream of American Dobermans. It was a time when dog fanciers were beginning to mobilize to combat legislation aimed at specific breeds—including the Doberman—that were accused of being vicious and dangerous.

The Schutzhund battle raged within the membership of the DPCA, and the club decided to

A breeding program aimed at producing family pets is likely to produce a different sort of dog than one aimed at producing protection dogs. (Alan & Jacquie Wendt)

Differences in culture are behind the differences between German and American breeding programs. (Rod Humphries)

included. A directive was sent to the DPCA, and the club dropped Schutzhund and even modified its Working Aptitude Certificate, which had been developed in the 1970s and required, among other things, that a dog show strong protection traits but no biting in confrontation with an aggressive stranger.

This marked another major turning point in the history of the Doberman in America. The Doberman community was split over the issue, and in 1990 a splinter group formed its own club, the United Doberman Club (UDC).

The twain are never likely to meet. Among other things, it is the culture of dog shows in America colliding with the culture of working dogs in Europe. It is not inconceivable that one day the American Doberman Pinscher will be officially declared a separate breed, just as other breeds have separated from their original homeland standards.

German historian and Doberman breeder-judge Philipp Gruenig, a man who believed that a dog allowed to be touched by a stranger had a faulty temperament, was clear about the evolution of this relatively young breed. "The creation of a breed can surely be termed a work of art and, like every work of art, it is subject to changes of viewpoint, of style and of the unconscious but creatively dynamic trend of the day."

The Doberman breed is still in the process of being shaped. It just happens to vary across the Atlantic, and even across the world.

hold a vote on whether to support Schutzhund. The debate never reached a vote. The American Kennel Club in early 1990 instituted a policy for its member breed clubs that barred them from endorsing or promoting any activity that included bite work. Schutzhund was not specifically mentioned, but there was no doubt that it was

(Lloyd Olson)

CHAPTER 4

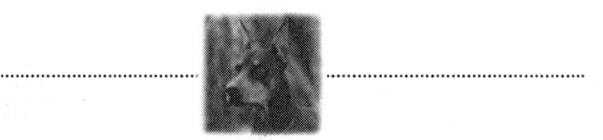

The Doberman Pinscher Breed Standard

The idea of breed standards originated in the last part of the 19th century in an attempt to bring uniformity to many breeds. A standard is a written description of how the ideal dog of a particular breed should look and act. It is a word picture of a mental image, not an engineer's blueprint. Therefore, the standard of any breed is open to some interpretation. That is how some breeders can develop a certain look that slightly distinguishes their dogs from those of another breeder, even though both dogs conform to the standard.

Although there are quite a few variations of the Doberman breed standard around the world, the American and German standards are the most widely recognized. The German standard was first written by Otto Goeller in 1899 (you'll find it in Appendix E) and has undergone dramatic changes in the last 100 years. The German standard is now written by the German Dobermann Verein and is used by the Federation Cynologique International (FCI), the governing body for dogs in about 70 countries. The American standard, written by the Doberman Pinscher Club of America and approved by the American Kennel Club, has been in existence since 1935 and has changed a number of times over the years.

THE FIRST STANDARD

When Otto Goeller drew up the first standard of the Dobermannpinscher in 1899, the physical aspects of the breed made it little more than a Rottweiler look-alike—and not a very good one at that. Dobermans were small by today's standards, with short legs and long backs, and were quite coarse overall. The Dobermannpinscher ranged from 18 to 24 inches at the shoulder and weighed only 44 pounds. The smallest bitches of today are bigger than the tallest males of Goeller's time, while the weight has more than doubled.

At the annual dog show in Apolda in 1899 the judge, Mr. Berta, was not impressed:

The Doberman still was coarse throughout, his head showed heavy cheeks, with a too wide and French front. In coat the dogs were too long and wavy, especially long on neck and shanks. A lot of dogs were built too heavy, appearing more like a Rottweiler. This was the first show where Dobermans were entered in every class. The first Dobermans were very sharp fellows. Straw yellow markings, white spots on the chest, sometimes appearing more gray in color than black, on account of heavy undercoats, they did not make the impression of a uniform and well-bred breed. However, exterior body deficiencies were made up by other splendid qualities.

Early Dobermans did not look much like the dogs we know today.

In that first standard, Goeller allowed only for deep black coats with rust markings, Two years later, undoubtedly under pressure from peers, he added two more colors: red (or brown, as it is known in much of the world) and blue. Ninety years later, the Germans would eliminate blues and accept only blacks and reds as the official colors of the Doberman. The Germans never accepted the fawn (or Isabella, as it is sometimes called), and neither did the Americans until pressure from within the Doberman Pinscher Club of America

The fawn, or Isabella, color is accepted in the American standard but not in Germany. (Mary Knueppel)

forced acceptance in 1969, making all four colors—black, red, blue and fawn—acceptable in the show rings in the United States.

The revolutionary changes in the breed after the turn of the century came in height, elegance of head and body, more defined markings and more tightly knit coat texture. The rough-coated small, ugly dog of the 1800s has been transformed into an elegant yet rugged individual. Slowly but surely, the breed has grown taller and the head has lengthened in proportion to the new body. It took breeders years to eliminate the low croups (the muscular area just above the tail) and the dippy and roached (hunched up) backs that persisted even 20 years ago. As the breed's second century begins, the commonly referred to "one-piece dog,"

which is square and compact with elegance and bone holds sway in the Doberman community.

GERMAN VS. AMERICAN

Today there are two distinct standards of the breed, the Americans having parted ways with the Germans in 1935 when the American breed club adopted its own standard.

The first obvious difference in the standards is in the spelling. The German standard retains the spelling of breed founder Dobermann's name, with two n's at the end. There are more substantial differences as well. The American standard today calls for bitches to be 24 to 26 inches (the ideal is 25½ inches) and males to be 26 to 28 inches (the ideal is 27½ inches) and says nothing about weight. But the German standard today allows males to be just over 29 inches and to weigh up to 99 pounds; and bitches may be a little over 27½ inches with a weight up to 77 pounds.

There are also distinct differences in how the two standards describe behavior and temperament, with the German standard requiring more hardness and insisting on working ability.

There are other important differences, as well. The Germans disqualify a dog missing any teeth, while the Americans will only disqualify a dog missing four or more teeth. The American standard allows red, black, blue and fawn dogs, while the German standard does not recognize blue or fawn.

There are important differences in the angulation of the fore and hindquarters, too, which we will explain later in the chapter. And this is only a brief overview of how the German and American standards differ. You'll find the complete German standard in Appendix E.

THE OFFICIAL STANDARD FOR THE DOBERMAN PINSCHER

The current American standard for the Doberman Pinscher follows, with comments in italics. The standard was approved in 1982 and was reformatted to comply with new AKC guidelines in 1990.

Because the standard is a written description of a visual image, a lot of specialized language has evolved to help clarify the descriptions. It's useful to be familiar with these special terms, but we'll certainly define them as we look at the standard.

GENERAL APPEARANCE: The appearance is that of a dog of medium size, with a body that is square. Compactly built, muscular and powerful, for great endurance and speed. Elegant in appearance, of proud carriage, reflecting great nobility and temperament. Energetic, watchful, determined, alert, fearless, loyal and obedient.

SIZE, PROPORTION, SUBSTANCE: Height at the withers: *Dogs* 26 to 28 inches, ideal about 27½ inches; *Bitches* 24 to 26 inches, ideal about 25½ inches. The height, measured vertically from the ground to the highest point of the withers, equaling the length measured horizontally from the forechest to the rear projection of the upper thigh. Length of head, neck and legs in proportion to length and depth of body.

The withers is the top of the shoulder. The Doberman of today is obviously on the top end of "medium," but the breed should not be so big that it becomes cumbersome. In football parlance, the Doberman is a runningback or a linebacker, probably with more of a linebacker mentality. It is not, however, an offensive or defensive lineman.

What is important to grasp here is the balance and symmetry among the parts. The Doberman should be square, with the length (from the point of the chest to the farthest point of the upper thigh) equal to the height (from the withers to the ground). The length equals the height, and the depth of brisket (chest) is in balance to the height of the dog. The depth of the brisket should be in proportion to the length of the leg—about halfway from the top of the withers to the ground. The shoulder and upper arm require an angle of 90 degrees and should match the rear angulation. The hip bone should fall away from the spinal cord at about 30 degrees. Other parts, such as the head and neck, are also balanced and flow with the overall dog.

HEAD: Long and dry, resembling a blunt wedge in both frontal and profile views. When seen from the front, the head widens gradually toward the base of the ears in a practically unbroken line. *Eyes* almond shaped, moderately deep set, with vigorous, energetic expression. Iris, of uniform color, ranging from medium to darkest brown in black dogs; in reds, blues, and fawns the color of the iris blends with that of the markings, the darkest shade being preferable in every case. *Ears* normally cropped and carried erect. The upper attachment of the ear, when held erect, is on a level with the top of the skull.

Top of *skull* flat, turning with slight stop to bridge of muzzle, with muzzle line extending parallel to top line of skull. Cheeks flat and muscular. *Nose* solid black on black dogs, dark brown on red ones, dark gray on blue ones, dark tan on fawns. *Lips* lying close to jaws. *Jaws* full and powerful, well filled under the eyes. *Teeth* strongly developed and white. Lower

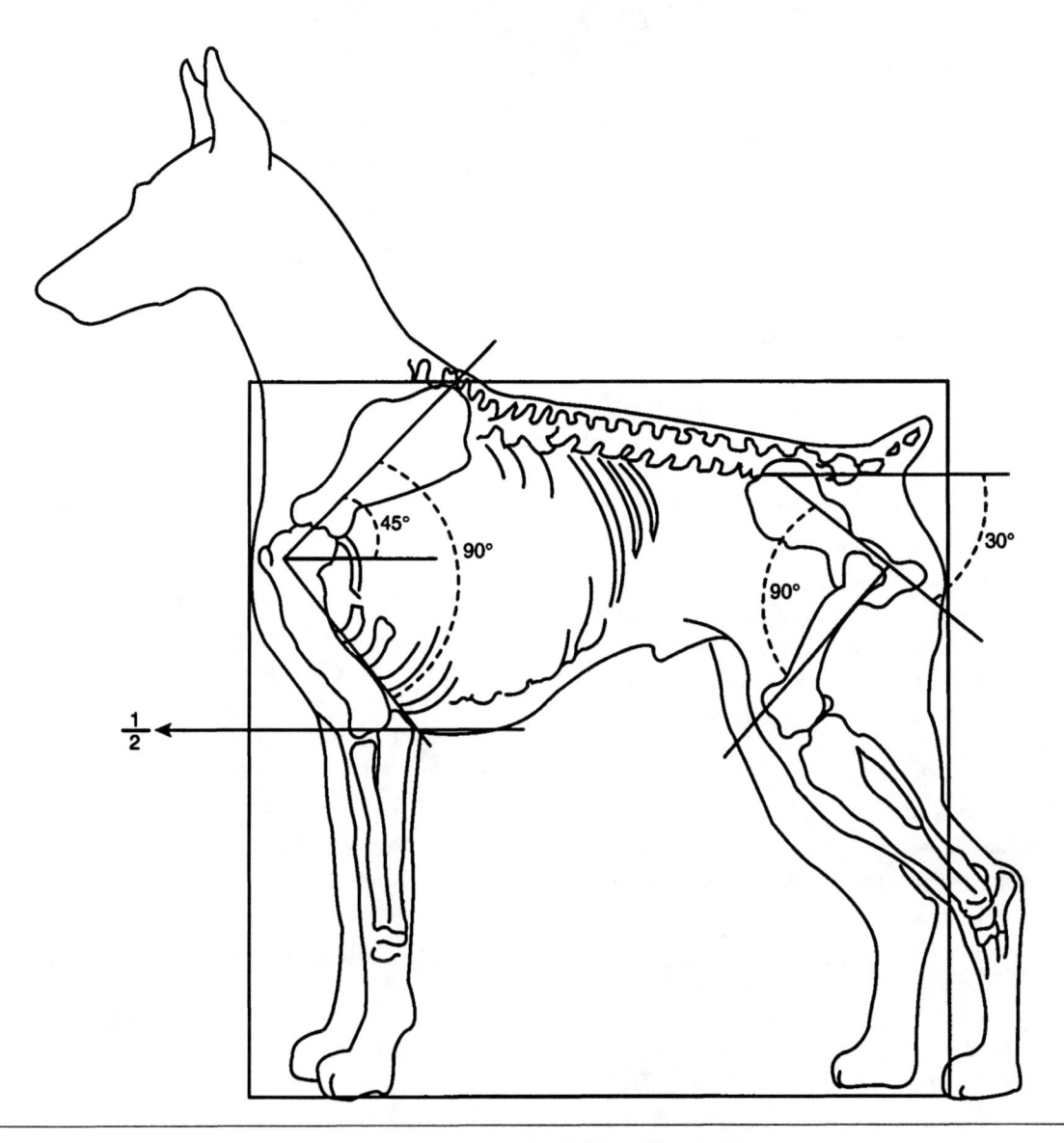

The parts of the Doberman should be balanced and symmetrical. (Fran Knueppel)

incisors upright and touching inside of upper incisors—a true scissors bite. 42 correctly placed teeth, 22 in the lower, 20 in the upper jaw. Distemper teeth shall not be penalized. **Disqualifying Faults**—Overshot more than ³⁄₁₆ of an inch. Undershot more than ⅛ of an inch. Four or more missing teeth.

The eyes are dark, the ears cropped and erect, the jaws full and powerful. (Joanna Walker)

The head of the Doberman is unique. A check of the standards of other breeds will show that many have a description of the body that is similar to that of the Doberman, but the gorgeous blunt wedge that is the true Doberman head is unique. The blunt wedge with a full, deep muzzle, strong underjaw, parallel planes of the top of the head and muzzle, interrupted by a slight stop (the place where the muzzle meets the skull), and no loose skin (that's what the word "dry" means) clearly distinguishes the breed. Newcomers should study the head diligently; watch for the wedge both straight on and in profile. A lot of Dobermans have no "filling" under the eyes, which destroys the wedge in a frontal view. And many lack underjaw, which ruins the blunt wedge in profile.

The Doberman is well-known for missing and extra teeth, and while there may be 42 teeth, they are not always correctly placed. Many of the variations occur in the premolars, where there may be extras or some missing. The Doberman is also known to have missing molars or incisors.

Although the standard allows for four or more missing teeth, most breeders of American Dobermans would not dream of showing a dog with a mouth full of gaps. Some

owners will show a dog with one missing premolar, or sometimes even two if the animal is otherwise a superior specimen. Such dogs have gained Championships with missing teeth. (Distemper teeth are teeth that are damaged or discolored due to incomplete or pitted enamel.)

"Overshot" means the top jaw extends past the lower jaw. "Undershot" is just the opposite. Too much of either will disqualify a dog from the show ring. Most good American breeders are producing scissors bites (the upper and lower teeth intermesh in front), and while there may be some level bites (the upper and lower teeth meet evenly in front) at times in the ring, overshot and undershot jaws are not prevalent. What is prevalent today is extra teeth— usually extra premolars in the upper jaw—which is not being heavily penalized in the show ring. Again, much depends on the overall quality of the dog. The teeth are just one part of the entire equation.

NECK, TOPLINE, BODY: *Neck* proudly carried, well muscled and dry. Well arched, with nape of neck widening gradually toward body. Length of neck proportioned to body and head. *Withers* pronounced and forming the highest point of the body. Back short, firm, of sufficient width, and muscular at the loins, extending in a straight line from withers to the slightly rounded croup.

Chest broad with forechest well defined. *Ribs* well sprung from the spine, but flattened in lower end to permit elbow clearance. *Brisket* reaching deep to the elbow. *Belly* well tucked up, extending in a

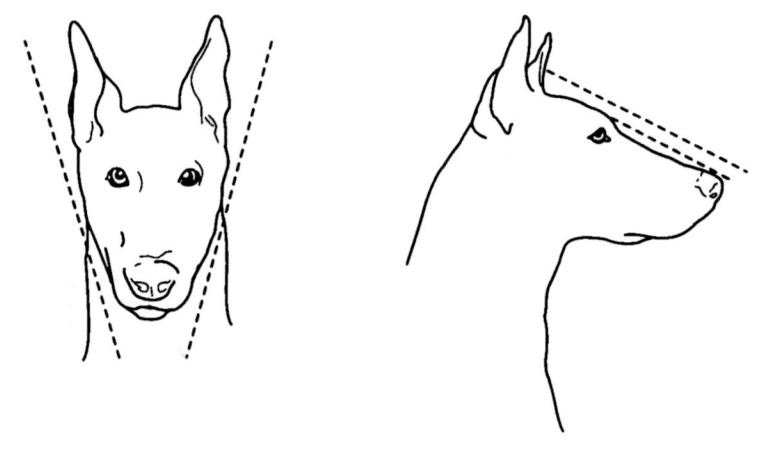

The head should be a blunt wedge when viewed from the front and in profile. The planes should be parallel, with a slight stop from the skull to the bridge of the muzzle. The eyes should be almond shaped and the neck well arched and gradually widening toward the body. (Fran Knueppel)

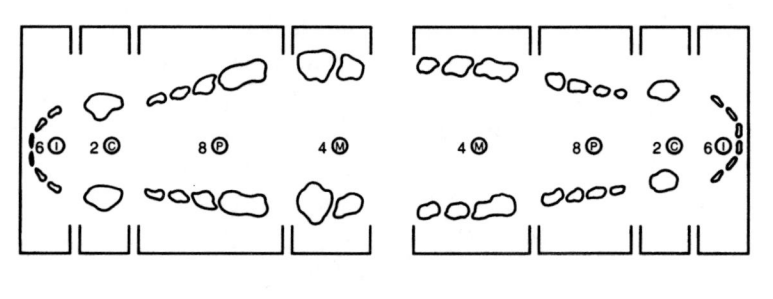

Upper 20 Teeth   Lower 22 Teeth

Ⓘ Incisors   Ⓒ Canine   Ⓟ Premolars   Ⓜ Molars

The Doberman should have 42 correctly placed teeth: 22 in the lower jaw and 20 in the upper jaw. The difference is additional premolars on the bottom. (Fran Knueppel)

curved line from the brisket. *Loins* wide and muscled. *Hips* broad and in proportion to body, breadth

of hips being approximately equal to breadth of body at rib cage and shoulders. *Tail* docked at approximately second joint, appears to be a continuation of the spine, and is carried only slightly above the horizontal when the dog is alert.

There has been a tendency in recent times to produce a swan-like neck, which can look spectacularly elegant in the show ring. But this is not practical, and many believe that the strong Doberman head atop a swan-like neck can cause neck problems.

The neck is a very obvious part of the flow of the Doberman outline, and if not correct it can jar the total picture. A long neck with a short back can give the dog a hyena look. Necks that are set too far forward are particularly prevalent. A good outline of the Doberman depends on the flow of the neck into the shoulders and a continuation to a strong, unbroken topline.

A good topline is a vital part in the overall picture, and thus is given heavy weight in the show ring. It is also important to stand over a Doberman to view the width of the dog, which should be the same at the shoulders, center rib cage and hips. There should be a discernible waist. If the body is straight from shoulders to hips, the dog is overweight.

FOREQUARTERS: *Shoulder blade* sloping forward and downward at a 45-degree angle to the ground meets the upper arm at an angle of 90 degrees. Length of shoulder blade and upper arm are equal. Height from elbow to withers approximately equals height from ground to elbow. *Legs* seen from front and side, perfectly straight and parallel to each other from elbow to pastern; muscled and sinewy, with heavy

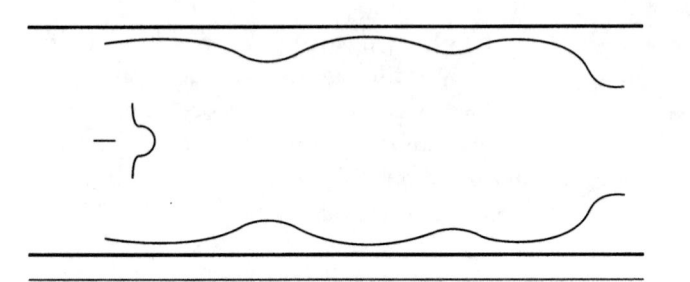

This top view of the Doberman shows the required balance of approximately equal breadth at the shoulders, rib cage, and hips. There should be a discernable waist. (Fran Knueppel)

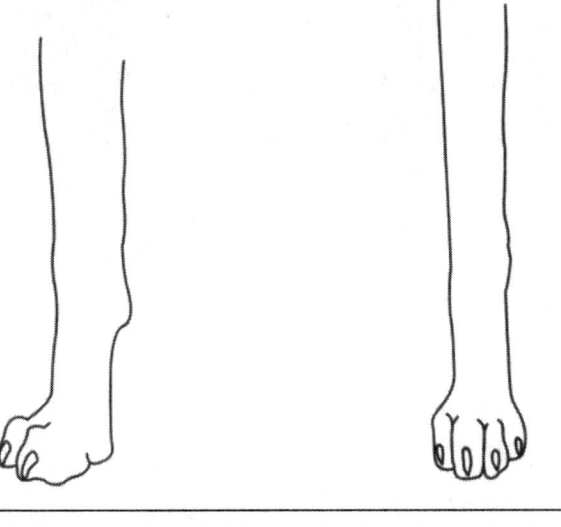

The feet must be tight like "cat feet," as the standard says. They must not turn in or out. (Fran Knueppel)

bone. In normal pose and when gaiting, the elbows lie close to the brisket. *Pasterns firm and almost perpendicular to the ground. Dewclaws may be removed. Feet well arched, compact, and catlike, turning neither in nor out.*

The 90-degree angle between shoulder blade and upper arm is controversial because critics say it is physically unattainable. The Germans are of that belief and have in their standard an angle of 105 to110 degrees. The Americans have a 45-degree slope of the shoulder blade and the Germans have a 50-degree slope.

American fanciers realize they will never see the perfect 90-degree shoulder, but they do not want to compromise by stretching it to 105 or 110 degrees. The Americans believe if they compromise now, future generations may stretch it even more, and straighter and straighter fronts will become the norm.

By the way, the pastern is the metacarpus; that is, the region between the wrist and the foot.

HINDQUARTERS: The angulation of the hindquarters balances that of the forequarters. *Hip bone falls away from spinal column at an angle of about 30 degrees, producing a slightly rounded, well filled-out croup. Upper shanks at right angles to the hip bones, are*

long, wide, and well muscled on both sides of thigh, with clearly defined stifles. Upper and lower shanks are of equal length. While the dog is at rest, hock to heel is perpendicular to the ground. Viewed from the rear, the legs are straight, parallel to each other, and wide enough apart to fit in with a properly built body. Dewclaws, if any, are generally removed. *Cat feet as on front legs, turning neither in nor out.*

The rear legs should be wide and muscled, like hams, indicative of this galloping breed. And they should be set on a good pair of wide hips. There are too many American show Dobermans today with weak rears—narrow in the hips and thighs (thighs are also called shanks).

The rear angulation is supposed to match the front, which means the hip bone and the femur, or thigh bone, should also meet at an angle of 90 degrees—another point of contention with the German standard, which allows for more angle.

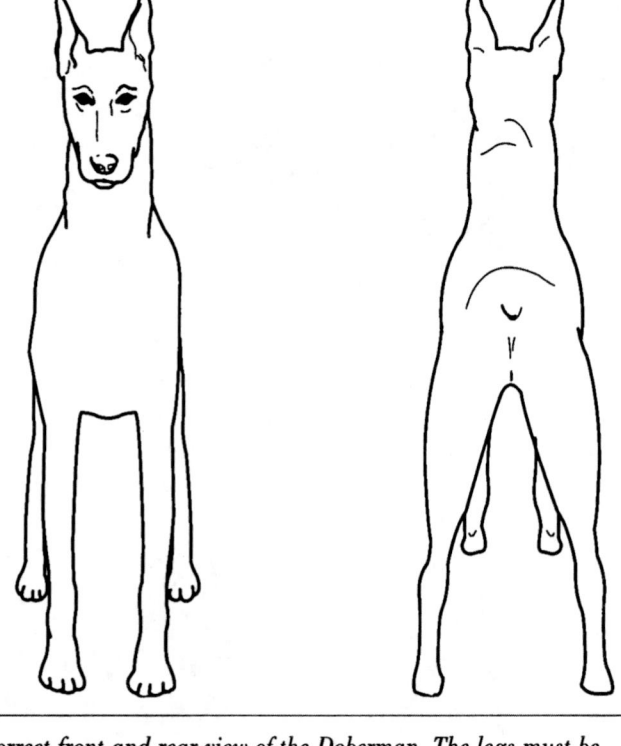

The correct front and rear view of the Doberman. The legs must be straight and parallel, the elbows must be tight to the brisket and the shoulders should not be too broad or overloaded. (Fran Knueppel)

The croup (the muscular area just above and around the point where the tail meets the body) can be confusing for novices, especially the statement that says the hip bone falls away at 30 degrees. People sometimes believe that means the tail set (how the base of the tail sets on the rump) is allowed to drop 30 degrees. Not so. The topline rounds off ever so slightly before the tail ("well filled-out croup"). The tail should be a continuation of that line, with a slight rise. The popular flat croup and erect tail in the show rings today are not correct and detract from the Doberman's flowing lines.

COAT: Smooth-haired, short, hard, thick and close lying. Invisible gray undercoat on neck permissible.

Cowlicks (raised tufts of hair) are prevalent on American Dobermans. The cowlicks can form a ridge on the neck, sometimes a slight ridge on the nose, or a swirl on the shoulder. They are not penalized on American Dobermans but are listed as a fault in the German standard.

Interestingly, the American Doberman standard of today still permits a half-inch-square white spot on the chest and what it amusingly refers to as "an invisible gray undercoat on neck." White spots, and sometimes large flashes, were quite common through to the 1970s and early 1980s. While recessive genes are surely still producing some white spots, their incidence is much lower. The gray undercoat, undetectable at times but certainly not invisible, was also appearing quite often through the 1970s. The undercoat was often straw-colored around the neck, and owners invariably had to brush for long periods to remove the unwanted hair.

COLOR AND MARKINGS: *Allowed Colors—* Black, red, blue, and fawn (Isabella). *Markings—* Rust, sharply defined, appearing above each eye and on muzzle, throat and forechest, on all legs and feet, and below tail. White patch on chest, not exceeding half an inch square, permissible. **Disqualifying fault—** Dogs not of an allowed color.

"Dogs not of an allowed color" is directed at the albino white, which has grown in popularity but is outlawed by the DPCA. White dogs cannot be shown, but the AKC does allow them to be registered because they are the off-spring of registered parents. The AKC tags all white dogs and those with white parents in their background with a "Z" on registration papers, to alert fanciers.

Marks-Tey D-Day. Pilot Dog Dede was raise by a foster home. She loved children and Jayne Siniard's granddaughter Hailey adored her, too. Dede now has her blind owner's grandchildren to play with.

Dogs with lighter rust or tan markings have been appearing with more frequency in the United States. If the gray undercoat is invisible, then we should not worry about something that is not there!

GAIT: Free, balanced, and vigorous, with good reach in the forequarters and good driving power in the hindquarters. When trotting, there is strong rear-action drive. Each rear leg moves in line with the foreleg on the same side. Rear and front legs are thrown neither in nor out. Back remains strong and firm. When moving at a fast trot, a properly built dog will single-track.

"Single-track" means that if a dog trotted along a sandy beach or a clean field of snow, all the pawprints would be in a single line. The authors are not sure there is such a thing as a perfect single track. Some dogs certainly take longer than others to hit their stride in a near-single-track trot.

There is an age-old argument about the Doberman's movement. It is a short-backed galloping breed, not a long-backed trotting breed, so a small show ring is not the best place to judge a Doberman. Often a slightly longer dog, which is not what the standard calls for, will trot better than a truly square dog.

One should expect good reach and drive when watching from the side ("reach" is how the dog's front legs reach

out when it moves, and "drive" is how its back legs push it forward) and clean movement without throwing elbows and paws sideways when moving to and from a judge.

TEMPERAMENT: Energetic, watchful, determined, alert, fearless, loyal and obedient. *The judge shall dismiss from the ring any shy or vicious Doberman.*

Shyness—A dog shall be judged fundamentally shy if, refusing to stand for examination, it shrinks away from the judge; if it fears an approach from the rear; if it shies at sudden and unusual noises to a marked degree.

Viciousness—A dog that attacks or attempts to attack either the judge or its handler, is definitely vicious. An aggressive or belligerent attitude towards other dogs shall not be deemed viciousness.

FAULTS: The foregoing description is that of the ideal Doberman Pinscher. Any deviation from the above described dog must be penalized to the extent of the deviation.

DISQUALIFICATIONS: *Overshot more than $\frac{3}{16}$ of an inch, undershot more than $\frac{1}{8}$ of an inch.*

Four or more missing teeth.

Dogs not of an allowed color.

(*Joanna Walker*)

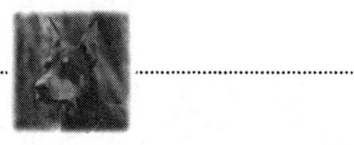

CHAPTER 5

How to Find the Right Doberman for You

When one considers the protection-dog history and the subtleties of temperament of the Doberman, would any prospective Doberman puppy owner look in the newspaper classified ads for a new family member? Would you trust someone who throws two Dobermans together and knows nothing about good breeding practices, proper temperament, dominance and how the pack operates, the breed standard, correct conformation, or health issues? Would you buy a used car or a Doberman puppy from this person? No!

There are two phases in the search for a new Doberman puppy. The first is the search for the right breeder, and then second is the search for the right puppy. Find the right breeder and everything else should fall into place.

Sifting through the options is not easy, and it will take time. The best approach is to always remember that you are obtaining a new family member for a decade or more. It is like going to an adoption agency. You are not going to take just any baby off the shelf, and the agency is going to check you out and place the right baby with the right family.

When you find the right breeder, chances are the rest of your questions will be easy to sort out. (Rod Humphries)

EVALUATING BREEDERS

So how do you find the right breeder? It should be relatively simple to spot what is commonly referred to as the "backyard breeder." He is the one who took little time in the study of his subject and then put any dog and bitch together, probably ones he owns, or maybe even a neighbor's male he thought was good enough to sire some pups. He may pull out a pedigree and show you a "Champion-filled pedigree," but he doesn't know much about genetics and doesn't have a long-range plan for producing excellent dogs that meet the breed standard.

This breeder—or, more precisely, this puppy producer—has probably cut corners and skimped on good veterinary care, food and so on. He will let the bitch nurse the puppies long after they should be on solid foods, and she is likely to look exhausted and undernourished. Shots, worming and ear cropping are, in his opinion, the buyer's responsibility. A check of the facilities will give insight into the cleanliness, care and grooming of the dogs and may be enough to deter any serious Doberman puppy buyer.

Then there is the next step up, the caring family that just wanted to breed little Tootsie one time before they spayed her. They might have even found a worthwhile stud dog and their care of the bitch and puppies may be exemplary. But they still do not know what they are doing when it comes to the intricacies of the Doberman breed.

The next is a breeder who actually has show stock and maybe even a Champion or two in the house. What you need to figure out is whether this particular breeder is totally involved in the Doberman as a breed and has its future and well-being at heart, or whether this is a glorified puppy producer with better stock. The latter is often more interested in the show ribbons he or she can accumulate which, in turn, allows them to sell higher priced pups. If you get the impression that this breeder relies on selling pups to make a living and is merely trying to offload a puppy, walk away.

THE TRUE BREEDERS AND HOW TO FIND THEM

True master breeders are indeed gems. They are the worthy heads of a bloodline, a canine family. They have planned breeding programs based on sound breeding principles, integrity and professionalism. They have studied the breed from top to bottom and use good breeding practices based on solid genetic principles. They know the good and bad of linebreeding and inbreeding, they can recite the Doberman standard and know how to apply it, and they know what it is to get down and dirty in the whelping box—cutting umbilical cords and clearing fluid from the lungs of a newborn.

They are not obsessed by show results or trying to be somebody on the board of this club or that. It is the dogs that count for these people. They are the true guardians of the breed who make enormous sacrifices in what they consider is their "watch" in the history of the Doberman.

True breeders care about where their dogs go to live and that they have a life that allows them to fulfill their potential. There is no sense of urgency when you buy a puppy from these people. They will always be there for you and the dog they planned and brought into this world, no matter what. These are the people who will not disappear if something unforeseen of dastardly hereditary nature befalls the dog, even years after the animal has left their kennel. These are breeders of character and substance. They build impeccable reputations which, even in the dog-eat-dog world of purebred animals, cannot be torn asunder.

WHAT ABOUT THE PAPERS?

The fact that the litter is registered with the American Kennel Club is important. If it is not, you cannot register your individual puppy. AKC registration is your guarantee that the dog you are buying is a purebred Doberman Pinscher.

But a registration certificate is not worth the paper it is written on if the dog is a poor specimen with health and temperament problems. The AKC itself has issued a statement that says registration papers are no guarantee of quality. Don't let anyone tell you otherwise.

So where do you find these people, these master breeders, these generational pillars of the breed? That's not an easy question to answer. The American Kennel Club is helpful with referrals, and the Doberman Pinscher Club of America has a nationwide service where names and addresses of club members can be supplied in your city or state. Both have informative Web sites on the Internet. Breed magazines are also an excellent source, because most of the top breeders are regular advertisers. (Contact sources are listed in Appendix A.)

Dog shows are another good starting point; most good breeders are involved in some way with shows because that is where the top conformation and working specimens of the breed can be found. You may find them at obedience or agility trials or flyball competitions, because they love their dogs to be involved in fun activities as an important part of their lives.

Some, like the authors of this book, are breeders who rarely visit dog shows anymore. They may send a dog out with a professional handler to gauge the quality of their current breeding stock, but the week-to-week grind of travel and crated dogs and long hours waiting for a few minutes of ring time can wear thin after 30 or 40 years. Ask about these breeders at dog shows and look for their names in magazines.

The best breeders have a long-term vision of how their breeding program will improve the Doberman breed as a whole. This is Cascade's Teegon of Tris Skor, MX. (Dwight Cash)

The breeder you like may not always have the puppy you want when you want it. Almost certainly he or she will not. Top breeders are not churning out multitudes of dogs. To get one of these gems takes time, and if you want the best you may need a lot of patience.

After you've asked your questions, expect to get as many questions in return. Good breeders want references. They most definitely want their pups to go to a home with a fenced yard. They do not want to get a call six months later telling them the puppy has been hit by a car. They want to know where the pup is going to live, the general lifestyle and the ability of the family to pay for the upkeep of one of these precious pups. Prospective puppy buyers should not be offended by these questions, just as they would not be offended at a baby adoption agency. In fact, they should be more worried if the breeder *doesn't* ask any questions!

ASKING QUESTIONS

Once you have found the breeder you think can best help you, start asking questions—lots of questions. Broad questions about the bloodlines and the breeding program should be followed up with specific questions about temperament, health, longevity and the various health tests carried out on breeding animals. Master breeders of long standing who care about the breed are more likely to spend more time answering your questions than a person who is just pushing a puppy. Ask questions, listen, learn, read and don't make any emotional or quick decisions about buying a puppy.

THE PRICE

If you are serious about getting a good dog, the last question should be the price. Breeders are always nervous when the first question out of a prospective puppy buyer's mouth is "How much?" Rightly or wrongly, breeders believe if money is the prime factor in purchasing a pup, then the buyer may not be worthy of owning one of their beloved animals. They feel that if you want a dog cheap, maybe you should get one out of the newspaper.

On the other hand, they also know that a good owner of their pups may not be able to afford the price in one payment, and many will offer a payment system. Normally, with a time payment contract you will get the registration papers when all the payments have been made.

The going price for a quality pup from a top breeder can range from $500 or $600 to $2,000 or more. Pet-quality dogs from a top breeder are usually excellent dogs that may have small flaws that will prevent them from winning in the show ring—but will certainly not prevent them from

A dog show is a good place to meet breeders. Most show their dogs to test the quality of their stock and to see how other dogs measure up against theirs. This is Ch. Rahdy's Sable v Deserae, the dam of 10 champions. (Jordan)

being wonderful members of your family. Sometimes a pet-quality dog from a top breeder is better than the so-called "pick of the litter" in a lesser litter.

While these prices may seem high, a good breeder rarely, if ever, makes a profit. The costs of bringing the kennel stock to Championship quality level—the stud fee (which can reach $1,000 for a top male); the shipping and handling of the bitch (often interstate) or the travel expenses when the breeder prefers to take the bitch to the stud dog himself; the veterinary bills; tail-docking and ear-cropping (ear cropping alone can run more than $150 a pup); shots; worming; top-quality food and numerous other incidentals—make breeding good dogs mostly a money-losing proposition.

Time is also worth money. Breeders put in countless hours whelping and raising a litter. Good breeders often sleep by the whelping box, help during birth and stay glued to the box for several

Top breeders don't always have bushels of puppies available. You may have to wait for the pup you want. (Joanna Walker)

The time, effort and expense that go into raising a litter properly mean breeders seldom see a profit from their efforts. (Jo Ann James)

days to ensure mother and pups are doing well. At three or four weeks, they start preparing four solid meals a day and scrubbing and cleaning to make sure that bacteria does not cause serious problems. The tail and ear surgeries are an horrendous time for breeders, physically and emotionally. Keeping stitches from being pulled, the seemingly constant posting and wrapping of ears and working to get them to stand erect, take an enormous toll. Then there is socializing the puppies—which is so very important for their future—some basic training and trips to the vet for shots and worming. And that is when everything goes according to plan! If there is sickness or puppies with health problems, the worry and time escalate.

PET OR SHOW?

A lot of prospective buyers who want a good dog will often tell a breeder that they want a show dog when they have absolutely no plan to show the dog. They want a good dog and think that unless they ask for a show-quality animal, they will not get a good puppy. But this is not the case.

If you go to a master breeder and ask for a pet, you will get a top-quality, handsome representative of the breed that will certainly satisfy your needs. As we've already mentioned, a pet in a top-quality litter is often better than the best pup in a second-rate litter.

Most top breeders want to be sure that their best animals find their way into the show ring to prove their worth and are then bred to continue their line. That's why these dogs are either sold on a co-ownership contract (so that the breeder can retain breeding rights for a litter), to hard-core dog show enthusiasts who have experience showing top dogs, or to capable newcomers who are willing to work with the breeder under some kind of contract arrangement. If you're serious about wanting to get a dog you can show, don't be frightened off by any offer to co-own or to retain some stud rights, as this is a regular practice in the dog sport. Obtaining a written contract spelling out all the details is absolutely necessary.

A pet-quality pup from a top-quality litter is a healthy, strong, stable animal that will be a fine addition to any family. (Marcha Shepperd)

Good breeders are also attracted to buyers who have an interest in training the dog for obedience, agility, flyball or some other organized sport and are willing to show it if it turns out well (sometimes gangly puppies can turn into stunning adults, and vice versa). First of all, the breeder is excited that the young dog will be trained, which is important for all Dobermans.

Second, the dog will get to do things with its new owners, and at the same time will expose the owner to the canine show world at large. Even if the owner is a complete novice when it comes to showing dogs, if an experienced person sees a good dog around a show or at training classes, he or she will often make suggestions and help the novice to show.

Actually, we find the descriptions "pet-quality" and "show-quality" to be quite inadequate. We have always said we would be proud to take any of our dogs into the show ring. Whether that dog can actually achieve an American Championship is another matter. There is such a great variation in the quality of show dogs that we prefer a more detailed description of pups being sold.

First, there is the "easy finishable dog," which means the animal is a shoe-in to finish its Championship if trained and handled correctly. Next is the "probable finisher," which means the puppy is likely to obtain a Championship but will need good handling and perseverance. The next level is the "possible finisher," which is a pup that, when it reaches maturity, may have a chance to gain a Championship. The last show category is one that breeders love to see trained for other activities and shown "if it turns out." Finally, there is the "pet," which has a slight flaw or flaws that would make it very, very difficult to gain a Championship. As we've already said, this does not make them bad pups. On the contrary, these are probably excellent specimens, just a notch or two short of Championship level. They still have that Look of Eagles that Doberman owners so love.

Breeders like to know their dogs are going to live with families that will train them to use their great physical and mental abilities. This is Ch. Royal Tudor's Wild as the Wind, UDX, ROM. (McNealy)

example, advises all prospective buyers that when he plans a litter it is to advance his breeding program, not to sell puppies. He chooses which pups he wants to keep either at his home or on co-ownership contracts with experienced show people, and then he sells the other pups that he does not need for his breeding program—not that he doesn't *want*, but that he doesn't *need*.

Top-quality breeders will spend time evaluating prospective buyers and understanding their specific needs. Then, when the right pup for those people comes along, it is offered. It's no good sending a big, rambunctious male who loves to run, bump and play to a retired couple who just lost their old dog. And you don't send a quiet female to a gung-ho ironman competitor who wants to run up mountainsides and through forests with his dog. When you find the right breeder, trust him or her to do the right thing in helping find the right pup for you and your circumstances. If the breeder takes you out to a kennel of pups and says, "Take your pick and take your time"—particularly with a

GOOD BREEDERS HELP CHOOSE THE PUP FOR YOU

You may not get a chance to pick your own pup if you go to a top breeder. You may be offered a particular pup from the litter, depending on whether you want a pet or a show prospect. Why would a breeder want to pick your pup for you?

First, the top breeders sometimes only breed once or maybe twice a year. Rod Humphries, for

Doberman—you may be at the wrong place.

There are more pups purchased sight unseen from top breeders today than ever before. A lot of buyers, including pet buyers, just cannot get the pup of their choice, or a pup at all in their immediate area, and go searching farther afield. It is not uncommon for the search to span the entire country. Most breeders would prefer that the new owners pick up their pups in person, but when it is a long-distance sale, this is mostly impractical and rarely the case.

If you surveyed America's top Doberman breeders, you would surely find that most of them sell an extremely high percentage of their pups to distant places, putting them on planes at early hours of the morning to arrive at the right time in the new owner's city. So don't be deterred if you find yourself buying a puppy from someone far away. If you are convinced that you have the right breeder, you must trust him or her. Ask for a video and still photographs of the sire, the dam, the pup in question, and its littermates. Make sure you gather as much information as you can.

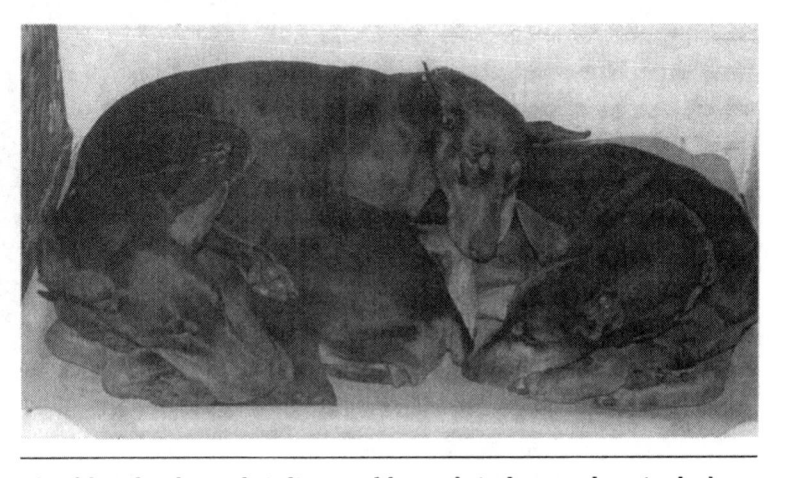

Good breeders know their lines and know their dogs, and are in the best position to pick just the right dog for you. (JoAnn James)

A good breeder will be able to match their dogs to the personality of your family. (Joanna Walker)

PUPPY OR ADULT?

Doberman puppies are great fun but a lot of work. They have a bull-at-a-gate, adventurous nature that can be cute to some people and a pain in the neck to others. They will chew through the teething stage up to about six months, and sometimes more, and quite often do not distinguish between the old shoe you threw down to occupy them and the expensive Italian loafers you foolishly left under the bed.

They need a lot of training, including house

training, and are extremely demanding of your time. But when they finally mature, which can be at up to 18 months in some cases, the end result is a wonderful family friend and protector. If you are a true dog lover who can take all a puppy throws at you, then this breed is a whole lot of fun.

Obtaining an adult dog, or a young adult about a year of age or more, can be equally rewarding. You may be happy to avoid the puppy stage. Breeders will sometimes have mature adults available that have finished their breeding or show careers and are better off in a home where they can be pampered pets and live out their lives in comfort.

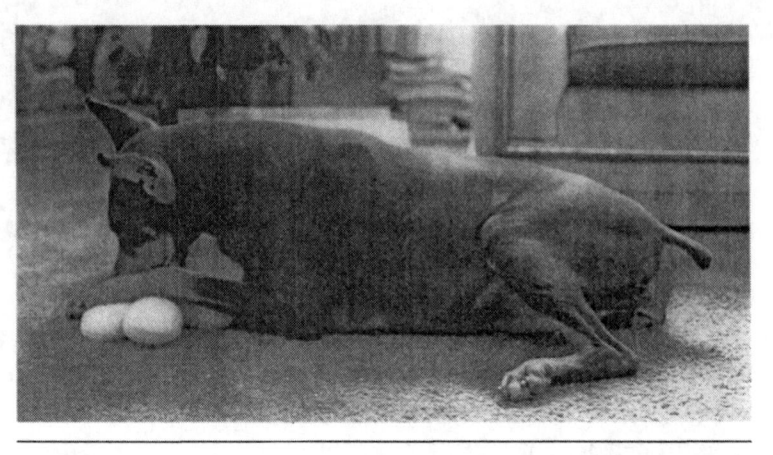

Getting an adult dog means you can avoid the difficult puppy stages. (Sue Korp)

These are not cast-offs. Master breeder Peggy Adamson pointed out many times that if the dog will get more love and attention in a pet home, then it is not uncaring of the breeder to let that dog go. Peggy said that while breeders care dearly about adult dogs, it would be selfish to keep a dog when it is one of many in a breeder's home. These dogs—usually well-trained dogs that are calm in a crowded dog show hall and settle quietly into a crate—can be a prize, indeed.

Young adults may also be available. Sometimes a breeder will keep a quality pup to see how it turns out. A breeder will then decide after four or five months that the dog cannot, for some minor reason, be used in the breeding program or gain a Championship. This animal becomes a coup for anybody searching for a quality dog. A lot of the early training has already been done and many of

the harrowing moments of the early puppy stages have been avoided.

If a dog is offered from a single dog family, then buyer beware. Make sure that you do a complete check on the animal's temperament before buying it. Ask a lot of questions, even if the person trying to sell you an adult dog insists that it is just because he or she is moving into an apartment or going through a divorce. There are obviously many legitimate situations which necessitate giving up a family pet, but a prospective buyer should do a lot of homework on adult dogs to be sure that the animal will absolutely fit into his or her family and lifestyle.

And, on the subject of adult dogs, why not rescue a Doberman in need? The many Doberman Pinscher rescue organizations do a fine job of screening and placing dogs in new homes. These groups take dogs from animal shelters, private homes and other situations, evaluate their temperaments and often give them some basic training, and work hard to find them permanent, loving homes.

The American Kennel Club and the Doberman Pinscher Club of America can help you find rescue groups in your area. You may want to contact a local rescue group to find out if a suitable dog may be available. You will have a dog that is veterinarian-checked and neutered, and an organization that stands behind the dog should you need any help with it.

Rescue organizations require an adoption fee that helps to defray their costs, but it is generally lower than the purchase price of a puppy from a reputable breeder. Plus you have the satisfaction of knowing that you took in a dog greatly in need of a home. Just remember that a rescue dog (or any other adult) comes with a history, which you probably won't know about. Be prepared to be patient until the new family member settles into your home and your way of life.

Cheryl Snyder and Brandy compete in agility. Brandy came from a rescue organization in Michigan. (Karen Taylor)

BLACK, RED, BLUE OR FAWN?

What about the color of your dog? Most people know the Doberman only as a black dog because that's what they see in the movies and on television. The authors especially love red dogs, and over the years have been privileged to share their lives with some unbelievable big red males, always descended from the poster boy in red who helped revolutionize the character of the breed, Ch. Dictator von Glenhugel. Dictator made red popular, and the authors can attest that his excellent temperament is embedded in the red dogs in this country.

Blues and fawns don't have widespread popularity with the Doberman fancy, primarily because of inherent coat problems that leave them with far fewer active hair follicles per square inch than the blacks and reds. While the colors may be attractive, especially as pups when the coats are fuller, the long-term problems make them hard for breeders to sell. These dogs are often full-coated through maturity and then begin to lose hair. Some have attendant skin disorders.

On the other hand, people who have lived with blues and fawns say they are most definitely

This is the classic black color. (Joanna Walker)

Am./Can Ch. Wingates's Leading Edge, CDX, CGC, TDI, ROM nicely represents the red color. (Ellice)

different, in a nice way, and some will argue that they may be superior in intelligence. Rod Humphries has a pet fawn male that he loves with a passion. The dog is very handsome, athletic, tough but not silly about it and has a high pain threshold. His intelligence level is definitely *magna cum laude.*

The white Doberman has been rejected by the Doberman Pinscher Club of America, and we feel adamant that it should not be encouraged and that prospective buyers should not be enticed by the so-called "rare" value. White Dobermans are albinos—a genetic mutation with some serious shortcomings in how they tolerate bright light and

High Halo's Calypso was one of the first fawn dogs to appear in the show ring. (Joan Brearley)

skin abnormalities, including cancer. Some of the early white dogs, in particular, had poor temperaments. This is a fad color that will never be allowed into the mainstream of American Dobermans. In fact, the American Kennel Club has tagged all dogs with white descendants with a Z on their registration number, so any novice wishing to avoid this mutation should check the registration number of the parents of a prospective puppy to ensure that they are not unwittingly purchasing a dog that carries the mutation.

THE IMPORTANCE OF A CONTRACT

It is incredible that people who buy, sell, breed and show dogs have so much trouble dealing with each other. People who have been friends for years may end the friendship simply because they did not take the time to discuss a deal and then put it in contract form. Verbal contracts have a way of being interpreted differently a year or two later.

Many top-quality puppies are sold on co-ownership or breeding rights contracts quite simply because the breeder cannot keep every one of his or her top pups at home. He or she is, in effect, widening the kennel activities to include people he or she trusts. Top-quality bitches are often sold with a proviso that the buyer agrees to allow the breeder to have one or two litters from the bitch. The breeder may contract for the pick-of-the-litter bitch or a split of the pups.

There are other kinds of puppy contracts, including time payment sales to good owners who cannot afford the entire price all at once. Joanna Walker has often contracted with trusted people who could not afford the price of a puppy at all by allowing them to take a bitch puppy on a breeding agreement. The contract calls for Joanna to choose the stud dog and take her pick of pup or pups, and then the registration papers are signed over to the owner.

Some breeders will have contracts in which they insist the pup be shown in the conformation ring, often by the breeder. There are also contracts with professional handlers where all the details of a show career for a dog are spelled out in a written agreement.

Why would anybody be interested in buying a pup with contracts and strings attached? Elementary, my dear puppy buyer. Good breeders are just not going to let their very best animals go without some assurance of being able to tap into that dog's

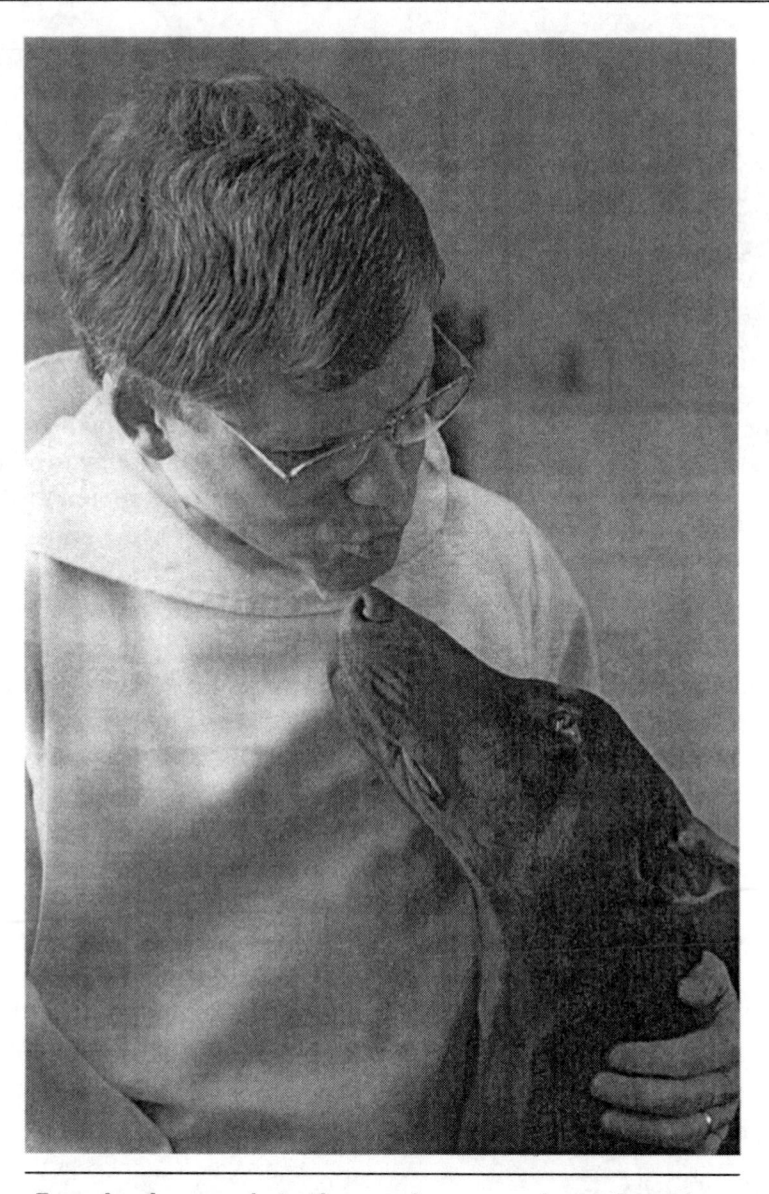

Every dog deserves a loving home and a contract that spells out the terms of endearment. Rev. Mark Showalter and his dog Marks-Tey Star of the Moment share a moment here. Joanna Walker has raised many Dobermans that have become Pilot Dogs for the blind.

AN EXAMPLE OF CO-OWNERSHIP

Rod Humphries has a standard co-ownership contract in which he sells a Championship-quality puppy bitch below market value and retains the option to breed that bitch once. He gets to choose the stud dog and to raise the litter at his kennel for reasons of quality control and evaluation. The owner, who has already gotten a top-quality pup for less than market value, receives one puppy other than the pick, or a cash payment after the litter is born. Rod pays for shipping and all litter costs. Nine times out of ten he will not call up that option, but it is there in case he needs it. As soon as the contractual agreement is fulfilled, either by a litter or a pass on the option, the bitch is signed over to the owner.

In the case of an outstanding male puppy he cannot keep at his home, Rod will sell for below market value price on a co-ownership, with the option to have a number of free stud services from the dog.

---

bloodlines in the future. So if you want the best from the best, you may have to sign a contract. It is certainly true that many a Championship-quality pup has been sold outright with no strings. But if a buyer is after the crème de la crème, then the odds increase with a contracted puppy from a top breeder. After all, if the pup was no good the breeder wouldn't be going to all that trouble. And for the prospective buyer, it will almost certainly be worth all that trouble.

Many breeders also insist on contracts for the sale of their pet pups. Don't be put off by them—they usually protect the buyer as much as the seller. Just make sure you read any contract carefully and make sure you understand every provision before you sign.

CHAPTER 6

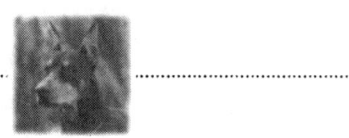

Understanding and Training Your Doberman

A ccording to scientists, the domestic dog is probably only 20 or so genes removed from its ancestor the wolf. Early humans domesticated the wolf, softening the temperament in the process, but while you can take the dog out of the wolf, you cannot take the wolf out of the dog. Every instinct that is observed in the domestic dog is straight out of its wild forebear.

It is essential that any individual or family that takes on the responsibility of a Doberman, or any breed, has a working knowledge of the basic hand-me-down traits in the canine. Your Doberman Pinscher is subject to an intricate system of instincts that are mostly triggered by key stimuli. For example, predatory instincts, often called prey drives, are triggered when another animal takes flight. Running children, joggers, a scurrying cat, a bicycle rider or even a car can set off a chase. Chasing may be mostly harmless, but sometimes it can end with a nip or a more determined bite by a strong-willed dog. Owners, parents in particular, need to understand such instincts and avoid the stimuli that may lead to problems. They also need to train the dog from an early age to distinguish between chasing a ball and chasing a child. Often all that is needed to satisfy this latent prey drive is to a substitute a ball or a Frisbee, coupled with some determined training by the owner.

THE PACK INSTINCT

Understanding the influence of *canis lupus*, the wolf, on today's *canis familiaris*, the domestic dog, begins with understanding that your new puppy's brain does not work like yours. The dog is a pack animal and, like any species of mammal that lives, hunts and breeds in a group, dogs must live by a social structure that facilitates ease of living for the group as a whole. That structure necessitates a social order where equality is non-existent and a pecking order is strictly maintained. Dominance is asserted by one pack member over another, and each individual is very aware of its place in the pecking order. With dominance there is sometimes attendant aggression, a subject important to all Doberman owners.

Pack life, with its attendant pecking order, is the underlying foundation of all a dog's motivation and instincts, and its human family becomes the surrogate pack for the domestic dog. In the wild, the puppy is trained by the older members of the pack in every phase of life, from hunting to survival. It is extremely important that members of the new Doberman's human pack become the substitutes to teach the pup all it needs to know to be a canine good citizen. This must include

Understanding your dog's instincts will enable you to channel them to constructive activities. Warlock and Duke are members of Missouri Search and Rescue K-9. (Irene Korotev)

setting boundaries for the pup. By that we do not necessarily mean physical barriers in rooms of the house, but boundaries of behavior in everything from barking to biting. The dog's brain is configured for the social structure of the pack, and training by humans serves both to guide the young animal and to establish the humans as higher-ranked pack members. This cements a valuable bond between the pup and its human pack members.

DOMINANCE AND THE PECKING ORDER

Dominance is an integral part of a dog's life. This does not mean that in the wild pack members are always jostling and fighting among themselves. Rather, the established hierarchy is a social rule that enables the pack to survive. The prime reason for a pecking order is to keep fighting to a minimum. Packs have to hunt, defend territory, share food and raise offspring as a team, so there have to be rules. There have to be cooperation and a minimum of conflict, injury and stress. That is the end result of dominance.

There is a myth that the top male in a pack (called the alpha male)

The pecking order is something dogs really understand. Dominance and submission enable them to cooperate in a pack.

dominates with constant aggression. This is simply not true. He does not need to use his obvious physical strength and aggression to control the lower-ranked pack members. Although this animal is often bigger and stronger than other pack members, he is very secure in himself and generally only has to posture to gain attention and keep control. Low-ranking animals rarely generate any problems for the alpha male because they are the more timid individuals. Most of the problems with fighting and jostling come from the middle of the pack, where there are young males with aspirations to lead and dominate, and others that are insecure about the animals below them.

We have watched for decades as the pecking order game is played out in our kennels.

Higher-ranked dogs have dominated younger animals by placing their entire mouth over the head of the youngster, often with a blood-curdling growl. The young animal sometimes urinates in fear and remains perfectly still. Often the underling lies on its back with all four feet in the air. When the superior dog believes it has made its point, it allows the subordinate to leave. Submission is very simple: Lie flat and do not move. After that first episode, there is generally no more need for the high-ranked dog to display aggression; posturing and a reminding growl will most often do the trick. Many Dobermans will "smile" by showing their teeth with a gurgling sound. The smile has long tickled Doberman owners, but it is nothing more than a gesture of submission when the higher-ranked family member returns home or enters the room. Dogs that lie down or urinate when their master comes home are often just doing the same thing, showing their submission.

THE PACK IN YOUR FAMILY

So what in the world does any of this have to do with you and your Doberman Pinscher? Plenty. When your young Doberman enters your home, you become its pack, and its instinct is to find its place in the pecking order.

Most often the man of the house is determined by the dog to be the leader. Depending on the dog's innate temperament, its strength of character, its ambitions, and how the woman of the house reacts to the new canine member, the woman will either be ahead of the dog in the pecking order or, ominously, below it in the mind of the dog. The children, often very young ones, mostly do not rate in the mind of the dog and are dismissed to the bottom of the pecking order—especially those born after the dog has matured. This scenario is played out millions of times a year when a family buys a pet dog. Statistics show that there are a million reported dog bites in the United States each year, and approximately 40 percent are due to dominance aggression. You can see why an understanding of basic canine instincts is so important when you bring a dog into your family!

The Doberman has a relatively high incidence of dominance aggression. That doesn't mean every Doberman has it, or even 1 in 10, or 1 in 50. Nobody can say with certainty just how often this occurs because people, including uncaring breeders who are often apt to hide things that may be detrimental to the sale of puppies, are embarrassed to talk about it. But it *is* there and it must be understood.

The Doberman is no different from other breeds when it comes to this phenomenon, which can manifest itself between the age of one and four years. Scientists believe it coincides with the age at which the wolf reaches maturity. The onset, which can bring overzealous guarding of food or a bed or just standing in a hallway growling at family members who dare to pass, may sometimes flare into seemingly unprovoked attacks on family members who thought they had a wonderful relationship with the dog. This is not true viciousness in the doggy sense of the word, but it is mostly dominance aggression where a middle-order pack member is trying to step up a notch or put down

When a young Doberman enters your home, its first instinct is to find its place in the family pack. (Alan & Jacquie Wendt)

what it considers to be a threatening subordinate. Still, it is often a shock for a family to have a dog that has never shown any signs of aggression suddenly exhibit a different personality.

Just as important is understanding the subtle maneuvers dogs use in the dominance game. For example, if a Doberman is very attentive and constantly wants to be patted, if it keeps pushing itself on a family member and that member always responds by patting the dog, the animal might begin to believe the patting is an acknowledgement of its dominant position in the pack. When the dog demands attention, it gets it. If this is the kind of dog that would back up its challenges, then the family is creating a problem.

Often the family makes things worse by not training the dog, and therefore allows the unruly animal to believe it ranks above humans in its pack. Untrained dogs allowed to sit on the couch or sleep on the bed often begin to believe that they are at, or near, the top of the family hierarchy. When commanded or physically removed, they will react with a growl, or sometimes more. The person who feeds the dog when it demands to be fed, or refuses to admonish the dog and will not retrieve a food item stolen from the dinner table, is asking for long-term trouble.

Training is imperative, and if all family members work with the dog it is likely to enforce their dominant position. Physical restraint is a major first step in teaching a pup to submit. The puppy should not be allowed to think that it can have its own way and dominate a human in the pack. We spend a lot of time physically restraining pups, sometimes just holding them back from things

There's nothing wrong with letting your dog up on the furniture, as long as the dog understands it's by your invitation. (Rod Humphries)

they want to do. They will struggle, sometimes very hard, and then finally resign themselves.

We also believe breeders should expose their pups to the real world of pack life before they are sent to their new homes. Some pups leave their mother at six to eight weeks without the discipline of pack life. The mother gives young offspring good lessons in submission and courtesy, but this is accelerated when a young pup is allowed to run with other big dogs before it leaves for its new home. Some breeders will coddle their pups and keep them isolated from older dogs for fear of them being hurt. But keeping a pup for 10 to 12 weeks before letting it go to its new home, and letting it be exposed to cranky old dogs who have little tolerance for the exuberance and silliness of youth, are valuable lessons. Woe betide any pup who thinks that the tennis ball or stick in front of the older male is fair game!

Dominance and its attendant aggression are not strictly a Doberman thing. They are an animal kingdom thing. Believe it or not, some of the most dominant aggressive breeds include the English Springer Spaniel, the Poodle and the Lhasa Apso. And this does not necessarily involve just *male* Dobermans, although they are more inclined toward this behavior. There are many cases of females who want to dominate. Still, the authors are always hesitant to sell a male to a first-time Doberman home with small children. Females, who often will tolerate more than males, are invariably a better proposition for a first-time Doberman family.

UNDERSTANDING DOMINANCE POSTURES

Among the many behavioral traits handed down from the wolf to the domestic dog is the greeting, a ritual in which the subordinate licks the mouth of the superior pack member. The Doberman is a boisterous greeter who will gleefully jump up on family members and even visitors who are well-known to the animal, often in an attempt to lick the face. While it can be cute for a little puppy to jump on a human, it is not so cute when a big male wants to do the same. It is not only unsatisfactory behavior, but it can cause alarm from

unsuspecting humans, who may trigger other canine instincts. A knee in the chest with a sharp "no," the favorite word of any puppy owner, should do the initial trick. The dog should then be trained to approach family and friends and to sit in front of the human to be greeted.

Face licking is also used by wolves and domestic dogs as a general form of affection. The Doberman is very affectionate with pack members and will persist with licks of the hand and face of higher-ranked family members. This "kissing" can be cute, but it can also cause serious problems if somebody forces themselves on the dog for a "kiss." Lower-ranked family members, mostly the children and non-pack members from the neighborhood, had best be very cautious when attempting to obtain a kiss from a Doberman, or any breed. Who would try to kiss an unfamiliar Doberman, you ask? Incredibly, many breeders will tell you that an amazing number of people have tried it—some with deep regret.

What some people do not realize is that dogs are very uncomfortable and are often stimulated to bite when a human throws two hands around its face, smiles—which can be construed by the canine as bared teeth—and gets right in the face of the dog. This can be perceived by the dog as an aggressive posture of stepping across the personal barrier, which instinctively draws a reaction of fight or flight.

Similarly, a higher-ranked wolf will show dominance by laying a paw or its head over the neck and back of a pack member. If the dog whose neck is being covered does not believe it is subordinate, then a fight could follow. When a human thinks he or she can hug a dog of any breed by grabbing it around the neck area, the result might be the same, even if the dog has allowed certain humans in its pack to penetrate its personal barrier. The neck is a vulnerable area and is the first target in a fight, so humans had better be very sure of the dog they are hugging, especially if they are approaching from the rear of the animal.

TEACHING CHILDREN ABOUT CANINE INSTINCTS

A Doberman Pinscher is not a toy for the kids. The old adage "Let sleeping dogs lie" is a profound one when dealing with the Doberman. You should never let the children jump on a resting dog of any breed. Rough play, including wrestling with a Doberman, is to be avoided by young children or unfamiliar adults. Any action or posture that could be construed by the dog to be a sign of aggression should be avoided at all costs.

For example, the Doberman, like the wolf, uses the "stare down" posture as a confrontation for dominance. The first dog to blink or to turn away becomes the subordinate. Years ago, Rod Humphries had a near miss with an untrained young boy who, while visiting his home, confronted a very steady male Doberman who had grown up uneventfully with Rod's trained children. The boy, who was only playing, stood about 10 paces from the dog, placed his hands on his hips, bent at the waist and stuck out his head toward the animal in a game he had no idea was a stimulus for the dog. The dog perceived

A Doberman is not a toy for children. Both dog and child should be taught how to behave around one another. (Joanna Walker)

the boy's posture as a real stare down, and when the boy began imitating a growling dog, the dog raised his hackles and growled in reply, while beginning to stalk the boy. The dog was intercepted, and after the situation was defused, the dog and the boy were introduced properly with absolutely no problem. Unknowing people very often confuse such behavior by the Doberman and other breeds as being "vicious." Not so. After the parents and the boy realized how little they knew about animal instincts and behavior, they were anxious to learn more.

READING A DOG'S BODY LANGUAGE

Body language and posture are vital aspects of the way dogs communicate. All dogs know each others' signs, and the humans who have a new Doberman pup should learn them, too.

A dog's body posture reveals much about its state of mind. This dog is alert and happy. (Rod Humphries)

A dog with the ears laid casually flat against the head and that stump of a tail wagging furiously in rhythm with the whole rear end is in a happy, possibly submissive mode. If the dog's ears are laid flat against the head and the facial expression is one of some fear, with the tail and rear end slightly tucked, approach cautiously.

Ears up and forward with the dog stiff-legged and pulled to its full height with hackles raised and tail erect means you are viewing the total aggressive stage. The dog who struts, has a confident posture and bumps and shoulders other family dogs or humans is one to keep an eye on for possible dominance aggression.

Owners should be aware of the three distinct stages leading to a dog attack. When it raises its hackles—the strip of hair down the neck and back—this is the first sign of agitation. Then there is the low, throaty growl, sometimes with a slight baring of the teeth, which is a warning shot across the bow, so to speak. Ignore it, and the dog will ratchet up to a full display of teeth with a more menacing growl, sometimes sucking in air and drawing noise from deep in the diaphragm. If the first two phases do not bring the desired back-off, the animal will attack with a mighty roar.

Small children are often the targets of aggressive dogs of all breeds, especially dogs with fear aggression, because they are unable to read those signals when an adult is not in the area. A child may have done something to the dog in a previous encounter: hurtfully pulled an ear, poked with a stick or even grabbed at the testicles. The dog may even have been severely admonished by an adult pack member for a low growl in that previous encounter. Now a child is about to step into the dog's personal space, the critical zone, and the reaction could well be dangerous.

THE IMPORTANCE OF SOCIALIZATION

We have talked about socialization earlier in the book, but it is so important that we don't mind repeating it here. We cannot stress enough that every puppy should be exposed to the whole gamut of life, from screaming kids to elderly seniors with walking aids. If you chose your breeder wisely, then the pup's temperament should stand up well. But puppies need to experience life, just as your children do, and the more experience you give them, the better they will handle situations as adult dogs.

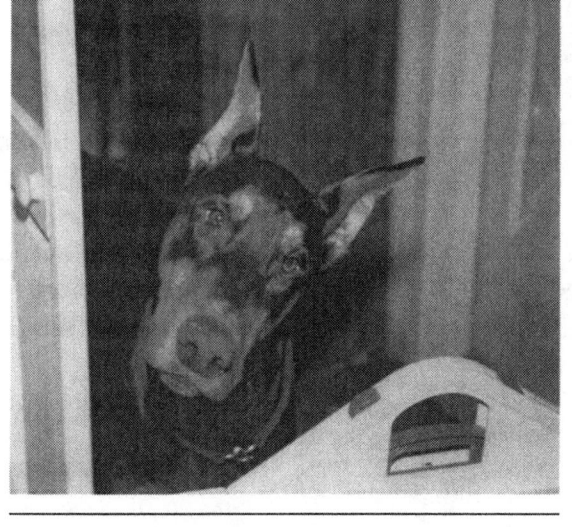

Young dogs need the widest possible range of experiences so that they will be able to handle all kinds of situations as adults. (Rod Humphries)

All wild animals have a kind of personal barrier, a "comfort zone" that they will only let other trusted pack members penetrate. Outside animals or humans who try to cross that invisible line will see the animal either fight or take flight. That personal barrier still exists in the domestic dog, but socializing your Doberman puppy aids in breaking down that barrier to allow not only the immediate family, but also other humans into that inner comfort zone.

It is critical that socialization begin in the early weeks of life and continue through adulthood. It is also critical that the young Doberman, like any other breed, be familiarized with situations and objects to reduce the fear factor later in life.

Imagine trying to deal with a fearful 90-pound Doberman! A dog afraid can hardly control itself, and that leaves *you* little hope of controlling it. Socialization will help here, too. Dobermans raised by breeders with children are always a good bet to be socialized and therefore well adjusted. Some breeders without children will invite neighborhood kids to help do the job. Taking pups on car trips and to places like shopping areas, plus exposing them to yelling crowds at children's sporting events or to the elderly and ill in senior citizens homes, are just some of the valuable socialization and conditioning experiences needed by young Dobermans.

Rod Humphries walks his young puppies in rain showers and storms, particularly when there is loud thunder, so that they will not fear loud noises. On one occasion, lightning hit a nearby tree with a deafening crack and set it afire on his property. The puppies quickly gathered around Rod's feet, but he played cheerfully with them before walking slowly back to the kennel. It was a very close call, but the pups were fine.

There are so many practical things that can be imprinted onto your baby puppy, and even your older puppy, if you just take the time. If you make a list of all the things your dog may encounter and

Senior citizens homes are a good place to socialize a trained dog. The visits can be very happy occasions for the residents, as well. (Gabriele Wentzel)

help the dog get used to them at a young age, then adult life with your Doberman will be much more simple.

Conversely, if there are things you don't want your dog to do in later life, start young in conditioning and training. A 20-pound puppy playing with you on the sofa or the bed may be fun, but it gets a little more difficult when a 70- or 80-pound adult wants to romp the same way. You had better set the ground rules from the beginning.

FOLLOW THE LEADER

Baby puppies seek the safety of proximity to their mothers or pack leaders by following them closely. Human pack members should take advantage of this instinct as the very first training for their little Doberman pup. Training a puppy to walk on a leash is obviously important, but off-lead training with a baby puppy also has its benefits. Too many puppy

STAND STILL, PLEASE

An integral part of socialization is allowing the young Doberman pup to stand for examination by all and sundry. Find people who, with your permission and guidance, will run their hands all over the pup. Make it a game at first, and give the pup lots of praise. You do not want a touch-sensitive adult Doberman who cannot stand for examination at the vet's office, on the grooming table, or in a show or obedience ring.

Joanna Walker's Ch. Marks-Tey Shawn, CD, was a big boy of 93 pounds, and on one visit to the University of Illinois the head of the small animal clinic told a room full of students to weigh the dog on the scales while he attended to some other business. All the students looked at the big Doberman and then at each other, not sure how to proceed. Joanna chuckled, told Shawn to get on the scales and, to the delight of the students, he weighed himself. Shawn's personality, coupled with his socialization and practical training, made him a delight to be around.

owners want to throw a permanent collar and leash on their pups as soon as they get them, when you can practically teach your pups to walk under your feet just by tapping into their desire to feel the safety of proximity to their pack leader.

Try this when you get your puppy home. Just put the little one down, encourage it to follow you around the house and watch what happens. If the pup is distracted by something and lags behind, call it by name and use the word "come." Throw your arms open to the pup when it suddenly realizes it is separated and wants to catch up. Presto! Your puppy is learning its name, and you are on the way to mastering the extremely important skill of having your dog come when it is called.

Imprinting this procedure when a pup is still instinctively seeking safety and security can prevent the problem of the older dog who has never been off lead suddenly bolting and ignoring calls to come.

You can also encourage this skill in slightly older pups with a retractable lead, so that they can have a lot of freedom to move and can also be encouraged to come with a gentle tug and a joyful tone.

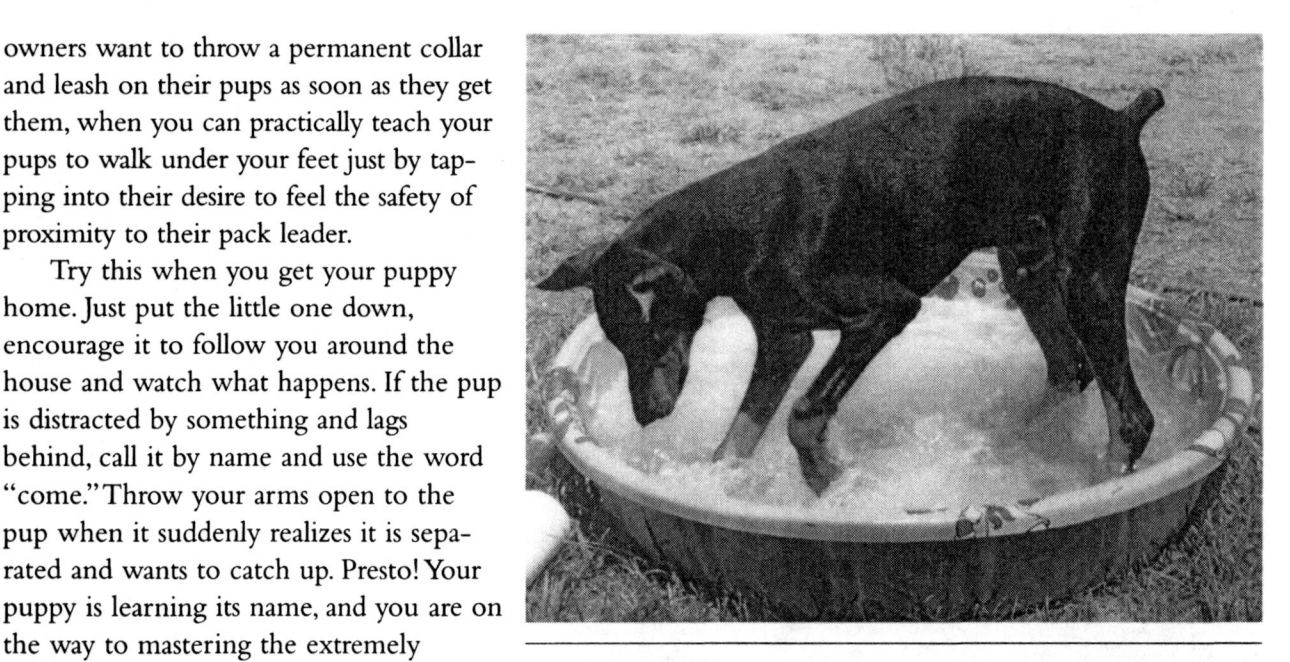

A romping puppy is cute, but a romping adult can be hard to handle. Let your puppy play, but be sure to set some ground rules. (Joanna Walker)

THE CRATE AS A HOUSE TRAINING TOOL

The wild dog is a den animal, and the domestic dog is most comfortable when it has a den-like place to reside. Enter the good old dog crate, the den within the family home. So many people see the crate as a cage, a prison, for the animal. But if your Doberman could speak, it would tell you that a crate is the perfect place—as long as you don't lock the dog in there for an inordinate amount of time. The crate is a haven from the bustle of everyday family life. It is a place to go when the kids are rowdy and the dog wants some peace. It is your dog's place, pure and simple. You can take it on the road and leave the dog secure in its crate in a hotel room and not cause undue agitation for the dog. A home away from home, so to speak.

Crate training is crucial at an early age, and that is why good breeders will expose baby puppies to

Teaching your puppy to follow you off lead will make leash training a lot easier later on. (Joanna Walker)

crates, often without a door, when they are still at the kennel. Dobermans, like all breeds, will avoid soiling their bed, which makes the crate an integral part of house training a puppy.

It is a good idea to crate a new puppy overnight, because the den instincts are strong and a pup feels safe in a cozy crate. As soon as morning comes and the puppy is ready to be released, take it outside to the very place where you would like it to relieve itself. You will probably get best results by carrying the pup to the spot, to make sure there will be no accidents en route.

The old idea of newspaper in the house is not the best way to house train a puppy, because all you are teaching your pup to do is relieve itself in the house. Yes, it's in a specific place, but why teach your pup a lesson you want it to unlearn later? It's easier to start off with the pup eliminating outside.

The secret is to make sure the pup gets it right each and every time. The crate will help with that at night. During the day, follow your baby puppy around the house and at the first sign of sniffing, circling or squatting, quickly pick up the puppy and take it outside to the designated area. It should be a matter of course to take the pup outside after it is released from the crate, after meals and after waking from a nap in the house. If you are diligent and consistent and use the almighty puppy word "No!" when you catch the puppy in the act—and whisk it outside for a chance to do the right thing—housebreaking should be a breeze.

Mind you, there will be times when your puppy will have an accident. Puppies are baby dogs, and they have limited bowel and bladder control. They also can get very excited and forget to heed the call of nature. Please understand this and don't scold your puppy for acts beyond its control. It's also important to know that dogs remember what they've done for about 10 seconds (we're not exaggerating!). That means if you come into the room and find a mess on the floor, it's no use at all dragging the puppy in to point it out and scold the tyke. The puppy will not have a clue what it did wrong. Just clean up the mess and resolve to be more vigilant. *The only corrections that have any impact on the puppy's learning are those made while it is in the act.*

FORMAL TRAINING FOR YOUR PUP

We strongly encourage every new Doberman puppy owner to train his or her dog. You simply cannot live with such a large dog untrained. To be a good citizen, every Doberman should learn the basic commands to come when called, to heel at your side, to sit and to go to a down position, and to stay in place when instructed.

Training begins the day you bring your puppy home. But we also encourage you to follow up with regular classes under the tutorship of a training expert. These will teach you how to teach your Doberman, will help socialize the puppy and will build a stronger bond between you, your dog and your family.

Puppy kindergarten classes are enormous fun. Puppies get a wonderful start and gain a lot of self-confidence as they learn to interact with dogs of other breeds. Most classes will take pups after 16 weeks, when they have received all their shots.

Come and Walk

As we've mentioned, if you can teach your baby puppy to come when it's off lead, then you are well ahead of the game. Using a long retractable lead is a good idea for slightly older pups who are a little more adventurous. If need be, use a long lead or rope and gently tug the dog and call it to come while using the pup's name. Heap praise, no matter how well the puppy does, because

punishing a dog for trying to please but not quite getting it simply teaches the dog that it can never please you, so there's no point in trying.

It is not wise to use food all the time when teaching a dog to come. The extra lure of food can be used far more successfully if it is saved for recalls with a dog who is not coming as fast as you would like.

Walking on leash follows naturally from the "come" command; the dog is learning to follow you closely. In early leash training, the reluctant pup should never be dragged but should be encouraged to follow with positive reinforcement and praise.

The pup that pulls your arm off as it heads down the road can be quickly trained to adjust if you give it slack on the lead and then do an about-turn and head the other way. The startled pup will not only be gently jolted, but it will quickly see the pack leader heading in the opposite direction and will hurry to catch up. Eventually it will get the message that remaining close is what you want and is what is best for the pup. An owner can walk closely along a fence or a wall with the pup sandwiched between to help the pup to learn to walk in a straight line.

Sit and Down

There are a number of methods you can use to teach your Doberman to sit and lie down, and each can be successful. Some instructors like to use food held in front of the pup's nose. When you move the food back over its head, the motion naturally shapes the pup into the sitting

Teaching your dog to sit can avoid all sorts of problems. For example, have your dog sit to greet guests and there will be no jumping up. (Nicole Baron)

position. Praise the dog for a job well done and let it eat the treat. To get the dog to lie down, the food is then moved toward the ground and forward to bring the pup all the way to the ground.

You can also work without food. Simply say "sit" and gently push down on the pup's rump to produce the sit. Don't forget the praise! When the pup is sitting, scoop a hand in front of its legs and gently lower it to the floor as you say "down." Some owners who train show dogs prefer to "collapse" the dog into a "sit" with a gentle push behind the knees. That way the dog won't be inclined to sit when a judge presses on the dog's rump in the show ring. Always remember to tell the puppy what you want, be clear about it, and praise it whenever it ends up in the right position, no matter how it got there.

Stay

Teaching a dog to stay takes more patience, because there are so many distractions for young Dobermans. This command actually starts with the breeder, who will use it to keep pups from rushing out of kennel gates and into dangerous situations. Often it just needs the universal stop sign—a hand in front of the face—with the word "stay" to keep a dog from moving. The stop sign with the command "stay" can later be added to sit and stay, so the dog learns that it must hold a command until advised otherwise. Just remember that young puppies can't stay still for long, and don't expect too much too early.

Repetition, repetition, repetition is the key in all training. Do a little each day. Don't make it boring and train with a lot of praise and some judicial use of treats to encourage your dog. Practice makes perfect.

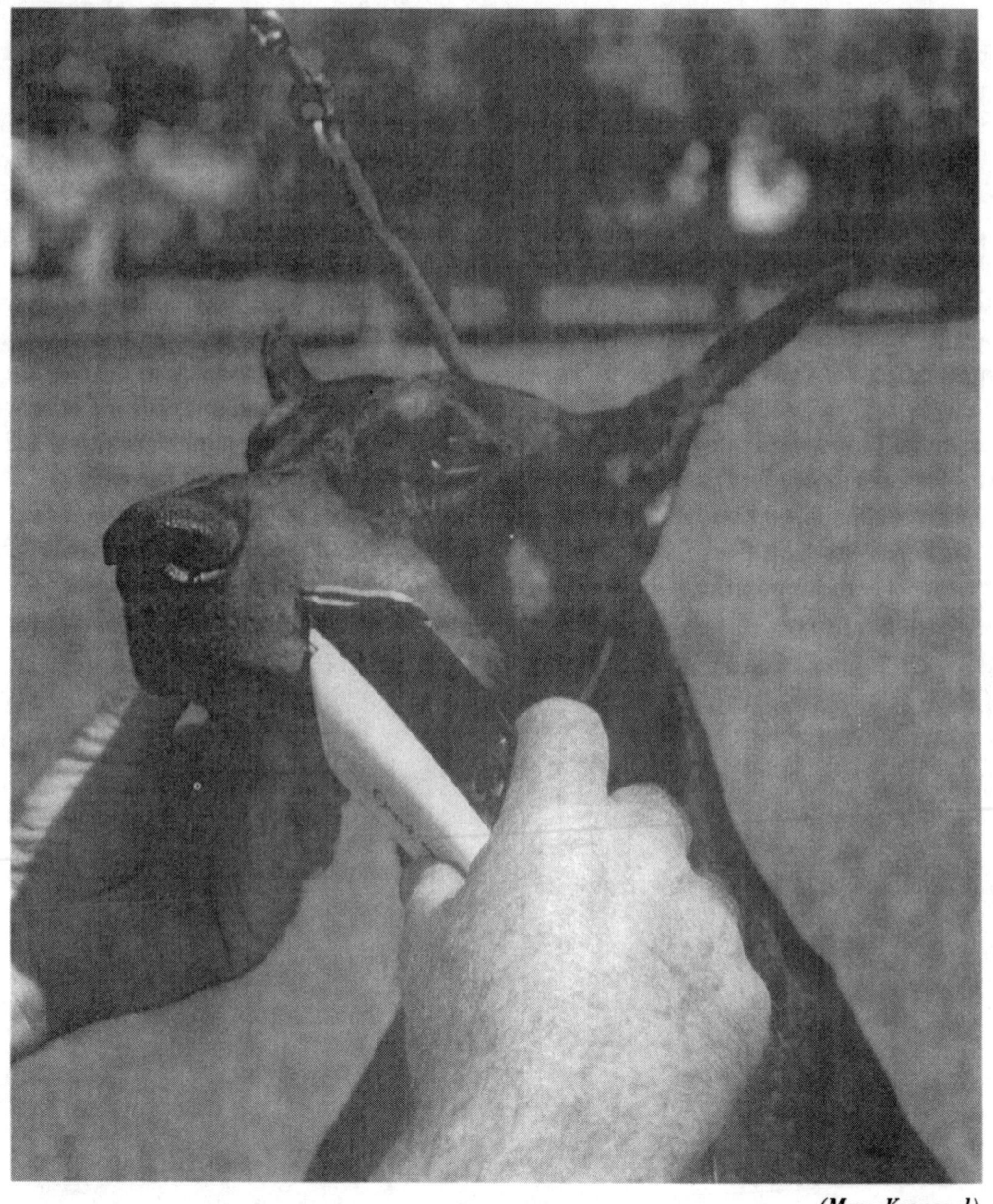

(Mary Knueppel)

CHAPTER 7

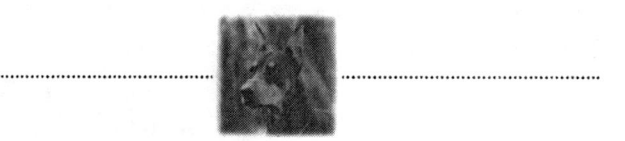

Routine Care of Your Doberman

You have heard it a thousand times: Eat a healthy, nutritious diet and get plenty of exercise. What is good for you is also good for your Doberman Pinscher. There is another important element as well: care in the form of grooming. The Doberman is an easy keeper, but there is basic grooming that must be done regularly.

CHOOSING A FOOD

Proper nutrition is the key to your dog's good health. If a dog is being fed a poor diet with inadequate nutrition, then all care and exercise in the world will be of little or no use.

America, which invented fast food, did a huge favor for dog owners worldwide by developing a fast food for canines: dry kibble that needs little or no preparation. However, this was not necessarily such a huge favor for our dogs, because over the years so many of the commercial dog foods—not to mention the avalanche of doggy treats—have been chemical time bombs.

The Chemical Feast

Dr. Wendell Belfield, author of *How to Have a Healthier Dog* (Orthomolecular Specialties, 1994), began his veterinary career as a meat inspector with the United States Department of Agriculture. He wrote that condemned parts and animals that are rejected for human consumption are commonly used in commercial pet foods. The so-called "4-D's"—meaning dead, dying, diseased or disabled animals—are also used for pet foods. Some pet food contains "chicken by-products," which means beaks, claws and feathers ground into meal, and "beef by-products" which means hooves, horns, skin, hair and organs rejected for human consumption.

Belfield also called commercial dog food a "chemical feast." He wrote, "Commercial dog food, like the master's food, has an ungodly array of chemical additives. Many of the same additives that are used in processed people's food are used in pet food. The standard daily menu of synthetic and manufactured nutrition that we place in our gullets has little or no resemblance to the food that nurtured the evolution of mankind."

Dr. Alfred Plechner, another noted veterinarian-turned-author, wrote in his book *Pet Allergies—Remedies for an Epidemic* (Very Healthy Enterprises, 1985), "30 percent of the ailments I treat in my practice are directly related to food." Skin problems caused by poor food and nutrition, including dry and scaly skin, hair loss and hot spots, are often just the tip of the iceberg, according to Plechner. He is convinced that many dog foods contain extraordinarily high amounts of protein, not always correctly

What's good for you is also what will keep your dog healthy: nutritious, wholesome food and plenty of exercise. If it's good enough for a service dog like Nixie, shown here, it's good enough for any Doberman. (Mardee Edelstein)

labeled on the bag, which, along with other impurities, cause a breakdown of the kidneys, liver and intestines. He believes two widely used preservatives, butylated hydroxyanisole (BHA) and butylated hydroxytoluene (BHT), "have been associated with liver damage, fetal abnormalities, metabolic stress and increased cholesterol in some laboratory testing. They also have a questionable relationship to cancer."

After years of research and practical experience in his practice, Plechner compiled what he calls The Allergic HIT (High in Trouble) List:

1. Beef and beef by-products

2. Milk

3. Yeast (foods and dietary supplements containing yeast and brewer's yeast are often given as a flea protection)

4. Wheat, wheat germ and wheat germ oil

5. Corn and corn oil

6. Pork

7. Turkey

8. Eggs, especially the whites

9. Fish and fish oils

There will no doubt be dog owners who will read this list and say, "I feed that to my dog, and he has no problems." What Plechner and other scientists are saying is that some animals are affected immediately, but most experience some cumulative effects from a lifetime of inappropriate nutrition.

Dogs are carnivores, right? So how could beef top the HIT list? Plechner explains, "It is unlikely you are feeding choice cuts to your animals. More likely you are feeding commercial formulations that include beef from condemned parts and by-products. These are the typical forms of beef generally processed into canned, semi-moist and dry kibble products, into pet snacks such as biscuits and bone treats, into rawhide chew sticks, and into meat sauce, meat meal and bone meal. These entities all have the beef antigen—the offending protein molecule—and it is literally flooding the digestive tracts of animals everywhere."

Until a few years ago, corn was the main ingredient in dry food produced by one of the premier dog food companies. Today most of the premier companies use chicken and lamb as a base. But if you scour the supermarket shelves, you will still see a lot of cheaper dog food brands that have corn as the main ingredient.

Looking for the Best Food

It is vital to the long-term health of your Doberman that you choose premium dog foods and spend time reading labels and asking questions. The dog requires a balance of protein, fat, fiber and a variety of essential vitamins and minerals. The food should be based on easily digestible, less-fatty lamb, chicken or even venison. It is best to choose foods that are preserved by natural and not artificial ingredients. Tocopherols (vitamin E), rosemary extract and citric acid are all natural preservatives that are used in some brands of dog food.

It is also important to select food from companies that tailor their product to various life stages and activity levels. For example, performance dogs, puppies and lactating bitches need more protein and more fat than a middle-aged or senior Doberman. A typical performance-puppy-lactation diet of lamb and rice has a minimum of 25 percent crude protein, a minimum of 15 percent crude fat, a maximum of 4.5 percent fiber and a maximum of 10 percent moisture. A maintenance diet of lamb and rice for the average adult Doberman typically has 20 percent protein and 10 percent fat (minimums), 4 percent fiber and 10 percent moisture (maximums). A senior diet for dogs over six or seven years typically has 16 percent protein and 8 percent fat (minimums), plus 10 percent fiber and 10 percent moisture (maximums).

The best-quality foods will usually cost more because these companies use better ingredients and spend more to ensure the highest quality. And what you spend on the food will be more than made up in other ways. Because better quality foods are more digestible, your Doberman will eat less. It will also have solid, easy-to-clean stools and your vet bills will be far lower.

Choose a food that is suitable for your dog's age and activity level. (Evelyn Stackpole)

What About Treats?

Those highly marketed, slickly packaged dog snacks and treats are often trouble waiting to happen. Not only do they epitomize all the problems we've been describing in terms of chemicals and additives, but they are so high in calories they will make your dog grow fat almost in front of your eyes. Those artificially colored, artificially flavored little time bombs can contain 20 calories in each small dog biscuit and up to 200 calories in the larger treats.

Some dog owners use these snacks for training, feeding them to their dog constantly throughout day. The irony is that the caring, methodical dog owner does broad research to find a good-quality kibble for regular daily meals, then blows it all by giving dry or semi-moist snacks that can be the equivalent of several additional measured cups of food per day.

We have heard scores of stories of Doberman owners who are puzzled by their dogs' excessive weight. "I only give him three or four measured cups of food a day," they say. But they never take into account the high-calorie treats the dog is munching on all day.

What's the solution? Avoid the packaged treats entirely. When you want to treat your dog, use natural foods. And make sure to count the treats when you are figuring how much to feed your dog for the day.

What About Table Scraps?

Just about all veterinarians, nutritionists, and breeders will tell you not to give table scraps and other family leftovers to your Doberman. Why not? First of all, you have to be careful not to create an unwanted nutritional imbalance in the dog's diet.

Also, table scraps are usually high in fat and in the items at the top of the HIT list.

And when it comes to table scraps, few dog owners count up how many calories they are feeding their dogs. Obesity is one result. Veterinarians see a lot of dogs suffering from vomiting and diarrhea after Thanksgiving and Christmas—the legacy of too much turkey and ham.

Rod Humphries gives his dogs some raw fruit and vegetables such as carrots, apples and pears, and they do eat a lot of nuts off the ground—particularly pecans, shells, and all. These are beneficial, but cooked meats off the table are another matter.

Table scraps are a random assortment of whatever you and your family are having, which is why they do not fit into a well-planned, well-balanced diet. However, a growing minority of dog owners is deciding to prepare natural meals for its dogs, using fresh, whole ingredients. If you have the time and the inclination to put your dog on a homemade diet, please talk to a canine nutritionist first. This way, you can be sure your dog is getting the right balance of protein, fat, carbohydrates, vitamins and minerals. Do your research before you begin, so you can be sure you are setting your dog up for better health, not more problems.

HOW MUCH IS ENOUGH?

The amount of food that's right for your Doberman varies with age and activity level. Your breeder should tell you what brand of food to use and how much to give your puppy when you first take it home, and also feeding information for when it is an adult dog. But remember, amount varies with activity level.

You could start with the levels recommended by the breeder or the amount suggested on the package and then do what most experienced Doberman breeders and owners do: Evaluate the condition and weight of your Doberman daily, and adjust its meals accordingly. When viewed from above, the Doberman should have a distinctive shape with width at the shoulders, a good spring of rib, a discernible waist and wide hips. If you look down on your Doberman and see a straight line from the shoulders to the hips, more exercise or less food, or both, are in order to get the dog back into shape. When viewed from the side, there should also be a steady tuckup from the lowest point of the rib cage to the stomach. If the tuckup is severe, the dog is not eating enough. If there is hardly one at all, it needs to lose some weight.

VITAMIN AND MINERAL SUPPLEMENTS

There is some controversy about whether vitamin and mineral supplements are necessary for dogs. The dog food manufacturers generally say they are not. However, many experienced breeders tell another story.

One must remember that there will be many scientific arguments for and against supplementation. Nutrition has not been a priority at medical or veterinary schools, and there is skepticism in this arena. We believe the proof is in the puppies. A high level of supplementation for Rod's

It's important to keep your dog at the proper weight throughout its life for optimum health. (Alan & Jacquie Wendt)

Dobermans over many years has improved their health to where visits to the veterinarian are generally restricted to annual checkups and the occasional injury. Rod's dogs run ruggedly over his six acres in Texas, and he is convinced that additional vitamin C produces good levels of collagen and therefore the connective tissue is strong and injuries and muscle strains are kept to a minimum.

If your dog suffers a twist or a pull and inflammation occurs, then additional vitamin C and shark cartilage can repair it very quickly.

Rod also increases the doses of vitamins C and E during pregnancy, which strengthens the uterine muscles and allows for quicker and easier births. Lactating bitches invariably suffer from dry, itchy coats because of the pressure of producing milk and feeding puppies. Not so at Rod's kennel, where the bitches maintain their coats through the entire process to weaning. These are just some of the benefits of vitamin supplementation.

Vitamin C

Vitamin C, or ascorbic acid, is necessary for life because both human and beast will die a slow death of scurvy within a few short months if deprived of vitamin C. Humans, along with apes and guinea pigs, are among the mammals that make absolutely no vitamin C in their bodies and must ingest it to survive. Dogs make about 40 milligrams of the vitamin per kilogram (2.2 pounds) of body weight in the liver. This sounds like a lot, until you realize that a rabbit produces 226 milligrams and a mouse makes 275 milligrams per kilogram of body weight.

What does vitamin C do for your dog (and you)? It is a long list. First, it is necessary to maintain the body's immune system and ward off all kinds of problems. One that is common in the Doberman is a blown coat, which means staph infection, hair loss, hot spots, pustules and so on. This is often due to a depleted immune system that has allowed bacteria on the coat to attack the hair follicles.

Second, vitamin C helps to produce collagen, a fibrous constituent of connective tissue, bone and cartilage—in effect, the cement of the body. Third, it is an antioxidant that helps the body fight free-radical molecules, which are a cause of cancer. And if that is not enough, consider that vitamin C is also an analgesic (pain killer), an antiviral agent, an antihistamine and an anti-inflammatory. It is truly a wonder.

Dog food manufacturers disagree that supplements are necessary, because they claim their dog food is a complete and balanced diet. They argue that because dogs make ascorbic acid in their liver, it is not necessary to include it in the dog food. Some actually include small amounts, but such small quantities have little additional benefit to the animal. They also do not take into account the fact that some dogs make less than normal amounts of vitamin C in their bodies, so they start behind the eight ball, so to speak.

The link between vitamin C and good health has been widely studied. Dr. Wendell Belfield, a disciple of two-time Nobel Prize–winner Dr. Linus Pauling, wrote, "Stress, in the case of our household pets, sorely taxes and depletes an already low vitamin C output. I have found that the liver of a dog or cat with high temperature makes little or no ascorbic acid. Dogs with skin disease have been tested and found to have low blood levels of vitamin C." There is some scientific evidence that the use of antibiotics depletes vitamin C. Cigarette smoking is also known to lower vitamin C levels in humans, and it's reasonable to assume that if the dog is inhaling secondhand smoke, it is also being affected.

Your new Doberman puppy is going to experience enormous stress, particularly in the first 18 months of life, and it is unlikely it can make enough vitamin C itself to cope. The puppy will be stressed when it has its tail docked at day two or three of its life; its ears cropped at about eight weeks and the ongoing cleaning and wrapping; early parvo shots and then permanent vaccinations; de-worming; separation from mother and littermates; traveling to a new home and settling into a new family pack; teething; and obedience training. Dogs that are going to be shown experience even more stress. Belfield's experience is that such stressful conditions place a demand on the dog for ascorbic acid that it is unable to meet naturally.

What happens when these vitamin C needs are not met? According to Belfield, the stage is set for a condition known as chronic subclinical scurvy. *Chronic* means the condition is always there. *Subclinical* means that symptoms are less severe and less identifiable than the signs of terminal scurvy. In other words, the body is getting enough vitamin C to remain alive, but not enough to ward off problems. As with humans, chronic colds, influenza, backaches, bad knees and other joint pain can be the result.

Vitamin E

Vitamin C's famous running mate is vitamin E, scientifically known as d-alpha tocopherol in the natural form and dl-alpha tocopherol in the synthetic form. Interestingly, the man who devoted much of his career to studying vitamin E, the late Dr. Wilfrid Shute, was also a Doberman breeder

Vitamin C can help a puppy cope with the many stresses of early life.

done on more than 30,000 patients. The Shute brothers believed unequivocally that vitamin E was a heart saver, and Wilfrid vigorously promoted his theories to all dog fanciers.

Sudden death due to heart problems has become a major killer in Dobermans. Wilfrid Shute wrote in his book *Health Preserver: Defining the Versatility of Vitamin E* that this problem is caused by a narrowing or blockage of a tiny blood vessel supplying the nerve mechanism in the heart that controls the heartbeat. He was sure it could be prevented with vitamin E.

Like vitamin C, vitamin E is also multifaceted. It is an antioxidant, it boosts the immune system, it aids in healing, it improves muscle power and stamina, it rejuvenates older dogs and it is an aid in improving the efficiency of other vitamins and minerals. "Its influence becomes clear when we see that sufficient vitamin E is essential to the most basic body systems, and when it is missing they are certain to break down," Shute wrote. "Increase vitamin E intake and the process is sure to be reversed."

Vitamin E can be found naturally in nuts, olives and leafy greens. How many of these do you think your Doberman is likely to eat in a day? That is why many top scientists and top breeders believe supplementation is vital to your dog's health.

The Antioxidant Team

Vitamins C and E are also the best fighters of free radical molecules. Free radicals cause oxidation of the cells—a kind of damage seen in cancer, heart disease, and other degenerative problems.

and judge and was a former president of the Doberman Pinscher Club of America. Shute and his brother, Dr. Evan Shute, were pioneers of vitamin E therapy, beginning in the 1940s with studies

This antioxidant team that daily battles the nasty free radicals includes two other important members: vitamin A and the mineral selenium. Selenium is also currently receiving wide attention for its role in fighting heart disease.

Vitamin A is also very good for the skin. The epithelium (the top layer of skin cells) and other parts of the body are strengthened and lubricated by Vitamin A. Dobermans are known for what is commonly referred to as "Doberman dandruff," but vitamin A should either eliminate it or keep the problem to an absolute minimum.

Vitamin supplements can help keep your dog's coat shiny and healthy. (Mary Knueppel)

Supplements for a Healthy Coat

The Doberman coat is a tricky part of overall Doberman health. While it may look sleek and shiny and easy to keep, it can pose some real problems. When the immune system is boosted by vitamins C and E, and when vitamin A is at work, there is normally little to worry about. Other supplements that help keep Doberman coats healthy are zinc (a mineral) and vitamin F (essential fatty acids). Zinc speeds healing and is important to the function of the immune system and the prostate gland.

The Dosage

The list of vitamins and minerals necessary for you and your Doberman is a long one, and it is not possible to give that entire list here. The aforementioned C, E, A, selenium, zinc, and essential fatty acids are all separate supplements that Rod gives his Dobermans daily. He covers the other essentials, including the B-complex, iron and potassium, with a doggy multivitamin available through most veterinarians and from many of the veterinary catalogs.

But how much should you give of each supplement? Let us begin by listing Belfield's recommended dosages for the major supplements, including the antioxidant team. These are in milligrams, micrograms and international units—the same way dosages are listed on vitamins made for humans.

The variations in vitamin C are based on activity level; the higher dose is for the most active dogs.

SIZE OF DOG	VITAMIN C (MG/DAY)	VITAMIN E (IU/DAY)	VITAMIN A (IU/DAY)	ZINC (MG/DAY)	SELENIUM (MCG/DAY)
Medium	1,500–3,000	200	3,000	10	25
Large	3,000–6,000	200	5,000	30	50

You can feed these supplements twice a day, breaking the dosages into equal amounts at each meal. Rod buys all his vitamins from a popular national supermarket chain to keep the cost to a minimum. Do look for the natural vitamin E (d-alpha tocopherol) rather than the synthetic product (dl-alpha tocopherol).

At Rod's kennel, the vitamin C dose rises steadily from drops of less than 1 mg at birth to 1,000 mg at 8 weeks, 2,000 mg at 12 weeks, and 3,000 mg at 16 weeks and continues to rise steadily to the adult dose of 6,000 mg a day. The levels rise with the pup's ability to tolerate the supplement; vitamin C, if rushed, will cause diarrhea. Rod increases the dosage to 8,000 or 10,000 mg a day if there is major stress or injury. Pregnant bitches go to 8,000 mg a day, while dogs on the show circuit normally get 8,000 mg a day because of the extra stress.

It is extremely important to understand that vitamin C will cause diarrhea if it is not introduced slowly to the system. So many Doberman owners give too large a dose when it is first introduced, which causes loose stools, and they completely drop the supplementation because they think their dogs are allergic to it. If a dog has trouble tolerating the acidity of ascorbic acid, Belfield recommends using sodium ascorbate, which is a slightly alkaline version of vitamin C.

Vitamin E should be introduced slowly at about 8 weeks. Rod pinpricks a softgel of the smallest vitamin E supplement he can obtain (100 IUs), and places one drop into the pup's food. That drop is roughly 30 to 40 IUs. The level rises to 100 IUs by 12 weeks, 200 IUs by 16 weeks, and then slowly to the adult dose of 400 IUs. This is increased to 600 IUs during pregnancy. Rod uses higher doses than those recommended by Belfield.

Vitamin A is also introduced very slowly, starting at about three months. Rod pinpricks a softgel of the smallest vitamin A supplement he can obtain (5,000 IUs), and gives one drop of about 500 to 1,000 IUs into the food. It is then moved up slowly but steadily to the adult dose of 5,000 IUs.

Zinc, selenium and multivitamin tablets are generally broken into quarters at about three months and then halves, rising steadily to the adult doses.

Vitamin C is water-soluble and passes quickly if not absorbed. Therefore, the dosage should be given throughout the day; at least twice a day with meals is better than just one big dose. Vitamin E and Vitamin A are fat-soluble and are therefore stored in the body. That is why extremely high doses are to be avoided.

EXERCISE FOR HEALTH

The Doberman is a high-spirited, high-energy dog, and for the health of the animal—and the peace of the home—regular exercise is a must. If you can find a large enclosed area such as a park, an unused football field or any place where it is safe to run your dog off a leash, this is highly recommended as the best form of exercise. The Doberman is a wonderful galloper and revels in wide-open spaces.

Wherever you exercise your dog, remember that many people are still very uninformed about the real temperament of the American Doberman today. You should be very careful not to upset other people walking or exercising dogs in the area. And you had better have your dog trained to come on command, or you are asking for trouble. Be a caring owner, and make sure your Doberman is a good canine citizen.

If you do not have access to open spaces, a two- to three-mile walk every day will keep your dog in excellent shape. It would be even more beneficial if you can break your day into two or three walks. Early leash training to avoid being

The Doberman is a high-energy dog, and it needs room to run. (Rod Humphries)

dragged around the neighborhood is obviously a top priority. Make sure your Doberman learns to heel correctly so that the walks are pleasant (more about that in Chapter 6). Once heeling is mastered, you can advance to a long retractable leash that allows the dog more freedom on walks. The retractable leash is a wonderful invention, but it needs to be handled with care, especially if you are walking on a sidewalk and you have enough slack on the leash so that your Doberman can still dart into traffic.

Doberman Pinschers have strong prey drives, so you can give them hard exercise by throwing tennis balls, Frisbees, sticks and other objects. Whatever form of exercise best suits your lifestyle and environment, do it regularly for the health of your dog, and make sure that the energy is directed into exercise rather than mischief around the home.

GOOD GROOMING

This is where the Doberman owner has a distinct advantage over owners of most other breeds. The weekly grooming time is minimal, and getting ready for dog shows is a breeze compared to many of the long-haired breeds. However, there is clipping and snipping and cleaning to be done, and their necessity should never be underestimated by the new Doberman owner.

Trimming Nails

You should trim a dog's nails regularly, perhaps once or twice a month. Some owners will use the guillotine nail cutters, and they work just fine. However, with these cutters you can cut the quick—that bundle of blood vessels and nerves inside the nail—causing the dog considerable pain. That's why experienced breeders and owners use nail grinders especially designed for canine toenails. Nail grinders allow you to work the nail back to the quick without causing bleeding or pain.

It's important to remember that the quick grows along with the nail, so if you don't trim the nail, eventually you will not be able to trim much off without cutting the quick and hurting the dog. We would like to say that we abhor the lazy practice of letting the nails grow excessively long and then having them cut off under anesthesia. It is not a difficult process to correct excessively long nails in just a few weeks by grinding back to the quick, waiting three or four days for the quick to recede, and then repeating the operation until the nails are normal length.

Many breeders introduce puppies to the nail grinder and to electric hair clippers when they are just a few weeks old. You can use the hair clipper

Nail grinders will enable you to cut your dog's nails short without causing any pain. (Mary Knueppel)

as a massager by running it all over the pup's body. The low noise and the vibrating action prove very soothing for young pups, and it teaches them not to be afraid. You can also supplement guillotine clippers with the noisy grinder at a few weeks,

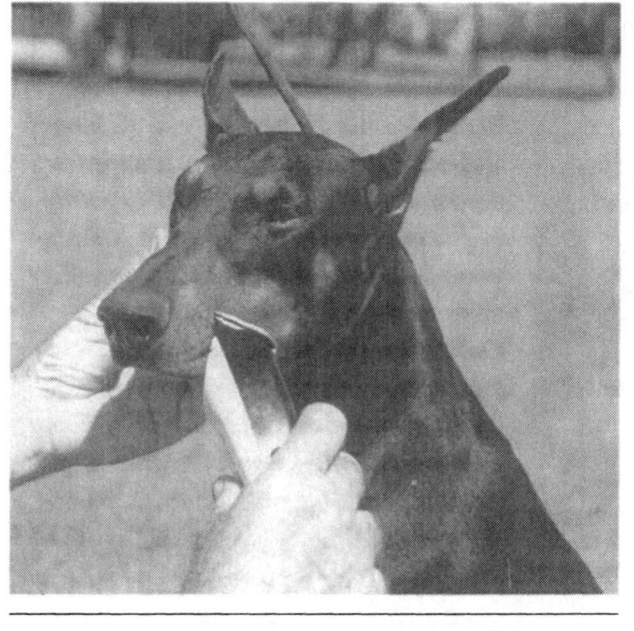

Trimming is easy for a Doberman. Just trim off anything that sticks out. (Mary Knueppel)

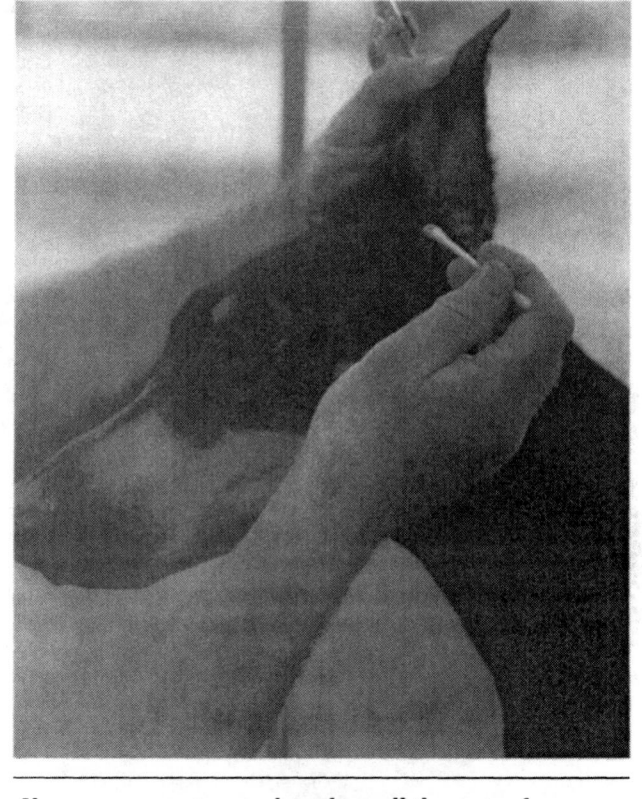

You can use a cotton swab to clean all the parts of your dog's ears that you can see. Never stick anything into the dog's ear canal. (Mary Knueppel)

merely touching the top of the nail and finishing the exercise quickly so as not to upset the pups. If the breeder has not used the electric tools, you can still have success if the tools are introduced slowly and with patience.

A Little Haircut

Dobermans have very short hair, and you might not think they need any trimming, but they do. When asked what hair should be removed from a Doberman, one long-time breeder-judge replied, "Anything that sticks up!" Use electric clippers to trim the whiskers on the muzzle and protruding hair above the ears and on the cheeks. Unsightly hair around the ears, under the tail, at the back of the legs and along the "skirts" of the tuckup is also removed. Some Doberman show owners will thin out the hair on the underside of the neck to give it a cleaner appearance. This routine requires a thinning blade so that the hair is not shaved right to the skin.

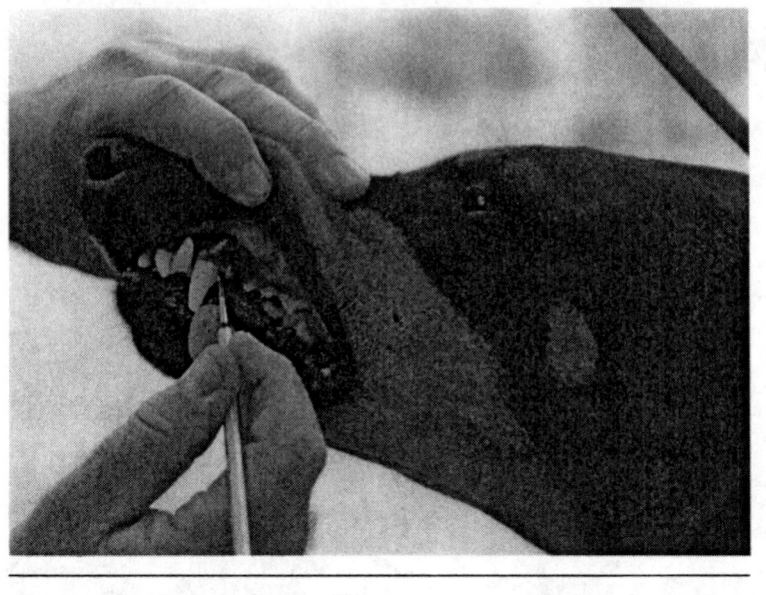

Your veterinarian can show you how to scrape your dog's teeth, or you can take the dog in for a professional cleaning. (Mary Knueppel)

Brush and Bath

You should also brush your Doberman regularly with a natural bristle brush. It's good for the dog, and it's good for you. When you groom your dog, check it all over for parasites, skin disorders and other problems that might otherwise go undetected. Sometimes a tick will lodge itself in the skin and be detected only at grooming time.

Ticks and other mites also get into the ears, so check your dog's ears weekly for any little hitchhikers and for a buildup of grime and wax. A dog's ears should look and smell clean. If they don't, put some rubbing alcohol on a cotton swab and clean all the parts of the ear you can see. Do not stick anything into the dog's ear canal.

Bathing your Doberman should also be a regular thing, but while some like to do it once a week, other owners have found that the Doberman can go longer without periods of bathing. It depends on the dog's activity level and exposure to places where it can get dirty. A shampoo made just for dogs should be sufficient to clean the coat, but many Doberman owners will use a coat enhancer, mink oil or a silicone-based liquid on the damp coat to give a glossy appearance. Please don't use your shampoo on your dog, because it can really dry out the skin.

Keeping the Teeth Clean

Regular checks of the teeth are important because tartar buildup, if unchecked, can cause gum disease and tooth loss. Dog food manufacturers will sometimes advertise that their dry dog food or biscuits will help remove tartar. If anything, we've found the opposite to be true.

Some owners are now using doggy toothpaste for clean teeth and breath. (Don't use your own toothpaste on dogs because they can't rinse and spit the way we can.) However, removing tartar is the main objective, and a good scraping tool used regularly can be of great benefit in avoiding teeth problems for the older dog. Ask your veterinarian to show you how to use one, and be very careful, as these tools are quite sharp. Never ask your dog to stand still for more than a few minutes of scraping. Just do a few teeth at a time.

Rawhides, bleached and chemically prepared for sale, are not good for your dog and certainly do not help to clean teeth, as they are sometimes advertised. Also, rawhides are difficult to chew, and many Dobermans try to swallow the moist hide whole, which can cause problems. Bones that do not splinter, such as large knucklebones, can be given sparingly to Dobermans to help control tartar, but for the most part it is up to you to keep your dog's mouth in good shape. Regular dental care, from either you or your veterinarian, will help you accomplish that goal.

(JoAnn James)

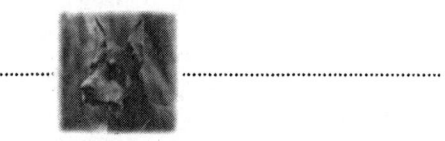

Keeping Your Doberman Healthy

T he health of a dog begins long before birth, when a puppy's breeder makes a myriad of decisions, not the least of all about the health history of the animals to be bred. Like all animals, including humans, the Doberman has its share of genetic problems, primarily the Killer C's: cancer, cardiomyopathy and cervical vertebral instability. A breeder has an obligation to the puppy itself, to the breed in general and to the people who receive that puppy, to avoid certain dogs or a family of dogs that have these problems. This is no guarantee that the puppy will have a disease-free life, but it is an enormous step in the right direction.

Sometimes it can be a most difficult decision, as the dog or dogs involved may be great show winners or wonderful working dogs who otherwise have all the important traits a breeder needs for the program. But breeders need to be strong in their conviction; they should take matters firmly into their own hands and be tough and diligent in eliminating a problem when it arises in their stock.

Today the awareness of genetic and general health of purebred dogs is much higher, and buyers are demanding more from their breeders. This is a good thing. It pushes puppy buyers to seek out responsible breeders who stand the behind the pups they sell with health tests and carefully planned breeding programs.

However, it's important to understand that a breeder can never be 100 percent certain that any dog is genetically sound. Genetics is both a science and an art, and both come into play whenever a breeding decision is made.

ROLLING THE GENETIC DICE

The quest to breed healthy dogs is one every responsible breeder shares. But breeders face a daunting uphill task that at times seems insurmountable. There are an estimated 300-plus genetic health problems in the canine world and science has genetic tests for only a handful of them. Incredibly, there is only one for Dobermans at this time, the DNA test for von Willebrand's disease. This means breeders are taking a lot of educated guesses when they try to breed away from other genetic conditions. It is so difficult for breeders because bad genes in recessive form can hang around for many generations, and most will only express themselves when matched with a like recessive gene.

Some breeders are very diligent, cutting affected dogs from breeding programs, while others are not so diligent and make compromises. Then there are the unknowing, the unwitting and the ignorant who just breed with absolutely no idea of what is behind the stock to begin with, which is just another reason why we have been so adamant

Genetics is both a science and an art, and both come into play whenever a breeding in planned. (McNealy)

that finding a breeder with deep knowledge and high integrity is crucial when buying a puppy.

Testing for the health problems that can be tested (hip dysplasia, thyroid dysfunction, von Willebrand's disease and others) is very important, but it does not tell the whole story. For example, there are no genetic tests for the Killer C's. It is also a myth that German dogs are freer of hereditary defects than their American counterparts. Dogs from top German kennels have succumbed to the same hereditary diseases, including widespread cardiomyopathy.

What this all means is that responsible breeders do their best, but there are no sure guarantees. If anyone tells you otherwise, be wary. While we hope your dog will live a long, healthy life, and we believe that dealing with a responsible breeder will increase that likelihood, you should know about some of the health problems that arise in Doberman Pinschers so that you can ask the breeder about them and recognize the signs if they ever do appear.

THE KILLER C'S

Cancer

There are no solid national statistics on the prevalence of cancer in dogs, but there is little doubt that it is a major killer in all breeds. Cancer is as insidious in the canine world as it is in the human world.

Scientists are still grappling with the causes of cancer, and just how much hereditary influence is involved is not known. Scientists refer to "family predisposition," and there seems to be some family connection with cancer that must be taken into account in both the human and dog worlds.

A high percentage of cancers in dogs can be detected at the surface of the body. Bone cancer has a high incidence in Dobermans and can, for example, be detected by lumps on the shoulders or legs. Dobermans that limp or have constant pain in their legs could well have bone cancer.

Mammary glands have a high incidence of malignant tumors, and veterinarians will recommend spaying females that will not be used for reproduction, to reduce the risk of breast cancer. Bitches spayed before their first heat have very little incidence of mammary cancer.

Dogs also have widespread cancer of the digestive system and the blood and lymph nodes. The incidence of undescended testicles, or chryptorchism, is fairly common in Dobermans (and across the board in dogs), and this is also associated with a form of cancer. The testicle that doesn't descend into the scrotum and remains trapped in the abdomen is at high risk for developing cancer. It should be removed, and the dog should be neutered as soon as possible.

The Doberman owner who grooms his or her dog regularly will be able to detect abnormal cysts, lumps and bumps early on. This could be a lifesaver for the animal. Surgery and chemotherapy are available to battle cancer, but because in most canine cases the cancer has spread before it is detected, the prognosis is not good for long-term survival.

Cardiomyopathy

Cardiomyopathy, a fatal heart condition, is a prevalent killer of Dobermans. It strikes down older animals but primarily those at four to six years of age. It affects both males and females, but most definitely has a higher incidence in males. Cardiomyopathy can bring sudden death in some cases, but is a slower process in others, where the heart muscle degenerates to the point where it cannot pump sufficient blood to the body.

The disease is definitely hereditary and there is no cure at this time. Scientists are searching for

Regular careful grooming will enable you to detect any lumps or bumps that need further investigation. (Mary Knueppel)

Some Dobermans are known to have a form of occult, or hidden, cardiomyopathy, without the obvious clinical symptoms. Tests show an irregular heartbeat and abnormal ultrasound, but there is a better prognosis for longer survival if this form of the problem is caught early and treated by a veterinarian.

Cervical Vertebral Instability

The Doberman is prone to a spinal condition known as cervical vertebral instability (CVI), or Wobbler's syndrome, which affects the last three vertebrae in the neck. The discs between the vertebrae are like waterbed cushions, and biological changes can cause them to weaken and push into the spinal cord.

The most obvious repercussion is weakening of the rear legs, which is aptly described as "wobblers." There can also be a stiffening of the neck, which gives the dog pain when it moves, or in the front legs where there is also pain. In severe cases the dog can be paralyzed in all four legs and lose control of bladder and bowel.

Not all disc problems are CVI. Just as humans have injuries or biological changes that cause ruptured discs, so too does the Doberman and other breeds.

The root cause of CVI is not known, but most Doberman breeders believe it has a hereditary component and act accordingly. There are theories that the development of the modern Doberman, with a heavy skull on a long, thin neck is a contributing factor to the problems with the cervical

answers, trying to identify gene location on the chromosomes and the mode of inheritance. In the meantime, breeders can use electrocardiogram and cardiac ultrasound tests for early detection, but are faced with serious and painful decisions on whether to risk using animals from certain families and lines that have had instances of cardiomyopathy.

The onset of the disease can be most subtle at first, with a slight cough or abnormal breathlessness or fatigue after exercise. Obvious weight loss is another symptom, along with fluid buildup in the lungs and abdomen. The heart enlarges and races irregularly. Drugs can be prescribed to control the heartbeat and the fluid buildup, but the prognosis for survival at that point can normally be counted in days and months.

vertebrae and discs. Some veterinary surgeons who specialize in laminectomy, the procedure to remove the damaged disc, say that heavy-handed lead work with pulling and jerking on a dog's neck from a young age is also a factor in later disc damage.

Interestingly, Dr. Wendell Belfield (the vitamin expert mentioned in Chapter 7) believes disc problems may be related to collagen weakness. Collagen, the cement of the body, is produced by vitamin C. This could well be lacking in the system of a dog that is struck down by disc rupture. Belfield also wrote that two special talents of vitamin E aid in disc problems: First, as an antioxidant; and second, by enhancing the transportation of nutrients through the bloodstream. "It may be bringing a better supply of nourishment to the spinal tissues and thus keeping them more robust and better able to withstand wear and tear," he wrote.

Normal X-rays will not necessarily pick up ruptured discs, and the dog needs a myelogram to obtain the total picture. Veterinarians will use

Careful selective breeding as part of a responsible breeding program is more likely to produce healthy dogs, but there are never any guarantees. This dog is not a show-quality Doberman, but works diligently as a service dog. (Irene Korotev)

steroids and other medicine to alleviate the problem, but this is not a cure. Some owners have had limited success with acupuncture in alleviating pain, but in some cases surgery is necessary.

Joanna has had wonderful results with acupuncture on several of her dogs. It is something she always does before considering surgery. It has saved the lives of several of her dogs. Two guide dogs were able to work again when they had before been in constant pain.

A laminectomy to surgically remove a damaged disc is a difficult operation because the proximity of the spinal cord requires top surgical skill. Some dogs bounce back quickly from such surgery, and some take months of recovery; some need a portable body sling to take them outside to relieve themselves. The surgeon will sometimes fuse two vertebrae together after removing a disc, or will allow the vertebrae to fuse on their own. However, when you take a link out of a chain, it does weaken the chain, and when a disc is removed, there is pressure on the adjoining discs.

OTHER DOBERMAN DISEASES

While these three are the top killers of Doberman Pinschers, there are other diseases you need to be aware of and discuss with your dog's breeder.

Hypothyroidism

Dobermans have a high incidence of low thyroid function, and good breeders will avoid breeding, or at least breed away from, Dobermans with thyroid test results that fall below normal levels. While it is true that daily thyroid medication enables an affected dog to lead a normal life, the Doberman would be far better off if breeders did not breed animals with defective thyroids. It should be a priority for all breeders to correct thyroid dysfunction in the Doberman.

To complicate matters, thyroid function varies with age, and a Doberman that has a normal reading from a blood test taken at one or two years may not be normal for life.

The thyroid gland, situated in the neck, produces hormones that have many functions for our dogs. One of the initial signs of poor thyroid function is a thin coat with brittle hair and a thickening and discoloration of the skin. There is also lethargy, obesity or sometimes weight loss, mental depression, weakness of the joints, a slowing of the heart beat, and inconsistent heat cycles and whelping problems in bitches.

Von Willebrand's Disease

Von Willebrand's disease is a blood disorder that has aroused enormous controversy in the Doberman world. Humans and dogs need good levels of a protein complex known as von Willebrand's factor, which is released into the blood to aid in clotting. The gene that enables this to happen was mutated somewhere early in canine history, because more than 60 breeds have been diagnosed with the problem. Some breeds have a severe form of von Willebrand's disease, while the Doberman has a mild form.

The canine version was first pinpointed in the 1970s, and the controversy has not ceased in more than a quarter of a century, primarily because in Dobermans von Willebrand's disease is a laboratory phenomenon and not a clinical phenomenon. In other words, the disease can be detected, but it rarely produces clinical symptoms. This is the only disease for which there is a DNA test for Dobermans, and the advent of the test has produced high numbers of affected dogs in the laboratory but still no widespread actual bleeding problems. There certainly are some dogs that bleed more than normal, but the incidence is relatively small.

Von Willebrand's disease has become a very emotional debate, because on one hand you have some veterinarians who are warning dog owners not to take their "affected" dogs any place where they might be bitten or cut since it might cause them to bleed to death. On the other hand you have some veterinarians who treat the whole situation with a deal of suspicion. Some Doberman breeders treat von Willebrand's disease as a major problem, while others see it as a minor ailment that needs to be monitored but that should not be allowed to dominate breeding decisions. Other biological factors, as yet undiscovered, may well be at work in minimizing the impact of von Willebrand's disease in the Doberman community.

Hip Dysplasia

Hip dysplasia occurs when there is a poor fit in the pelvic ball and socket joint, caused by a malformation of either or both parts. A loose fit causes calcification, pain and lameness. There are varying degrees of dysplasia, and a variety of techniques, from medication to surgical hip replacement, are used to alleviate the problem.

Hip dysplasia plagues the larger breeds, and although Dobermans have a low incidence, breeders and buyers should not be complacent. Some scientists say the disease is genetically based, but there is an argument that nutritional factors and the environment may be the major culprit. Most likely, hip dysplasia develops as the result of the subtle interplay of all three factors.

Good breeders have been vigorously guarding against the disease in Dobermans for decades by having their dogs' hips X-rayed after two years of age. The X-rays are inspected by a specialist and are given a rating of excellent, good, fair or dysplastic by a panel of examiners at the Orthopedic Foundation of America (OFA). More than 90 percent of Doberman X-rays submitted to the OFA have been passed.

A newer technique developed at the University of Pennsylvania Veterinary School is also catching on, although it is still not as widely used as OFA. PennHip measures joint laxity, which can be measured as young as 16 weeks of age because it doesn't change as the dog ages. Any Doberman X-rayed for PennHip measurements is compared only to other Dobermans, not to other breeds. Your dog then receives a joint laxity distraction index (DI) number. PennHip suggests that only dogs in the top half for their breed (in other words, those with the tightest joints) be used for breeding. Those dogs that fall into the lower half, or that have the loosest hips, have a greater chance of developing hip dysplasia in the future.

Always ask your breeder if the parents and grandparents of your pup have had their hips tested and what the results were.

Copper Toxicosis

The Doberman breed is known to have an apparent hereditary defect that prevents dogs from jettisoning unwanted copper from the body. A buildup of copper in the liver can lead to chronic hepatitis and, eventually, to complete liver failure and death.

Regular blood testing can help analyze liver enzymes and possibly give an early warning of copper toxicity. Diets low in copper, steroids and supplementation with vitamin C all help to lower the level of copper in the body.

YOUR ROLE IN ROUTINE HEALTH CARE

Your breeder should do everything possible to give your puppy a good start in life. We've just discussed some of the factors a breeder must consider in making breeding decisions. Chapter 12 outlines what breeders do to keep their pups healthy and robust after they are born.

When you take your new puppy home (or when you adopt an older dog), the responsibility shifts to you. All the good work of the breeder can be undone in an instant if you are not caring and diligent.

Good breeders will provide a complete medical report on vaccinations, worming and so on, written and confirmed by the breeder's veterinarian. They will also give a list of instructions. Often the new arrival is not old enough to have had the second adult set of vaccinations or a rabies shot, or to begin heartworm medication, so it is imperative that you be totally attentive to these matters.

It is an excellent idea to take your new pup to your veterinarian within a week. This way your veterinarian can review the health records you got from the breeder and map out a plan of good preventive health care.

Your dog also needs an annual checkup. Each year the Doberman should have its normal vaccination boosters, which include DHLPP and rabies. Some veterinarians prefer to give kennel cough and coronavirus only to adult dogs that spend a lot of time at dog shows. Discuss your vaccination options with your veterinarian, and make a plan.

You should also ask the vet to give your dog a comprehensive physical checkup each year. This can include blood tests to determine thyroid and

When you take your puppy home, the responsibility for its care falls to you. (Rod Humphries)

liver function, right up to electrocardiograms and ultrasound to check the heart.

PESTS AND PARASITES

Where there are mosquitoes there will almost certainly be heartworms. Where there are fleas there will almost certainly be tapeworms. And your dog can pick up roundworms, hookworms and whipworms in the blink of an eye, as early as in the uterus, and later from eggs in the ground.

Scientists have done a marvelous job of combining preventives for so many of the insects and parasites that plague our dogs into one monthly medication. You can now buy, through a veterinarian, a once-a-month tablet called Sentinel that prevents heartworm, controls adult hookworm infections, removes and controls adult roundworm and whipworm infections and, if that is not enough, also controls flea populations by breaking their life cycle. Although this medication does not kill adult fleas, the eggs and larvae are prevented from maturing into adult fleas.

Fleas

Fleas have coexisted with dogs since the beginning of dogs and fleas. They were once the source of constant scratching and chewing, which created skin problems and introduced tapeworms into a dog's system. But these pests are a lot easier to control now, thanks to three products on the market that are safe, easy to use and deadly only to fleas. Program is a pill that is taken monthly and works by blocking the reproductive cycle of the female flea. Eggs are laid, but they are sterile. No viable eggs, no new fleas.

Two other products, Advantage and Frontline, are liquid solutions placed on the dog's skin where the neck and back meet, and on the back above the tail. The solution spreads over the dog's body. When a flea bites the dog, it is killed. The liquid products should not be used on breeding animals, but they have no other restrictions.

Studies vary as to how long these products are effective, but both provide excellent control and continue to be effective even after a dog swims or is bathed. It is always important to read the directions and follow a veterinarian's advice when using any such product.

If Program is used, it may be necessary to use another method of flea control to kill fleas that might get on the dog when it travels. Some veterinarians recommend the using both Advantage and Program at the same time for total protection and elimination of the problem. But even using just one of these products often solves the average flea problem completely.

Of course, the old-fashioned flea sprays are useful in controlling fleas for a short period of time. Also, if fleas are living off other animals or are constantly being transported onto your property or home, you will have to back up the flea cycle buster and other medication with commercial sprays in infested areas. Flea collars and regular sprays and dips, however, are no longer necessary.

Ticks

Ticks are common in many parts of the country and are the cause of several serious diseases. Lyme disease is the one of most concern, as it has spread nationwide. The disease is transmitted to the dog when it is bitten by tiny, infected deer ticks. If you live in an area where this is known to be a problem, or if a dog is exercised or trained in an area infested with ticks, be sure to prevent the problem. There is a Lyme Disease vaccination on the market, as well as tick collars, sprays and preventive medications. However, the value of vaccinating a dog against Lyme disease is debatable. It may not be completely effective, and once a dog has been vaccinated, it will test positive for the disease in the future. Discuss all these options with your veterinarian, who will be most familiar with the conditions in your area.

Whenever a dog is in an area where ticks may be present, it is a good idea to examine it thoroughly. Ticks are often found on and around the head, as they gravitate there in search of fluids.

Ticks can be removed by dabbing the skin with alcohol and using tweezers to pull the parasite from the skin. Grasp the tick firmly as close to the skin as you can, and pull steadily outward. Make sure you get the whole tick, and don't leave any part of the head or mouth embedded in the dog. Dab the area with a mild antiseptic.

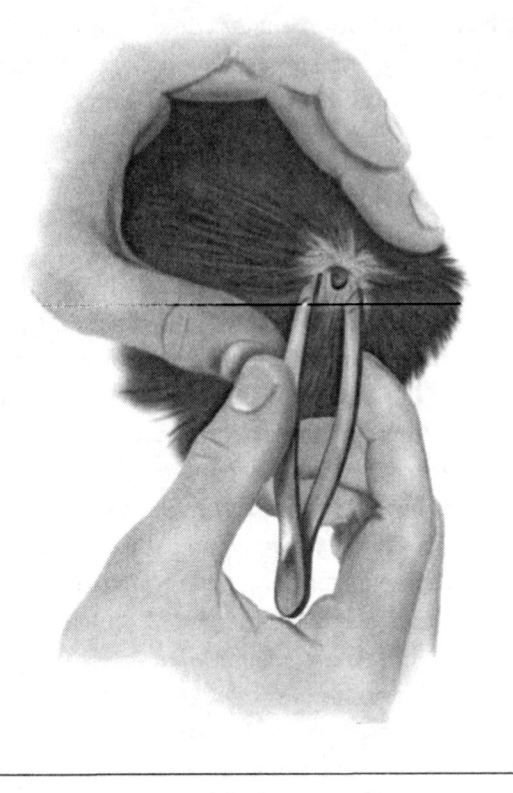

Use tweezers to remove ticks from your dog.

Since tick diseases can also be transmitted to humans, dispose of the tick by putting it in an empty jar. Then add a little alcohol and seal the jar up. This is the only way you can be sure of killing the tick without coming into contact with its toxins.

Worms

At your puppy's first veterinary checkup, bring along a fresh stool sample. As a dog matures, stool samples should be periodically checked. Unless it is possible to actually see worm segments in the stool, this is the only way the presence of worms of the intestinal tract can be confirmed.

Roundworms (*Ascarids*) are the most common types of worms found in puppies. These worms pass from the dam to the puppy during pregnancy. They are easily removed and may have already been treated by the breeder. The roundworm has little effect on the adult dog, but in puppies it may cause poor weight gain, diarrhea and vomiting.

Tapeworms (*Cestodes*) live in the small intestines and look like grains of rice in the stool or around the dog's rectum. The tapeworm is carried by fleas and is passed to the dog when it swallows a flea. If fleas are on the outside, tapeworms are almost always on the inside. Watch the stools and the areas around the anus, because adult tapeworms break off into small white segments that look like crawling grains of rice that can be easily spotted in feces.

It is best to be rid of these parasites, because they, too, can cause weight loss and a poor coat. The medication to eliminate tapeworms from the system is simple to give and works well, but if the flea problem is not addressed, the tapeworms will be right back.

Whipworms (*Trichuris vulpis*) and hookworms (*Ancylostoma*) are seen less frequently and are acquired primarily through contaminated soil. Whipworms are long and thin and attach themselves to the wall of the large intestine. They are responsible for diarrhea and weight loss. Hookworms are thin and short. They inhabit the small intestines and primarily affect young puppies. Weight loss, anemia and diarrhea are frequent signs. Diagnosis is made by the presence of eggs in the stool.

Both diseases are treated and eliminated fairly easily with specific drugs from a veterinarian.

Heartworm

The most dangerous internal parasite is heartworm, (*Dirofilaria immitis*). The adult worm actually lives in the right side of the heart, although it can later travel to the lungs and the liver. A dog is exposed when bitten by a mosquito carrying the larvae. These then enter the bloodstream, developing into microfilariae, which eventually enter the heart and mature into worms.

A dog may have heartworm for six months or more before any signs are seen. Usually the first signs are shortness of breath and a persistent deep, soft cough. Progressive symptoms are the same as those seen in congestive heart failure. Left untreated, a dog with heartworm will die.

Heartworm can be avoided by placing the dog on a preventive that is taken orally. In the past, this was usually a small pill taken daily and marketed under several names. Now most people prefer a chewable tablet such as Sentinel or Heartguard that is given monthly.

Before beginning any heartworm prevention program, a dog must always be tested to make sure it is heartworm-free.

MORE COMMON PROBLEMS

The list of all the diseases and health problems that plague dogs is a long one, and there is no way we could mention them all. Your dog's annual checkup, and your regular grooming and examinations, will help keep your dog healthy and give you early warning of any problems that develop. However, there are a few other conditions that crop up often enough to deserve special mention, if only so you can be on the alert for their signs.

Panosteitis

One of the most frustrating puppy problems in the breed, panosteitis, or pano as it is popularly called, is a kind of growing pain in our young dogs. This is a bone disorder that causes lameness, sometimes shifting from one leg to the other. In fact, it is sometimes called wandering lameness disease.

Pano can last for days or months, and in severe cases the affected dog will completely avoid exercise. It can also cause the pup to tuck its back legs into the body and can produce a fever. Pano is prevalent in larger breeds that grow quickly, and it appears to run in families.

The good news is that pano is not permanent and is self-correcting. For that reason, there is little emphasis or research into the problem in the veterinary world, and most of the time owners just have to ride it out. X-rays can identify panosteitis in the bones, and a hard squeeze on the affected bone will elicit obvious pain.

There is no known cure for pano, and most of the medical attention is aimed at alleviating the pain. Symptoms usually disappear by the time the dog is 20 months old. Analgesics prescribed by your veterinarian can be given to relieve pain. If the dog is severely affected, restrict exercise.

Dr. R.M. Brown, the veterinarian who wrote the popular book *The Doberman Owners' Medical Manual*, has had some success in quickly aiding young dogs with a sulfa antibiotic. Rod took his advice on one severe case and had instant success.

Demodectic Mange

A red mite called *Demodex canis*, which is passed to pups by their mother in the whelping box, lives in the pores of the skin of almost all canines and normally causes little or no problem. However, some dogs have a particular sensitivity to the mite and develop a reaction.

This is a puppy problem that's more common in breeds with short hair and oily skin, including the Doberman. The presence of this mite is particularly evident with stress and at puberty. When the stress depletes the ascorbic acid in the body and the immune system is not at full strength, the mite is free to attack the hair follicles and causes small patches of baldness, usually on the face and muzzle, around the eyes and on the chest and front legs. This usually causes no itch or irritation for the animal. Skin scrapings under a microscope can positively identify the mites.

Doberman breeders are very familiar with the irritating problem, but it can be quickly treated by a dip of the drug Amitraz, which can be swabbed onto individual spots on pups. However, if the localized form of the mange is untreated, it can spread into a generalized form over the entire body, which can be a long and involved process to correct.

Please do not be alarmed by veterinarians or literature that suggests you should not breed a bitch that has had demodectic mange. All dogs host this mite, and some females pass on a higher incidence to their offspring. But if the breeder and owner are diligent and watchful and know what they are looking at when they see tufts of hair missing around the front of their young dogs, they can eliminate it easily with a topical dip and it is most unlikely to ever appear again.

Lick Granuloma

Veterinarians will tell you that *acral lick sore* is the correct name for this prevalent Doberman condition, but the dog fancy commonly calls it lick granuloma, so we have labeled it the same way. This is essentially a lifestyle problem. The Doberman needs activity to expel energy and to relieve stress. If a dog has a lifestyle that is without exercise, and boring, chances are the Doberman will begin licking itself on the front leg near the wrist or on the hind leg at the hock. This is a continuing cycle of itch-lick that opens the skin and causes a thickening of the immediate area. This can have serious consequences if left unattended.

Treatment begins with a lifestyle change and medication to alleviate the itch and to speed up healing. Wrapping the wound is recommended, because topical medication is often licked off by the dog—which defeats the whole purpose.

Rod Humphries had a male who became stressed and began a lick sore on his hind leg when bitches were in season at his kennel. Rod's veterinarian prepares an anti-pruritic mixture that has proven to be a winner in eliminating the problem.

EAR CROPPING AND TAIL DOCKING

The centuries-old practice of cropping ears to stand erect and the docking of tails to two or three joints has become a highly volatile and emotional issue across the world. The European Community in the late 1980s voted to ban ear cropping, and most member countries have complied with the vote. The United States, which has 14 cropped breeds, is one of the last places where it is permitted, but some veterinarians have taken strong stands against it.

There has also been a push against tail docking, and some countries have banned it, although there does not appear to be strong enough support at this time for widespread prohibition. In the United States there are 42 breeds with docked tails, nine of which are also cropped. Those nine are the Doberman Pinscher, the Boxer, the Miniature Pinscher, the Bouvier des Flandres, the Brussels Griffon, the Affenpinscher and the Giant, Standard and Miniature Schnauzers. The other five breeds that are cropped are the Boston Terrier, the Great Dane, the American Staffordshire Terrier, the Manchester Terrier and the Briard.

Animal rights groups worldwide have been the driving force behind the bans, which have changed the look of some breeds in Europe. Britain has not allowed cropping since the early part of the 20th century, when the Royal Society for the Prevention of Cruelty to Animals, prompted by a

Ear cropping is a controversial subject among dog owners and veterinarians. (Rod Humphries)

royal patron who disdained cropping, was successful in obtaining a ban. British Commonwealth countries such as Australia and New Zealand followed in prohibiting cropping in the early 1900s.

Continental Europe saw dramatic changes in the 1990s, especially when Germany succumbed and the softer, long-eared look became official. Breeders tried to circumvent the rules by having litters born in, or dogs imported from, countries that still allowed cropping, but as the cropping ban widens that loophole is closing. Cropping is banned in another of the great pioneer Doberman countries, Holland, and there have been reports of a major drop-off in breeders and breeding. Tail docking was banned in Sweden, and there are reports that breeders could not sell their pups, which many people felt no longer looked like Dobermans.

The United States has become a battleground between the animal rights groups, supported by the American Veterinary Medical Association (the AVMA, which has 52,000 members, has long held an official position that the AKC should prohibit showing dogs with cropped ears), and the dog breeders, dog clubs and the AKC. There are, of course, fanciers and breeders on both sides of the issue. There are also veterinarians on both sides: Some agree with the animal rights activists that the practice is "cruel and barbaric," and others agree with breeders and fanciers that the practice is not cruel, is not strictly cosmetic and does have some practical applications.

On May 12, 1993, 24 national breed clubs in America, representing 29 breeds agreed to form the National Breed Club Alliance to "ensure that cropping and docking bans would not occur in the United States." The consensus of this group is that there should be freedom of choice. There is nothing to stop an uncropped Doberman from being exhibited at dog shows in America, and at least one uncropped dog has attained

An uncropped Doberman has a softer look. (Carole Watson)

its Championship. To be honest, judges are not used to seeing uncropped dogs in the ring, and there is no doubt that it is more difficult to win with one. But it has been done.

Mirroring the divisions of opinion in the United States, the authors of this book are also divided on their ideas about ear cropping. Rod, who grew up in Australia with mostly uncropped dogs, believes the Doberman should most definitely have cropped ears, and he has been very active in opposing any ban on cropping and docking. Joanna, who was born and raised in Britain, does love the Look of Eagles that comes with cropped ears, but has learned to appreciate the uncropped look. Joanna says she finds the general public likes the natural look and is less afraid of an uncropped Doberman. She finds this particularly so with the guide dogs she trains.

The argument against ear cropping is simple: It is cruel and unnecessary. The argument for ear cropping is rather complex: Proponents say it is not cruel and is really only a discomfort for the dogs. Wild dogs have naturally erect ears for a reason, and it was humans who took a mutation millions of years ago and developed floppy ears for their own satisfaction. Flexible, erect ears are natural and allow any guarding breed to hear better. While the Romans may have begun docking in the

Many breeders have their pups' ears cropped before they go to new homes, so you may not have a choice. (Rod Humphries)

misbelief that it prevented rabies, in later times guarding breeds were cropped and docked to remove "handles" for attackers, human or animal. Erect ears, totally controlled by the dog, give telltale signs of moods and instincts that are not possible with uncontrolled, floppy ears, a fact that is especially important for protection breeds. There are also arguments that erect ears are easier to keep clean.

The Doberman was originally developed to have cropped ears and a docked tail, and proponents of cropping and docking believe strongly that the historical appearance of the breed will be lost if there is tampering with the original look. The other side of the argument is that many European and Pacific countries have banned cropping, and the breed continues in those places.

On the question of how much pain it causes the dog, many people claim to speak for the dogs, but we can only guess. Some breeders and veterinarians who deal with cropping and docking regularly will tell you it is a minor discomfort, at worst. Other breeders will tell you they believe puppies suffer a lot of discomfort from the taping and untaping required after the surgery.

Tail docking surgery is done at two to three days without anesthesia, but the pup's central nervous system is not fully developed until two weeks, and scientists have argued that the pain level is minimal. Some breeders use the sheep docking method of tying a taut rubber band around the tail, which causes it to merely drop off in time because of a lack of blood flow. Ear cropping is done with anesthesia at about seven or eight weeks, and the ears often must be taped for several months.

Do I Have a Choice?

Quality breeders generally crop their litters before puppies are released to their new homes. Ear cropping is an art, but it is covered very briefly in most veterinary schools across America. Few veterinarians do the surgery, and fewer, still, know how to cut the ears to suit the size of the dog, the length of the head and so on. So top breeders will often travel long distances, sometimes out of state, to find a suitable ear cropping surgeon.

Because top breeders go to so much trouble to get a good ear crop, and because it must be done before they can truly evaluate the worth of each puppy, it may be difficult to obtain an uncropped puppy unless it is obviously pet quality. Evaluating puppies is an ongoing process that can stretch way past the ear cropping age of seven or eight weeks, so making a decision on particular pups at ear cropping can be a tricky business. While uncropped dogs can compete in the show ring, it is difficult to win against the cropped dogs.

There is also not a high demand for uncropped ears. Breeders will mostly crop show-quality pups in any case, and some will certainly consider the non-cropping of pet-quality pups. A prospective buyer may find breeders who are prepared to set aside a pup to leave it uncropped—especially if the buyer and the breeder are close friends and there is no chance that the buyer of the uncropped puppy will renege, leaving the breeder with an uncropped puppy that will be difficult to sell.

What Happens During Ear Cropping?

Most cropping is done while the pups are still in the care of the breeder, giving the breeder control over the length and shape of the ear. Breeders will often choose a particular veterinarian because of the type of cut he or she performs.

The sutures should be removed at 7 to 10 days by the breeder or the breeder's veterinarian, not by the new owner. At the time of the surgery, the ears will be dressed in one of a number of ways. These include being attached to specially designed racks, glued to Styrofoam drinking cups or even just taped over the top of the head (this last method was popular in the early days, and some veterinarians still use it). Whatever the method, the aim is to train the ear cartilage to grow upright. The cartilage is the key to getting the ear to stand.

The new puppy buyer should reasonably expect that the breeder will have removed the original apparatus used at surgery, and have the ears cleaned and posted separately when the puppy is handed over. The posting, which can be best likened to football goalposts complete with a tape crossbar, is done in a variety of ways, and the new puppy owner should receive

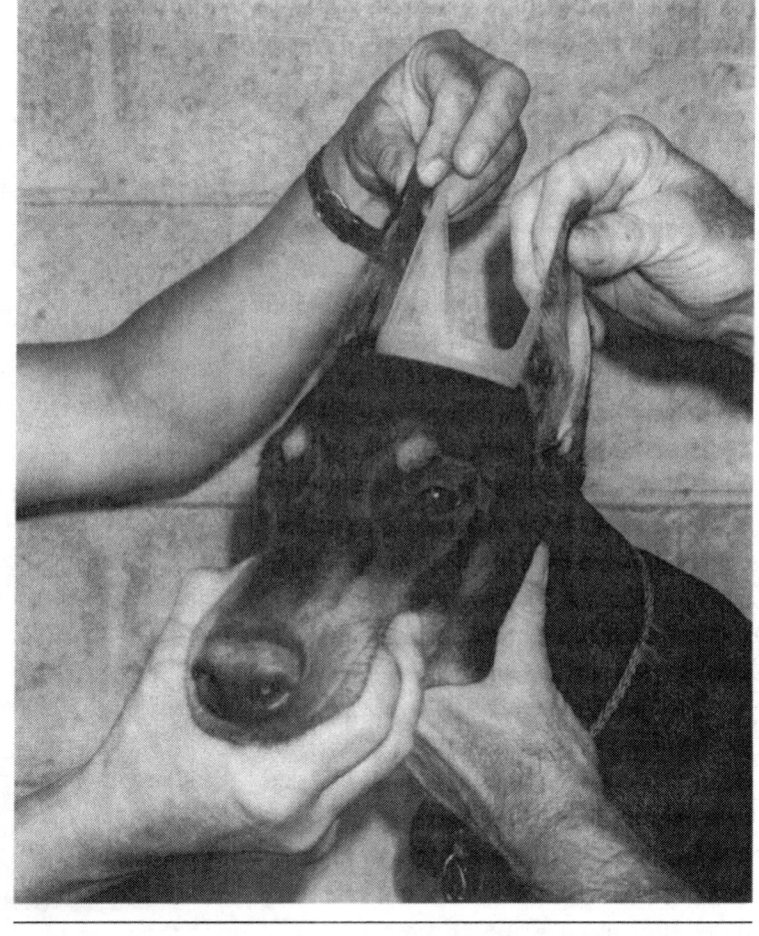

Chris Thomas' puppy wears the wolf rack. Adhesive is applied to the rack and to the backs of the ears.

a full course in posting and taping at the time the dog is handed over. The ears will have to be posted and taped for several months to ensure that they stand upright. As so many pups are sent to new owners in other states, the paperwork from the breeder should include a written explanation of the taping procedure and, if possible, some drawings to clarify how it is done.

The actual post, which must fit well into the bell of the ear opening and is then taped to the ear to give solid support, can be made of many things. The authors have seen various methods including sections of thick paper towels rolled tight like a cigar, Popsicle sticks, solid three-quarter-inch caulking from the hardware store, and even tampon applicators. All of these are wrapped, barber pole style, with the sticky side of the tape facing outward so that it will grip the inside length of the ear. To keep the ears even and help provide support, a brace made of tape is stretched between the two ears.

The postings can be kept on for four or five days, or longer if they remain clean and erect. However, it is always safe to let them down after four or five days, clean the inside of the ear where glue from the tape will build up, and re-post them after some airing. If the ears are standing when the posts are removed, there is no need to re-tape. Only if there is sagging should the posts be reapplied. Never leave a floppy or dropped ear for more than 24 hours, as the cartilage may be permanently affected.

The question every new Doberman owner asks is, "How long will I have to post and tape the

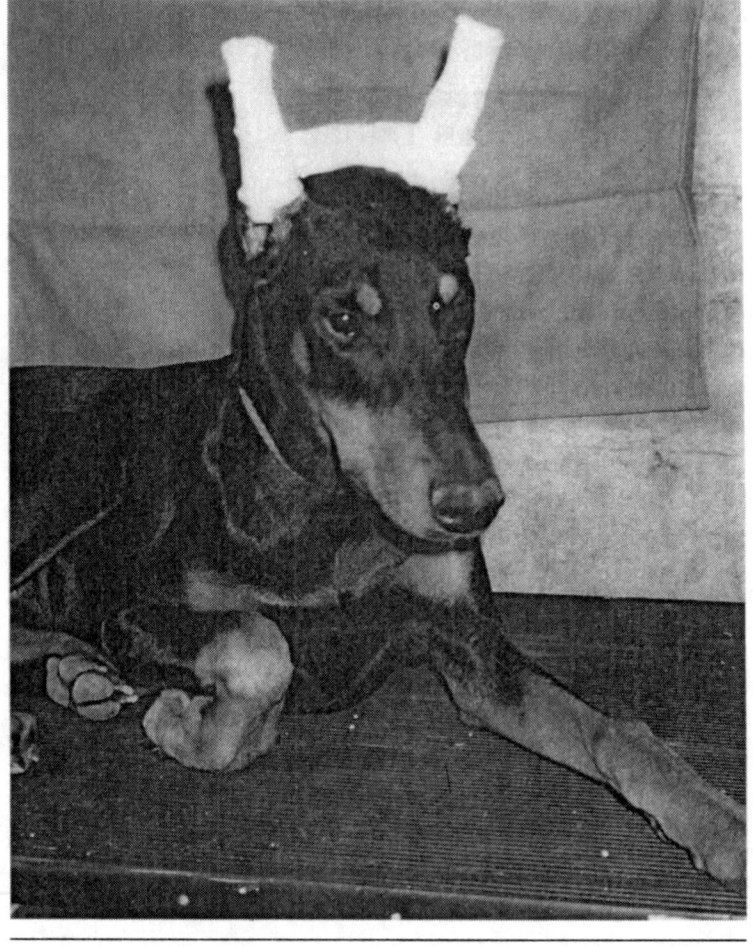

Many months of posting and taping may be required before the ears stand on their own. (Joanna Walker)

ears?" There is no hard and fast rule. It depends on the thickness of the leather of the ear, the length of the crop and the diligence of the breeder and the new owner. Some pups are out of braces at three months, while others take nine months to a year. If

Dobermans are sensitive dogs that need intelligent handling. This is Ch. Rahdy's Sable v Deserae. (Joanna Walker)

The Look of Eagles is evident in Ch. Bikila's Jet Setter of Marks-Tey. (Jordan)

Agility competition is a good outlet for your Dobe's energy. This is Cascade's Teegan of TrisSkor, MX. (Bill Newcomb)

Chris Thomas' puppy wears the wolf rack. Adhesive is applied to the rack and to the backs of the ears. (David Whittfield)

Lorelei gives us an innocent puppy smile. (Rod Humphries)

James Fendley and Tripper enjoy a hike. Your Doberman will be happiest when it's with you. (Joanna Walker)

Dobermans can be trained to do almost anything, as Roeckl's Black Jake demonstrates. (Kevin Roeckl)

If it's springtime, there must be puppies! (Rod Humphries)

A good breeder will be able to match your family up with a dog that mirrors your personality. (Joanna Walker)

Some people think uncropped ears present a softer look. (Carole Watson)

Schutzhund combines protection work with obedience and tracking. This is Ch. Chalmer's the Big Red One, SchIII, guarding the helper at the UDC National. (Gay Glazbrook)

Great dogs come from responsible breeders. This is Am./Can. Ch. Datelis That's Enough Alisaton, CDX, ROM.
(Joanna Walker)

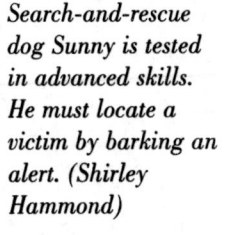

Popping through the tunnel in agility. (Tien Tran Photography)

Scudmore Khax Quidam, CGC at 11 weeks, already showing fine form. (Finn

Search-and-rescue dog Sunny is tested in advanced skills. He must locate a victim by barking an alert. (Shirley Hammond)

Dobermans are among the breeds used most often at Pilot Dogs. Rev. Mark Showalter and Star navigate the winter streets. (Joanna Walker)

Ch. Elhaus New Age Girl v Deco thinks the tire jump is a breeze. (Lewie)

Ch. Freedom's Perpetrator, a disaster search-and-rescue dog, is hauled to the top of a building. (Tess Lynch)

From the left, these pups are blue, red, black and fawn—the four acceptable colors of Dobermans. (Lloyd Olson)

you are worried by slow progress, consult with your breeder first, then a veterinarian who does ear cropping.

One problem that has emerged is the excessively long cut; this may personify the Look of Eagles, but unfortunately it takes an inordinate amount of time for the ears to stand—*if* they can be trained to stand at all! Unfortunately, the long cut sometimes requires a second surgery to re-trim, often when the pup is in the home of its new owner. The re-trim can be as expensive as the original crop. A buyer who wants a cropped dog but does not intend to show can most certainly ask the breeder to try to ensure that his or her pup will not have an excessively long cut. This will make life easier in getting the ears to stand.

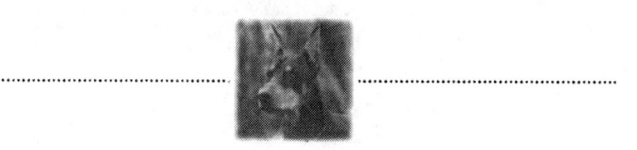

Showing Your Doberman

British entrepreneur Charles Cruft had a dream when he organized the first dog show in England in 1859, but he could never in his wildest dreams have envisioned the massive worldwide sport that dog showing would become by the end of the 20th century. One hundred years ago in America there were a dozen or so all-breed shows a year. Today the American Kennel Club oversees about 1,300 all-breed and 2,000 breed specialty conformation shows a year. That, of course, does not include the 1,500 match shows that do not offer championship points.

THE RIGHT PUPPY

A good show puppy is not just a well-conformed animal, but one who has the three P's: Personality, Presence and Pizzazz. Too many people forget that it is a dog *show*, not just a conformation contest. The dog not only has to look the part, but it has to ooze showmanship.

When you're looking at a pup and trying to decide if this animal has what it takes to make a top show dog, setting up the dog in a show stance with all feet in correct position (which we call *stacking*) and baiting it with a treat, pulling it this way and that and molding the outline, is not the best way to make your decision. Rather, you must evaluate the pup as it moves freely around the yard or kennel. Showmanship is evident in the natural stack, with all four feet landing in place without your help. It is that arrogant flick of the head, the arch of the neck and the alert expression and body language when the pup spies some curiosity. It is about a puppy who knows what it wants and most definitely knows how to get it.

To pick a good show prospect, watch the puppy move naturally. Showmanship will be evident in the dog's natural stance. (Rod Humphries)

You need to take the time to train your dog to work well in the ring and stack freely. (Rod Humphries)

A good breeder will have done at least very basic conformation show training for a promising Doberman pup before it is handed over to its new owner. Stacking is a constant in the life of such a pup, and the breeder will evaluate the puppy often on a grooming table from three or four weeks of age. In the stacking procedure, the breeder will use some tantalizing bait, which is another step toward training a show dog.

You need to take the training further, getting the dog used to walking on a light show lead, stepping easily into a stack (we call this *free stacking*), posing for the judge and gaiting at a trot in various patterns around the ring.

Never take an unruly dog into a show ring. It's not fair to the other competitors or to the judge. Take the time to train your dog, and wait until you are both ready.

BEGINNING IN THE SHOW WORLD

The AKC, the Doberman Pinscher Club of America and its local charter clubs across the country are the key places to make the first step into the world of showing. The AKC publishes an *Events Calendar* as a supplement to its monthly magazine *AKC Gazette*. The calendar lists upcoming dog shows nationwide, the judges at each show, entry deadlines and where show entries should be sent. Shows are always sponsored by dog clubs, but they are often organized by superintendents. Superintendents are agents who are AKC-approved, and they organize entries, catalogues, show materials and so on. Entries are generally made through superintendents, and once on their mailing list the new exhibitor will find that entry forms will arrive regularly in the mail.

Membership in a local Doberman club is a must for a new show puppy owner, as there will be many caring people who will give advice. In addition, the clubs often hold show training classes for newcomers. The Doberman Pinscher Club of America can provide contacts at chapter clubs across the nation. Among other important breed activities, these clubs conduct championship shows and non-championship puppy and fun matches where the owner and puppy can get their feet wet.

Fun puppy matches are extremely important because they give the puppy exposure to the show atmosphere, to working around other young dogs and to the process of standing to be examined by a judge. It is wise to socialize a puppy in all kinds of situations and at fun places, and to have men and women, old and young, run their hands over the dog and open the mouth and examine the teeth. Good preparation for the show ring will make life much easier when you are sweating inside the ring.

Before tackling your first show, a novice should attend as many championship shows as possible to study ring procedure, which can vary from judge to judge. Watch the professional handlers and their actions and reactions at various stages of judging,

Fun matches give pups and young dogs a chance to learn the fine points of showing. Practice does make perfect, so don't pass them up. (Booth)

study the way they are dressed and think about what clothes best complement them and their dogs in the ring. Walk around the grooming area and obtain as many tips as possible on how to groom a Doberman. Observe and ask questions. It will all be invaluable on "game day."

GROOMING FOR THE RING

A Doberman is without doubt one of the easiest dogs to keep looking well-groomed. The most important consideration is that your dog must be in top condition in order to have that gleaming coat and look of vitality.

The routine care of nails, coat and teeth are discussed in Chapter 7. If you keep up with these regularly (and you should for all your dogs, whether they are going in the show ring or not), you will not have much extra to do on show weekends.

The day before the show, your Doberman must be trimmed to look its best. This is easiest if you have a grooming table, so you do not have to bend over and so the dog knows it must stand on the table in place while you work.

Show trimming is simply a matter of trimming off any long hairs that stick out to spoil the lines of the dog. Start with an electric trimmer and a pair of curved scissors and closely trim the whiskers and eyebrows, as well as the long hairs under the chin and on the side of the face. You will find that your dog has a way of pulling its whiskers in, so be sure to cut them very short to give the muzzle a clean look.

Next, take your electric clippers with a fine blade and clip the hair along the edge of the ears. Use your scissors to clean out the hair on the inside of the ear, starting at the top and going down to the base. The hair should be cut very short to give a clean look.

Then take your clippers and trim the long hair in the loin area. Take off any excess hair on the

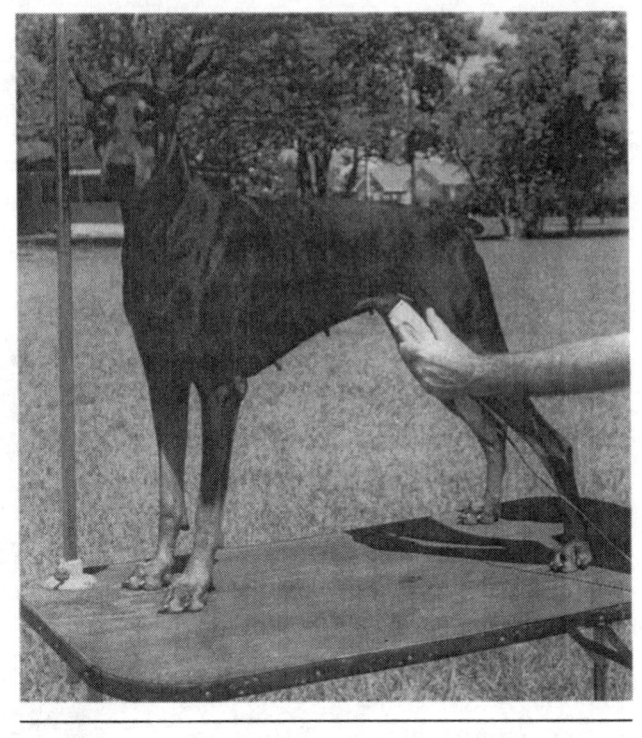

Show trimming is simply a matter of trimming off the hairs that stick out. A grooming table will make your work easier. (Mary Knueppel)

stomach around the nipples on a bitch and around the penis on a dog. Some dogs have quite a bit of hair on the backs of their hind legs, while others have very little; this, too, should be neatly rounded. Some people like to trim the hair on the backs of the pasterns, but unless this is very long, it is not really necessary. You can likewise trim off any long hair on the backs of the front legs. If your dog has a cowlick on the back of its neck, this also should be trimmed down, along with any cowlicks on the side of the dog's neck.

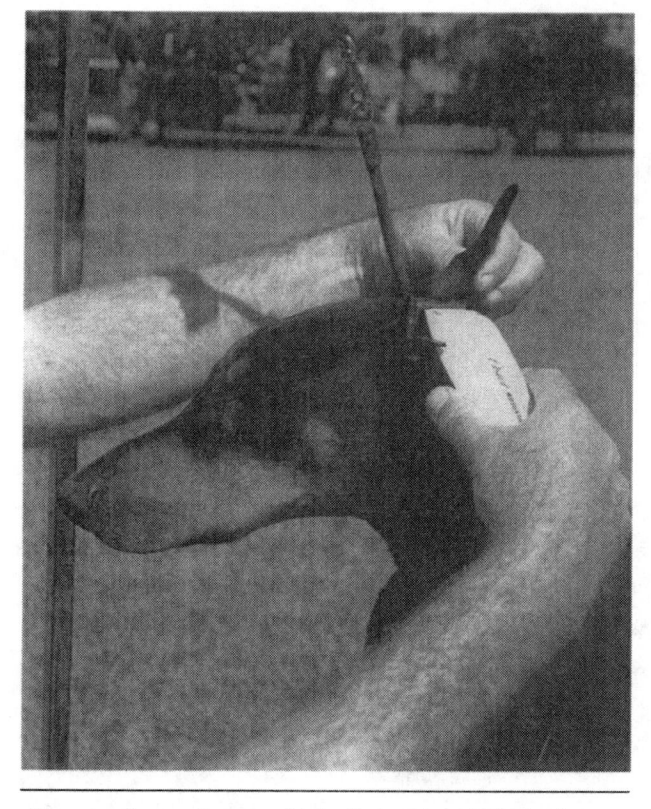

Electric clippers do a good job of trimming the hair along the edge of the ears. (Mary Knueppel)

The muzzle should have a nice, clean line, minus the whiskers. (Mary Knueppel)

On show day, give your dog a good grooming with a rubber-bristle brush, wipe the dog off with a towel, make sure the eyes are clean and remove any matter in the corner of the eye with a soft tissue. Your Doberman is ready to go into the ring!

WHAT SHOW JUDGES LOOK FOR

At its most basic, dog show judges compare each dog in the class to the official standard of the breed, and then rank the dogs according to how closely they embody the standard. The standard, as we explained in Chapter 4, is a detailed description of how a Doberman should look, but it is not an intricate blueprint drawing of the breed. That means there is room for interpretation by breeders, and by judges. And while certain styles and a specific "look" may be appealing to some, they may not be as appealing to others. That's one of the reasons why the same dog doesn't win every dog show.

Then there is the elusive *breed type*, a time-worn phrase that means different things to different people. What is breed type? It's the overall aspect of the dog—the subtle things that make a Doberman a Doberman, and not a slender Rottweiler, or a black and tan Greyhound, or any other breed. Recognizing breed type takes years of experience, and only then will the mind's eye instantly recognize a dog that epitomizes breed type. One of the hardest things for judges who started out in other breeds is to determine true Doberman breed type. Old-timers and breeder-judges from within the Doberman breed have a much better vision of what type means for the Doberman, which is why a lot of exhibitors prefer to enter under breeder-judges.

Breed type, The Look of Eagles, is hard to define but easy to see in Ch. Carosel Make My Day. (Jordan)

What else do judges look for? Movement is of paramount importance. Judges will ask that dogs be moved in a straight line and around the ring to determine whether the structure observed in the stack is still evident when the dog moves. When a dog is standing, you can place its feet to hide little structural flaws, but on the move everything is out in the open. There is an old adage: "If it is built right, it will move right."

When the dog moves straight away from the judge, the judge is watching for single tracking (which means the left and right paws converge under the body, to eventually leave a single trail of footprints) and clean movement of elbows and pasterns (the region between the wrist or ankle and the foot). In side movement, they look for reach and drive of the legs (how far the front legs reach out ahead and the rear legs follow up under the body) and a level topline when gaiting.

Last, but certainly not least, the judge is looking for personality, presence and pizzazz. After all, this is a dog show, and the dog has to show itself off to the judge.

DOG SHOW CLASSES

Unlike some countries where dogs that are not Champions have to compete against Champion dogs, the American Kennel Club separates the two.

To obtain an AKC Championship, a dog has to compete against non-Champions of the same sex and the same breed.

Puppies can begin entering Championship point shows at six months of age, and judges sometimes will award Championship points to young pups if they are of extremely high quality. It is not unusual for outstanding dogs to earn their AKC American Championship from the Puppy class.

Puppy classes are normally for dogs 6 to 12 months of age, and therefore there can be a wide discrepancy in size and experience, from the baby puppy at its first show to the developed pup at almost 12 months. At some shows, especially breed specialty shows, the puppy class is split into 6–9 Month and 9–12 Month classes.

Next comes the relatively new 12–18 Month class. As a rule of thumb, this class is for young animals that have just entered the age group and may still be learning, or those the breeder or owner thinks are not mature enough to tackle the older dogs. This is followed by the Novice class for dogs that have no championship points and have not won three Novice first-place ribbons or a first prize outside of the Puppy class.

Next is the Bred-by-Exhibitor class, where the handler or a member of his or her immediate family must be the breeder of record. The American-Bred class is next, designed to showcase homegrown talent. This class began way back when there were many, many imports, sometimes dominating the ring. It is now geared for advanced animals that the breeder or owner believes are not yet ready to tackle the very mature Open class dogs.

And finally there is the Open class. In Dobermans, the Open class is split into two classes: Black and Any Other Allowed Color (AOAC), where red, blue and fawn dogs are eligible.

Winners Dog and Winners Bitch

All of these classes are divided by sex, so there will be Puppy Dogs and Puppy Bitches, Novice Dogs and Novice Bitches and so on. After all the dogs are judged in the classes, the winners of each of the classes, from Puppy through Open, are brought back into the ring to decide the Winners Dog. The same procedure occurs at the end of the bitch judging to decide the Winners Bitch. These two are the only animals that win championship points at a show. The judge also chooses a Reserve Winners Dog and a Reserve Winners Bitch in case either of the Winners is later determined to be ineligible or is disqualified by the AKC.

After being awarded the points, the Winners Dog and Winners Bitch then join the Champions in the Best of Breed class to determine who will be the top Doberman at the show. The Winners Dog and Winners Bitch then go head-to-head to determine Best of Winners. What difference does it make? Well, it can add to the points a dog wins. As the box on page 125 explains, dogs get points based on the number of competitors they've defeated in the ring. If there are, say, many more bitches than dogs at a particular show, the Winners Bitch will get more points because she has defeated more rivals in the ring. But if the Winners Dog is named Best of Winners, he has now defeated all the dogs, plus all

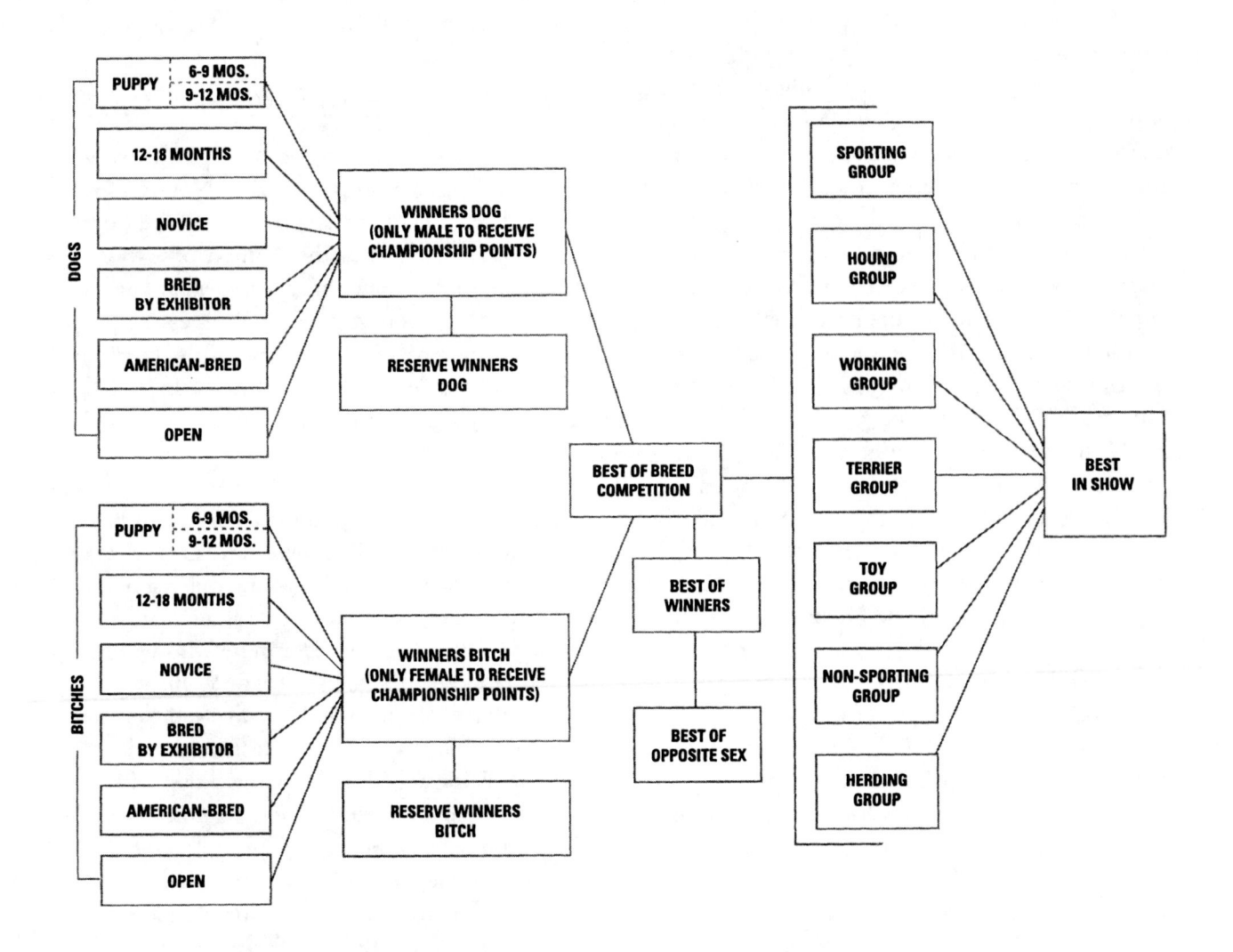

HOW A DOG BECOMES A CHAMPION

A dog needs 15 points to become a Champion, and when that's accomplished we say the dog is *finished*. At any show, only one dog and one bitch (in each breed) will be awarded points toward their championships. The number of points these dogs win is based on the number of dogs and bitches they defeat in competition. There is a point scale printed in the front of the catalog at every show. It is different for every breed and it can change from year to year. The point scale is reevaluated by the AKC every year based on the average number of dogs that are shown throughout the year. The country is also divided into regions, and the point scale varies from region to region. The point scale for all breeds is printed each May in the *AKC Gazette*, the official magazine of the American Kennel Club.

Depending on how many dogs are entered at a show, the Winners Dog or Bitch can receive anywhere from one to five points. A win of three, four or five points is called a major. To become a Champion, a dog or bitch must win a minimum of two majors under two different judges and at least one point under a third judge. The rest of the points needed to bring the total to 15 may be won under those same three judges or several different judges. In other words, it would have to be the opinion of at least three judges that a particular dog is worthy of becoming a Champion.

For example, a dog may win three three-point majors under three different judges and three two-point wins under three other judges, totaling 15 points. Once in a while a very good dog comes along and finishes with three five-point major wins.

The points awarded are automatically recorded and owners can conveniently keep a tab on their dog's championship progress through a computerized telephone service at the AKC. The AKC automatically acknowledges a Champion by sending a certificate to the owner.

the bitches, and he will be awarded the higher points. For example, if the Winners Bitch scored a three-point major and the Winners Dog had only two points, the Winners Dog would also be awarded a three-point major if it beat the bitch for Best of Winners. Dog show people call it a *cross over*, and alert show judges will often use the Best of Winners to award majors in both sexes on a day when there was only one in the regular classes.

THE CHAMPIONSHIP CHASE

All of this may sound relatively simple if you have a good dog and there is an abundance of majors in your particular area. Unfortunately, the majors are spread thin across the entire North American continent, and it could be a long haul to nail them down. The first nine (non-major) points, referred to as the *singles* by the show-going set, may not be that difficult to obtain with a good dog at smaller local venues. But the majors are a different matter, and an owner may have to be prepared to travel long distances, staying overnight in hotels, to chase them.

Because the majors are not designated in advance, and because points are allocated only by the actual number of dogs entered, there can be dilemmas for owners when they receive the show entry form in the mail and the entries listed in the catalogue are right on the bubble for a major. The owner knows you need 32 bitches for a three-point major in that area and there are 32 entries. Sometimes it is one or two over, but the question is: Do you take that trip hundreds of miles away in the hope that every entered dog actually shows up and makes the major? Or will the major "break," to use show parlance, and waste your time and money. If a dog already has nine singles, it is absolutely worthless to enter it in a one- or two-point show because it cannot advance further to its Championship, and other owners get very upset if a dog with nine singles is entered in a two-point show, potentially blocking animals who actually need the singles.

Chasing majors can be very expensive, time-consuming and most definitely frustrating. And then you have to win against a slew of the best dogs in the country who may have also traveled hundreds of miles to secure that major. The quality of dogs in America is very deep, especially in the Doberman rings; with so many people chasing so few majors, the competition is fierce.

It's not always easy to find shows with enough Dobermans entered to win the majors needed to make a Champion. (Bernard W. Kernan)

THE SPECIALS CLASS AND BEYOND

Once a dog finishes its Championship, the question then is whether to *special* the Doberman—to continue to show it past its Championship. Is the animal an outstanding specimen and does it have what it takes to compete at the all-breed level? Simply, is it *special?* There are many good dogs that obtain their Championship, but a rare few have the entire package required to go head-to-head and win against the best dogs of other breeds.

Once it's a Champion, an animal competes in the Best of Breed class. The winner of each breed moves on to compete in its respective group—the top Doberman moves to Working Group judging. The Group judging (there are seven groups) is like the semifinals of a major sporting event. Four placements are given, but only the Group winner moves on to the Best-in-Show contest. There, the top seven animals still left in competition vie for the highest award at a conformation

Very few dogs have what it takes to go beyond a Championship. Ch. Brykis Red Badge of Courage finished when he was seven months old— a record for the breed. Owners Harner and Carolyn Friedman. (John Gilbert)

show that may have started with several thousand entries.

It's the dream of a lifetime to win Best in Show, and many very fine breeders and very fine dogs never do. In terms of what a dog can contribute to its line and its breed, the breed judging is a much more important measure. But in terms of the glory, Best in Show is the ultimate. Dogs at that Best-in-Show level are normally involved in a myriad of national competitions, which include all kinds of point systems to determine Breed Dog of the Year, Group Dog of the Year, All Breeds Dog of the Year, the X-Brand Dog Food Dog of the Year and so on. You get the picture.

DO YOU NEED A PROFESSIONAL HANDLER?

Author Rod Humphries successfully handled his own dogs in a long career in Australia in the 1960s and 1970s, winning a number of prestigious Best-in-Show awards along the way. After all, everybody showed their own dogs in Australia in those days. When he moved to the United States and truly got into the swing of the show world in America in the early 1980s, he decided to again do his own handling. He was moderately successful, picking up points here and there. Two things finally dawned on him: 1. You spend a lot more time and money in the United States traveling long distances if you want to attend shows regularly; 2. He was unknown, and the professional handlers, who have the skill, longevity and recognition, were normally the big winners at shows. It did not take Rod long

to figure that if he sent out his dogs with professional handlers, especially for shows far from his home, he would actually save money and get his dogs to their Championships a whole lot quicker.

It was very hard at first for Rod to give up his own handling, and more particularly to send his dogs away for days, weeks and sometimes months with a professional handler. It is no doubt just as hard for any owner doing the same thing for the first time. But the dogs do adjust, and they actually get an education because they are exposed to so many things. If a dog is living with a handler preparing for shows and is traveling with the handler in a motor home or van, it learns about traveling and living at different places and gets to meet and play with other dogs and other people. Actually, Rod has found that his dogs return much more experienced and rounded in their outlook.

Still, if sending your Doberman away for weeks or months seems unthinkable, you can try to put the Championship singles on your dog yourself by personally handling it at the smaller shows. Then, if the going gets tough for the majors, you can hire a professional handler the rest of the way. The pro is set up to travel long distances, sometimes thousands of miles to shows you would never contemplate attending.

Handlers may charge $75 for one dog in one ring, plus daily boarding and maybe even a percentage of the gasoline on a trip. Professional handlers generally have a written contract that spells out all the conditions. The contracts can vary enormously, depending on the level the dog is being shown at. Some handlers have an increasing

Blind minister Mark Showalter's Star is with him 24 hours a day.

to present a dog and frame a perfect picture for the judge. Good handlers will frame the strength of an animal—maybe an excellent head—and lead the judge's eyes to that part of the dog. They have the hands, the magic touch that brings the best out in an animal.

The other side of this is that professional handlers can only make a living from winning, so unless they consistently get good dogs, they will fail. They will mostly only take dogs they can finish, which is yet another reason you see them winning. Judges may recognize their faces, but at the end of the lead is a quality dog being presented at its best.

scale of fees if your dog wins the points, the Breed class, the Group or Best in Show, because each win means an additional trip to the ring. Some handlers will even consider taking a flat fee, say $5,000 or more, and guarantee to finish a dog. To special a nationally ranked dog is a whole different scenario, often with guaranteed money contracts and incentives.

One will often hear disgruntled owners complaining that professional handlers get preferential treatment in the show ring. Sometimes they do, but probably not as much as is claimed. Professional handlers can ask for money for their services because they have the experience to properly train a dog for the ring, the ability to show a dog at its best on game day and the expertise and drive to win. They are experts in the breed and know how

DOING IT YOURSELF

Having said all this, we still think it's a great idea to show your own dog. Every professional handler, and every top-notch owner-handler, started as a novice. There are no exceptions. Even if you are not feeling particularly ambitious about how far you want to go with your dog, everybody should try showing because it can be a positive experience for both you and your pet.

Being at shows is also a great way to meet other Doberman owners and to learn more about your breed. If you are considering breeding your dog, then showing it is important. As we explain in Chapter 12, only the very best animals that have something positive to contribute to the breed should be bred. One way you test your dog's

There's no reason you can't show your dog yourself. Gwen was 17 when she won the points here from the Bred-by-exhibitor class at the DPCA National Specialty in 1973. Alisation's Kinderwicke leaps into her arms with joy.

potential contribution is in the ring, competing against other dogs.

You will also be able to meet mentors at dog shows—experienced people in the breed who will help you learn more about showing and breeding. Everybody needs mentors, and dog shows are the place to find them.

THE CHANGING DOG SHOW WORLD

The authors cut their teeth on dog shows in the 1950s and 1960s, when shows were more of a social gathering for breed lovers who would enthusiastically try to whip each other in the ring and afterward sit around the barbecue and drink a beer or two in a wonderful spirit of camaraderie. A newcomer could get a breed education in no time, as the Doberman elders would discuss a wide range of subjects in colorful sessions.

In those days, shows were a weekend family affair, but now show circuits run three, four and sometimes five or more consecutive days in some places. There is still some of the old charm about certain shows and circuits, and there are still times when people sit around chewing the fat and talking about the breed and telling war stories. It is just harder to find these days.

For better or for worse, showing dogs is now a multibillion-dollar business that attracts people from all walks of life and all income brackets. We say "for better or worse" because the sport has lost much of its old-world charm in this new era, and at the very top levels is dictated by money and influence. There have always been stiff competition, professional handlers and advertising, but today in the penthouse of the sport, where the nationally ranked, multi-Best-in-Show-winning dogs dwell, it has become almost entirely the domain of the wealthy. The small breeder just cannot keep up with deep-pocketed, often high-profile owners and financial backers who get little in return other than bragging rights for pouring hundreds of thousands of dollars a year into dogs; sending the animals criss-crossing the country—sometimes in private jets—in a bid to qualify for national rankings and historical breed and all breed records. It is hard for the little breeder to run with the big dogs.

There are many levels at which you can compete in dog shows, and there is room for everyone who wants to get involved. (Gay Glazbrook)

While the space is very limited at the summit of the dog world, the owner of a show-quality Doberman pup who wants to have fun should not be deterred. The grassroots of the show world is at the breed level, where owner-handlers are in abundance and the road to an AKC Championship for a quality dog will not necessarily break a tight family budget. You just have to understand the system and decide to which level you want to take your dog.

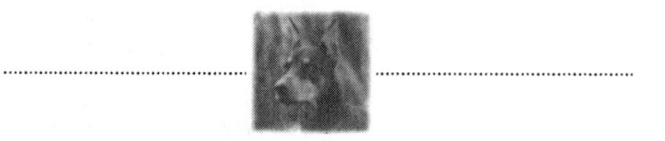

CHAPTER 10

Performance Sports for Your Doberman

The Doberman is an athletic dog, full of energy and intelligence. Like most large breeds, it was originally developed with work in mind, and work is what it loves. This is a breed that wants and needs something to do. And it's your job to put your dog to work.

There are many sports you can get involved in with your dog. All will offer you a chance to deepen the bond between you, as you train together and work together as a team. You can get involved just for the fun of it, or, if you are of a competitive nature, you can take your dog to the very pinnacle of the sport you choose. No matter what level you decide on, your active, well-trained Doberman will be a better pet for it.

SCHUTZHUND

Dobermans were originally bred for police work. To maintain that trait in the breed, Germany and other European countries require a Doberman to earn a Schutzhund ("protection dog," in German) title before it can become a conformation champion. So passionate are the Europeans in maintaining working ability in their dogs that Schutzhund titles are also demanded of breeding animals before offspring can be registered.

Schutzhund is a German sport that grew out of the activities of the German Shepherd Dog Club, which began in 1899—the same year the first Doberman Pinscher club was formed in Germany. Competitions today have three phases: obedience, tracking and protection, with titles of increasing difficulty simply called Schutzhund I, II and III.

In Schutzhund I, the tracking phase requires the dog to locate two objects on a rectangular track about 300 to 400 paces long. The obedience work in Schutzhund is not unlike trial work used in AKC obedience competition, with two main exceptions that test the stability of nerves: heeling and stopping in a sit position in a group of people, and firing two gunshots behind the dog, who is then heeling off-lead and moving away from the group of people. If the dog reacts fearfully by shying away from the handler, it is automatically dismissed from the trial.

The protection phase includes a series of confrontations with a trained helper (called an agitator) wearing a protective sleeve.

In Schutzhund I, the dog must seek out the agitator from behind a series of blinds and then bark to keep the agitator in place. When the dog cannot see the agitator, he moves to another blind and, when the dog and handler approach, the agitator simulates an attack on the handler. The dog should react without command, launching its own attack with a powerful bite on the sleeve. The agitator will drive at the dog and twice strike the dog with a cane stick. The judge will call for the agitator to stop fighting and the dog is commanded out of the exercise.

A great Schutzhund dog shows both courage and control during its confrontations with the agitator. (Gay Glazbrook)

The final phase is the pursuit and courage test, in which the dog is sent after the agitator, who is required to turn and charge at the dog with menacing actions. The dog is expected to engage the agitator immediately and hit the sleeve with force and purpose. The agitator will "fight" the dog for several seconds, and then is required to halt all aggression toward the animal. The handler, who is still 30 or 40 yards away, commands the dog to release and then, with the dog still in full attention, searches and disarms the agitator. The dog is then expected to walk between the handler and the agitator as they march him to the judge.

Obviously, the tracking, obedience and protection phases increase in difficulty for Schutzhund II and III. But all three levels require the dog to exhibit exception athletic ability, control and courage. Dogs that refuse to bite when required are failed, as are animals that are out of control or that continue to attack and bite when they are commanded or expected to stop.

Schutzhund competitions are held all over the United States, and many American Doberman owners participate. The activity has always been hugely popular in Europe and has developed a solid band of devotees in the United States since the first trial was held in California in 1963. However, the sport has limited appeal overall. One reason is that the AKC does not permit its member clubs to sponsor Schutzhund events. This is because the protection phase of the sport includes bite work (the dog bites a person who is heavily padded and protected). The AKC is obviously worried about an increasing number of vicious dog laws, the national statistics on dog bites and the image of certain breeds that have traditionally been used for protection work, and just does not believe it is prudent to promote or sanction a sport that trains a dog to tap into its natural aggression.

The AKC decision spawned a breakaway national Doberman club, the United Doberman Club, which conducts Schutzhund trials under the auspices of the American Working Dog Federation.

The AKC does promote and sanction other important breed-specific events that acknowledge breed function, such as field trials and hunting tests for sporting dogs, herding trials for herding dogs, lure coursing for the sighthounds, earthdog trials for the terriers and coonhound hunts for the coonhound breeds. But protection breeds such as the Doberman are never going to have AKC approval for an activity that has dog biting man, even if it is on a protective sleeve.

However, there are plenty of other sports, AKC-sponsored and otherwise, for Dobermans and their owners to get involved in. The AKC offers obedience, tracking and agility, which are open to all breeds. And other canine organizations run competitions in Frisbee-catching and flyball, the athletic relay race of the dog world. In fact, flyball is a big favorite among Doberman owners.

LURE COURSING FOR DOBERMANS?

Author Rod Humphries has always believed Dobermans make good hunting and coursing dogs and could perform well in lure coursing. Rod actually ran some of his dogs in all-breed fun races on Greyhound racetracks in his native Australia. The matriarch of American Dobermans, Peggy Adamson, was in attendance at a Sydney racetrack when a six-month-old red bitch bred by Rod, later to become an outstanding Best-in-Show winner, placed third behind an Irish Wolfhound and a Boxer.

Peggy agreed that the Doberman, which has some Greyhound in its background, would be an interesting participant in regular coursing events. If the AKC can allow Rottweilers and Samoyeds into the herding trials, there seems no reason why Dobermans cannot compete with the sighthounds in lure coursing.

The sleek figure of the Doberman, combined with the Greyhound in its background, make it a natural for lure coursing. (Rod Humphries)

There are many lure coursing clubs that have fun events in which dogs of any breed can participate. The AKC has a list of local lure coursing clubs.

OBEDIENCE

Apart from the obvious difference between conformation and obedience, what truly separates obedience (and most other performance events)

from conformation shows is that, in its basic form, obedience is about the handler and dog achieving personal goals, regardless of who else is competing. In other words, a handler and his or her obedience Doberman can compete in trials and earn titles without ever having to beat another dog.

An analogy from sports is the difference between tennis and golf. In tennis you actually have to beat an opponent; in golf you have no real opponent except yourself and the course. As with golf, obedience trials do have a level of competition, but the basic idea is that you seek personal goals, and technically there is no head-to-head competition.

To quench the competitive thirst of the human spirit, however, there is competition. Some handlers will strive for the High in Trial awards and placings in Open and Utility competition, which count toward an Obedience Trial Championship (OTCh). Also, there are breed and national obedience Top 10s and Top 20s for the consistent winners, including the Obedience Top 20 in Dobermans, which has its finale every October at the Doberman Pinscher Club of America National Specialty. But the very essence of obedience is setting personal goals, and this allows for a less tense atmosphere and often more fun than in the head-to-head world of conformation shows.

Getting Started

If you want to get started in obedience trials, there are plenty of breed and obedience clubs that offer lessons. Newcomers should choose their instructors wisely, as everybody claims to be a professional

There are also plenty of obedience matches to prepare a young animal for novice work. The AKC *Events Calendar*, which lists the conformation events, also lists obedience trials with information on the host club, show site and address, entry closing date, the trial secretary or superintendent and the addresses where entries must be posted. If you belong to a club or a training group, your instructors and fellow handlers are also likely to know when trials and matches are coming up.

How High Can You Go?

AKC obedience trials offer three levels of competition—Novice, Open and Utility—and titles are awarded at each level (Appendix C lists all the titles a dog can earn in obedience and other sports). The exercises at each level get progressively more difficult. To get a title, the dog must earn three "legs" under three different judges at three different trials at a given level. A leg is a passing score of 170 out of 200.

The Novice title is CD, for Companion Dog. It's aptly named because Novice consists of exercises that are basic to good dog behavior in everyday life. At this level the dog is expected to heel by the handler's left side both on and off the lead, moving at different speeds and in different directions as commanded by the judge. On lead, the dog is expected to heel in a figure-eight pattern around two people. Novice animals must stand for examination by a stranger; do a recall from the sit position on the other side of the ring, with a finish in the heel position; and do a group exercise in which the dog must remain in place on a one-minute

The deep bond between dog and handler is apparent in this heeling off-lead obedience exercise. This red male, Ryan, was the winner of the Obedience Top 20 in 1998. Owner Kathy Rambo. (Ellice)

dog trainer but there are no licensing bodies. Look for a trainer who has long-time experience with dogs and has personally taken dogs to advanced obedience titles.

sit-stay and a three-minute down-stay. In the group exercise, the dog is surrounded by other animals while the handlers stand at the other end of the ring.

The level of difficulty and the range of exercises increase as the animal moves to Open and then Utility. In Open, the basic obedience work is similar to Novice, but the dog is required to work only off-lead and for considerably longer periods. Open exercises also include high jump and broad jump exercises and retrieving skills. In Utility, the dog is expected to perform all these exercises at an even higher level of precision, off-lead and with hand signals only. The Utility level also requires scent discrimination tasks where the dog must retrieve two objects scented by the handler and placed in a group of 10 identical articles.

A relatively new title, Utility Dog Excellent (or UDX), is now being awarded to dogs that secure qualifying scores in both Open and Utility at 10 trials.

The title of Obedience Trial Champion (OTCh) is earned by accumulating points finishing either first or second in Open and Utility B classes. (B classes are for experienced handlers, while A is for beginners whose dogs have no titles.) When a UD dog has earned 100 points and at least one win in Open and Utility competition, the AKC awards it the OTCh.

The AKC publishes a booklet listing the rules of obedience trials, and no prospective competitor should be without one.

In this group exercise, the dogs are required to remain sitting until their handlers return.

TRACKING TRIALS

This is for the athlete with a good nose, and the Doberman qualifies on both counts. Tracking tests and titles are offered at three levels: TD, or Tracking Dog; TDX, or Tracking Dog Excellent; and VST, or Variable Surface Tracking Dog. A dog must pass the tracking test just once to achieve the title.

At the TD level, a complex track about a quarter of a mile long with two turns and one object to find is laid about 30 minutes or more before the event. The TDX track, which is laid about two hours before the event, is roughly half a mile long, with multiple turns and four objects to be found by the dog. The TDX track is older and much more challenging in that it shifts over different terrain and there are cross-scents to fully test the animal. The VST dog must work in urban settings on a track that is roughly half a mile long and is often

At a tracking test the handler must completely trust his dog because the handler does not know where the track will lead. (May & Arnold Jacobson)

more than three hours old. The dog is asked to track a scent that could lead through a building, around walls and fences and across vacant lots while locating four objects.

Because scent tracking is a natural instinct for dogs, training for these tests can start at a young age, and it is not unusual for dogs just over six months old to earn their TD title. The equipment is very basic: a working harness and a tracking line 20 to 40 feet long.

The AKC can help you find tracking clubs and other training clubs that do tracking. The AKC also has a booklet on the rules, and tracking tests at all three levels are listed in the monthly AKC *Events Calendar*. Be warned, though, that clubs set very small limits on the number of dogs that can do tests. Because of the time involved and the intricacy of the tracks, track tests are mostly limited to less than a dozen animals—often just three or four at each venue.

AGILITY

Author Joanna Walker visited her homeland of England in the 1970s and watched an impressive red champion Doberman male win Best in Trial at an event that resembled an equine hunter jumper contest for dogs. With handlers running alongside their dogs and urging them on, canine competitors of all breeds flew over and under a variety of obstacles, dodging time and fault penalties. Joanna was so enthusiastic that she took photographs and had an article published in *American Doberman* magazine about the fun new sport. Interest at the time was underwhelming.

How times change! The sport of agility, which began as a filler specifically created by a dog show committee to kill time between the obedience championships and the conformation group judging at England's most prestigious show, Crufts, finally came to America in 1986. Agility today is the fastest-growing performance sport in the world of dogs. There are clubs and trainers all over the country teaching this crowd-pleasing sport, which is often the highlight of any doggy get-together.

What makes agility so appealing is that owners get to basically run and play with their dogs in a most enjoyable competition. While conformation and obedience events can have all the "shushing" quietness of a golf tournament, agility is helter-skelter noise and mayhem.

Dobermans revel in agility, which is basically an obstacle course where dogs, with the clock running, must negotiate a series of jumps, scale a six-foot A-frame, weave quickly through a set of poles, scamper through tunnels, traverse a narrow elevated dog walk and conquer an old-fashioned see-saw. Dogs of different sizes are tested at different heights on the jumps, and there are contact zones that a dog must touch as it enters and exits obstacles. The contact zones are there to protect the animals who, without them, might be inclined to throw their bodies down from halfway up an obstacle, possibly causing injury.

This is not a sport for older animals, and dogs must be at least a year of age to compete. It is important that competitors have some basic obedience work, because the dogs run

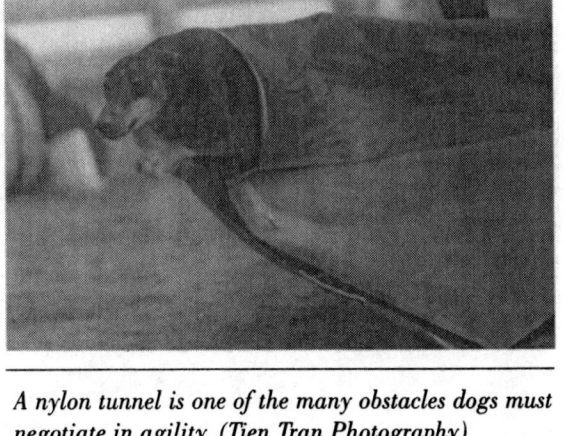

A nylon tunnel is one of the many obstacles dogs must negotiate in agility. (Tien Tran Photography)

Dobermans really enjoy agility, which takes advantage of their natural athleticism. (4U2C Photography)

off-lead and need to be under control.

There are four organizations sanctioning agility trials in America today, and the latecomer, the AKC, conducts the most. The others are the United States Dog Agility Association, the North American Dog Agility Council and the United Kennel Club.

FLYBALL

This is a sport in which the athletic Doberman excels. In fact, the first dog to earn 20,000 flyball points was a Doberman named Onyx. Now the North American Flyball Association (NAFA) gives the Onyx Award to dogs that also reach that magic number.

Flyball is a four-dog team relay race held over a 51-foot course. The course has four hurdles, with the height set 4 inches below the shoulder of the smallest dog on the team. At the end of the course is a spring-loaded box that

The flyball hurdles are pure enjoyment for an active Doberman. Skylark (dog), owner Alice Abdullah. (Juli Carralejo)

at the same time. The team with the best time is the winner.

NAFA offers a point system based on the finishing time of a team in competition. It starts at one point per team member if they finish under 32 seconds. If a team runs a heat under 28 seconds each racing dog earns five points; under 24 seconds the points per dog jumps to 25. NAFA keeps a record of points for all dog competitions and awards titles based on points.

Wow! And to think this all began with some guy in California in the 1970s with a tennis-ball-crazy dog who built a contraption that enabled the dog to flick the ball into the air. When flyball first began, the box would spring a tennis ball 10 feet in the air and the dog would fly high to get it. That is where the name of the sport came from. But today the spring-loaded boxes are so sophisticated, and the dogs so quick and smart, that they nail the tennis ball just as it is released.

contains a tennis ball. The dogs negotiate the hurdles and hit the box with their feet to pop a tennis ball into the air. They catch the ball in their mouth and race back over the hurdles to the starting point. Four dogs touch and go, and two teams race

Like agility, this sport is growing fast in the United States as well as internationally.

FIRST IN
GROUP

SNAKE RIVER CANYON
KENNEL CLUB
OF IDAHO

SPRING 1996

(Carl Lindemaier)

CHAPTER 11

The Headliners

After World War I, American breeders were ready to make an unprecedented run at securing the best Dobermans in the world. They had the drive and they had the money. And their money spoke volumes to a devastated Germany.

Two of the first big purchases were the black Siegers from the hallmark 1922 show in Berlin: the red Benno v Burgholz, who arrived here in 1923; and the black Benno v Roemerhof, a Dutch-bred dog who was the first foreign competitor to win a German Sieger title, imported in 1925. Each year in Germany there is a major Sieger show, which is akin to a national specialty. Sieger titles are given to the best black and the best red male, and the best black and the best red female.

For two decades leading up to World War II, there was barely a handful of Siegers or Siegerins left in Germany. The custom was for the Germans to breed their dogs for retainable offspring and then sell them to Americans. Those two imports were just the beginning of a relentless buying spree that began in the Roaring Twenties and that proceeded through the Great Depression to the beginning of World War II.

THE ROARING TWENTIES AND THE IMPORT WAVE

One of the key players was George H. Earle III, a Philadelphian of great wealth and stature who was an envoy to Austria in 1933, the governor of Pennsylvania from 1935 to 1939 and the United States minister to Bulgaria for two years before America's involvement in World War II. Earle bred Dobermans under the well-known prefix of Red Roof. In 1921, when he was in his early 30s, he was a prime mover in the

Benno v Roemerhof, born in 1920, was one of the first major imports to the United States. He was brought here by big spenders Francis Fleitmann and Howard Mohr.

formation of the Doberman Pinscher Club of America. There had been a loosely knit organization of the same name before the war, but in 1921, with the heightened interest and imports starting to arrive, fanciers met at the Westminster Kennel Club Show in New York and decided to bring everybody together and register the new club with the AKC. Earle was designated to obtain the official German standard, which had just been rewritten in 1920 in the first major overhaul since the turn of the century.

In the same year, Earle led the new invasion of German imports when he purchased a two-year-old black dog, Ch. Lord vd Horstburg—one that Gruenig said was the first German dog of

outstanding beauty to travel overseas. Earle also imported several good German bitches; one, Ch. Bella v Stolzenberg, was a full sister to a German Siegerin. She was bred to Benno v Burgholz to produce the bitch Red Roof Rilda, who won the historic first Doberman Pinscher Club of America National Specialty Show in Philadelphia in 1924.

Lord was the top-winning Doberman at Westminster in 1922—the first import to topple the old guard from the early days of the breed. The early dogs in America were of the old type, smaller and coarse and lacking the height and elegance of the new dogs that dominated the scene after the war. The post-war dogs were the prototype of the Dobermans we know today. The Americans had been isolated from the German gene pool for a good number of years, and it must have come as quite a surprise to see these new-look dogs appearing in the 1920s. Eventually the old-style dogs were swamped genetically and in the show ring as wave after wave of imports hit these shores.

So frenetic was the chase for European dogs that many poorer specimens were also foisted on naive American buyers. One of the prominent importers, Howard Mohr, said that even registration papers were falsified by the Germans. People were warned, but they bought anyway. And many fanciers who did land the big prizes had an interest in the breed for only as long as the fame of their import lasted.

The high rollers in this big-stakes game were two wealthy businessmen who joined forces not only to skim the best from Europe, but also to travel to Germany with American-bred dogs and challenge them in the show rings on their own turf: Francis F.H. (Hermie) Fleitmann of the Westphalia kennel in Far Hills, New Jersey, and Howard K. Mohr of the White Gate kennel in Philadelphia. The two men apparently became involved with Dobermans around 1919, but the interest escalated as Fleitmann regularly traveled abroad for his huge family textile business in New York. He was highly regarded on both sides of the Atlantic, and it is interesting to note that he obtained a judge's license in the United States and judged in Germany, reportedly judging at a Sieger show in the 1920s. In his later years, Fleitmann moved to Switzerland, where he died in 1976.

Fleitmann and Mohr built the foundation for the magnificent dogs we have in the United States today. In order to educate new Doberman fanciers in this country, they also helped arrange for a host of German judges to officiate in the United States. They also were the instigators, financial backers and copyright holders of Philipp Gruenig's definitive book *The Dobermann Pinscher, History and Development of the Breed*, which they had published by the Orange Judd Publishing Company in New York in 1939.

Fleitmann and Mohr began their buying spree in 1923, and within three years they were successful in purchasing so many Dutch and German winners that Mohr was moved to write in 1926, "The combined kennels contained, probably, the greatest collection of Doberman dogs and brood bitches in the world." It was no idle boast.

Howard Mohr (left) and Francis Fleitmann with some of their early dogs. Their great Dutch and German imports consolidated the breed in the United States after World War I.

The Dutch were neutral in World War I and had an opportunity to boost the Doberman breed because many German breeders had sheltered their dogs there. Many of Fleitmann's early imports came from the top Dutch kennels of Koningstad, Grammont and Roemerhof. The Dutch dogs, which were apparently raised differently, were still sharp but were not as belligerent as the German dogs. They had developed a head type in Holland that was a little more full-muzzled and that appealed to the American fanciers.

Fleitmann and Mohr secured an entire package of top studs and brood bitches from Holland in the early 1920s. The black male Prinz Carlo vd Koningstad (born in 1919) and the Grand

Champion of Holland, a red bitch named Angola v Grammont (born in 1917) were two of the greatest Dobermans of their time. They were bred together in Holland in 1921, producing three more stars: the red male Prinz Favoriet vd Koningstad; the red bitch Prinzessin Ilisa vd Koningstad; and the black bitch Prinzessin Elfrieda vd Koningstad. This star-studded family of five was shipped to the Westphalia and White Gate kennels in 1923.

Together, the Koningstad dogs produced 24 American champions—15 by Favoriet, who was the most successful of the early sires. Ilisa made history when in 1925 she became the first Doberman to win the Working Group at Westminster. It was another 14 years before another Doberman would match that feat.

With the German dogs making a strong recovery from the war, Fleitmann and Mohr then jumped to the best of the German-bred animals. These included Claus vd Spree, chosen the best black at the 1923 Sieger show but unable to be declared the titleholder because his owner was not a member of the German Dobermann club. Instead the title went to his half-brother, Lux vd Blankenburg. Both Claus and Lux were sired by Burschel v Simmenau, a black male of obvious great hereditary strength that was born at the outset of the war in 1914 and managed to survive the horrors to play a major role in the breed's resurrection in Germany. Then Fleitmann and Mohr purchased Lux's son, Ari v Sigalsburg. Another significant coup was the purchase of the junior Siegerin of 1925, the red bitch Bajadere v Zinsgut.

Prinz Favoriet vd Konigstad was the most successful of the early sires in America, producing 15 champions in the 1920s.

Buoyed by their successes, especially in producing quality stock from the mix of Dutch and German animals, in the late 1920s Fleitmann and Mohr hatched a plan to challenge the Germans on their own turf and made four trips to the Sieger shows between 1926 and 1930. A litter sired by Claus out of Prinzessin Elfrieda vd Koningstad in 1925 had some remarkable pups and three of them—Koningstad Amerant, and Asta and Algarda of White Gate—along with the red bitch Fleitmann had imported from Germany, Bajadere, were entered for the 1926 Sieger show in Berlin. The men spared no expense, taking along one of Americas top handlers, Ben Lewis, and his wife on the 3,500-mile sea journey. At a stop in Hamburg, Fleitmann decided he wanted to purchase a dog he had been watching with interest in recent trips to Germany. The party left Hamburg with a black male, Fedor v Butersburg.

The show was a smashing success for the Americans. The German-bred Bajadere brought the party much excitement by winning the red Siegerin title. The newly purchased Fedor, apparently flourishing under the expert guidance of Americas best handler, finished in a dead heat on points for the black Sieger title with the heralded German dog, Claus vd Sigalsburg. According to Mohr, the judge asked the president of the Dobermann Club what he should do about the tie, and he refused to give him any direction. Finally, the judge gave it to Claus. Lewis, who was highly acclaimed by the locals, also succeeded in winning the red Junior Sieger title with Amerant. The two young bitches took first and second in their junior classes to cap a great show. Mohr noted, "This writer has experienced the thrill of seeing his dog awarded best of all breeds at a big show, but the honest-to-goodness thrill of winning with your own breeding at a foreign show, in fierce competition, makes the former thrill pale into insignificance."

A number of Fleitmann's dogs, accompanied by his manager Ellie Buckley, made a reasonably successful trip to Germany in 1928, but the next year Fleitmann achieved the unthinkable: He took a red bitch from a breeding of Claus and Prinzessin Ilisa vd Koningstad, the beautiful Princess Ilisa of Westphalia, to the 1929 Sieger show in Hanover and came away with the red Siegerin title—the only American-bred Doberman ever to win a national Sieger award.

Princess Ilisa of Westphalia, an outstanding red bitch, was the result of a 1926 union of two Fleitmann imports. Three years later, Fleitmann did the unthinkable: He returned to Germany to win the national red Siegerin title with Ilisa. No other American Doberman has won an open Sieger title in Germany.

A great friend and rival of Fleitmann was Glenn Staines of the Pontchartrain kennel in Detroit, Michigan. The two had very different opinions about how a Doberman should look, and even though they were fierce competitors in the show ring, they stayed at each other's homes and showed their animals under one another in the ring. Staines used Fleitmann's Dutch import, Favoriet, and the German dog Claus with great success, and then made a significant move by importing Claus's half-brother Lux.

Lux was born in 1918 and was an old dog who had been shunted from home to home in Germany before arriving in Detroit in 1926. His temperament had been described as vicious, and he reportedly had bitten a number of owners. Some said he was being offloaded to the United States. When Lux arrived, Staines cleared the shipping office room and immediately muzzled the dog when he took him out of the crate. Staines did not kennel him, believing that Lux should become accustomed to family and friends. "After a week we saw no signs of anything but extreme affection. He did not like guests and did not greet them, but soon as they were seated he was satisfied to let them alone," wrote Staines.

Lux played a significant role in the development of the Doberman in Europe and America, siring the winners of six Sieger and Siegerin titles in Germany and 19 American champions. A number of his famous offspring, including the 1925 and 1926 black Siegerin Mia v Stresow, and Claus, who had beaten Fleitmann's Fedor, also found their way to America.

Lux vd Blankenburg, born in 1918, was imported by Glenn Staines in 1926 when he was already an old dog. But that didn't stop him from playing a significant role in the breed's development in America, siring 19 American champions.

In his later years, Staines spent more time developing his Path Finder organization, which trained Dobermans as guide dogs for the blind. You can read more about him in Chapter 14.

THE IMPORTS KEEP COMING

The 1930s saw an equally dramatic influx of German stock into the United States. The demographics of the Doberman breed in America were changing, and top kennels were no longer all situated in the Northeast. The Midwest made two huge coups in the 1930s with the import of the 1932 black Sieger Muck v Brunia by Owen West in Chicago, followed in 1937 by Muck's son Troll vd Engelsburg, bought by Ernest Bornstein of Peoria,

Illinois. Many Doberman fanciers believe Muck was the most influential sire in the shaping of the modern American Doberman. His son Troll, a striking black male who won the Sieger title in 1935, was the leading stud dog in Germany in the mid-1930s. In fact, in 1938 some 50 percent of the contestants at the German Sieger show were sired by Troll.

Another Muck son, Blank vd Domstadt, was overshadowed in the show ring by his brother Blitz, but Blank outstripped him enormously as a stud dog. Blank sired the 1937 Sieger Moritz v Roedeltal and then came to America where he gained his Championship and sired 15 American Champions, including the immortal red male Dictator v Glenhugel. Moritz followed his father to America, where he too became an important sire, producing seven Champions. Blitz was one of the few Sieger titleholders to remain in Germany.

In the late 1920s, the German breeder John Zimmerman settled in Detroit. He brought with him a black male, Kurt vd Rheinperle, who was later registered here as Kurt vd Rheinperle-Rhinegold. Kurt became an American Champion, but his ability to reproduce far outstripped his show career. He was the first sire in America to achieve 20 Champion offspring. Fleitmann, obviously a master breeder, saw the potential in him and also in one of his sons, Pericles of Westphalia, who was a double of his famous Ilisa. He helped forge Kurt and Pericles into worthy foundations of the new American Dobermans in the late 1930s and early 1940s.

Fleitmann was still breeding top dogs during the height of the Depression in the 1930s, but his business interests took much of his time. By the mid-'30s he was itching to go after further top German animals, and he pulled off probably the greatest coup in breed history when he secured what many described as the greatest bitch of all time—maybe the best Doberman of either sex—the 1937 black Siegerin Jessy vd Sonnenhoehe. She was a classic Doberman, a large bitch whom the late judge Herman Felton said was probably 27 to 27½ inches at the withers (the top of the shoulders). She combined elegance with good bone, which did not detract from her femininity. She had a beautiful head and moved like a dream.

Jessy vd Sonnenhoehe, born in 1934, won both the black German Siegerin and the American National Specialty in 1937; she is one of the pillars of the modern American Doberman.

But Jessy's temperament was less than desirable. "As was true of most of the Dobes of that era, especially imports, she was rather sharp—one would not take too many liberties with her, but she was quite manageable," wrote Felton. Jessy did not have a Schutzhund title, which the Germans considered a must for good temperament. (Schutzhund is a three-part competition that tests a dog's ability in tracking, obedience and protection work.) According to observers, Jessy won the Doberman Pinscher Club of America National Specialty show shortly after her arrival with a curl on her lip, but to be fair she was unaccustomed to the show techniques in the United States.

Before leaving Germany, Jessy had a litter to the top stud, Troll vd Engelsburg, himself exported to the United States the same year as Jessy. They produced a mighty pair who followed in their parents' pawprints: Ferry and Freya v Raufelsen. Ferry was a big black dog, 28 inches at the shoulder, sharp as could be and a dog of great presence. Fleitmann had apparently tried to buy him when the professional handler McClure Hailey was sent to Europe to find a dog to win Westminster by the powerful niece of John D. Rockefeller, Geraldine Hartley Dodge of the Giralda Farm in Madison, New Jersey. Dodge most definitely wanted Ferry and apparently outbid Fleitmann, paying the incredible price of $10,000. Ferry was shipped to New York, arriving on January 20, 1939, just days before the Westminster show.

Ferry was a take-no-prisoners kind of dog. The story of his legendary sharpness is told in Chapter 3. The big black dog made history by being the first Doberman to win Best in Show at Westminster, but he did so without any of the judges laying a hand on him.

Ferry's mother, Jessy, was not shown extensively in the United States but was put to the test as a brood bitch, where she excelled once again and became the matriarch of so many of the great Dobermans in the era after World War II. She produced six champions by the imported dog Kurt vd Rheinperle, and six more by Kurt's son, Ch. Pericles of Westphalia. Her two outstanding sons from those unions—Ch. Westphalia's Rameses (from Kurt) and Ch. Westphalia's Uranus (from Pericles)—became two of the seven home-bred foundations of American Dobermans, the immortal Seven Sires, ensuring that Jessy was a dominant factor in the decades that followed.

Forever inextricably linked to Jessy will be her red counterpart, the 1937 red Siegerin Ossi v Stahlheim. John Cholly of the Glenhugel kennel in Canton, Ohio, bought Ossi, an elegant bitch that was smaller than Jessy. Contemporaries said Ossi had a better temperament. The Muck v Brunia line was brilliantly consolidated in the United States by twice breeding Ossi, a Muck granddaughter to a Muck son, Blank vd Domstadt. From that breeding came another two of the Seven Sires: Domossi and Dictator.

Of all the Seven Sires, Dictator was very, very special. A good-size red boy about 27½ inches tall, Dictator had, like so many of his red progeny, a stable, people-friendly disposition that was a breath of fresh air after the vicious Ferry. And it didn't go unnoticed in the media, especially when Dictator

THE SEVEN SIRES

The Seven Sires, the first significant wave of American–bred dogs in the 1940s after the German imports ceased, were the rocks upon which the very foundation of the breed was formed through the second half of the century.

Peggy Adamson wrote an historic article in 1951 called *Illena and the Seven Sires*, which chronicled the dogs and their careers. All eight produced more than 10 Champions apiece at a time in history when that was a very difficult accomplishment.

"The Seven Sires were responsible for an era in American Dobermans which was as exciting and colorful as the dogs themselves," wrote Adamson. "They towered over the Doberman world like mighty Titans and the competition among them was brisk, awesome—and sometimes fierce. The dog magazines fattened on their advertising, the like of which the breed had not seen before or since. Their names were familiar to the most inexperienced

continued

Ch. Favoriet v Franzhof, born in 1941.

Ch. Westphalia's Uranus, born in 1940.

novice, and their offspring could be found in the remotest hinterlands. Each had his loyal partisans, and the legends concerning them were inexhaustible. With their passing, passes an era. History will not soon see the time when seven males of such stature live contemporarily again."

The Seven Sires were Ch. Domossi of Marienland, Ch. Emperor of Marienland, Ch. Dictator v Glenhugel, Ch. Alcor v Millsdod, Ch. Favoriet v Franzhof, Ch. Westphalia's Rameses and Ch. Westphalia's Uranus.

Dictator was by far the most successful of the seven historic stud dogs, producing 52 champions, over half of which were red. Dictator's full brother, Domossi, also red, was the sire of 20 champions. The other red of the group was Favoriet, sire of 13 champions. Alcor (26 champions) and Rameses (11) were both dominant black dogs. Emperor (18) and Uranus (14) were both black with a red recessive, meaning they could produce black and red offspring. Dictator and Alcor were the only ones to win the DPCA national specialty show, Dictator in 1944 and Alcor in 1946 and 1948.

Ch. Alcor v Millsdod, born in 1941.

Ch. Emperor of Marienland, born in 1941.

Ch. Dow's Illena of Marienland, a black bitch who produced only black offspring, was linked with the Seven Sires because she had produced a remarkable 12 champions.

One of the most telling statistics from Adamson's article was that at least three of the seven died of "heart attacks." They were Domossi at seven, Emperor at eight and Alcor at nine. Favoriet, who lived to be 10, is also believed to have died from a heart problem. These heart statistics on America's first home-bred foundations appear very relevant today, when cardiomyopathy is a major killer of our Dobermans.

won the Working Group at Westminster in 1944 in the same ring where Ferry had been untouchable just five years before. He was purchased as a pup by Peggy Adamson and her husband, Marine Captain Bob Adamson, originally of California but later of Long Island, New York. It was so charming, and different, to see the petite Peggy handling that big dog in the ring.

In time, Peggy followed Fleitmann as the most influential person in the breed. Most kennels are built on great brood bitches, but Peggy was unique in that she parlayed an outstanding stud dog into a fabulous breeding program under the kennel prefix of Damasyn. She became the breed's foremost authority and judge, architect of the later breed standards, and president of the DPCA.

One of Peggy's good friends and the co-author of the standards was Eleanor Rhys Carpenter of Jerry Run kennels in Pennsylvania. Carpenter, who obtained her first Doberman in Greece in 1931, closed the chapter on German imports in a remarkable adventure to Germany in 1940. The war in Europe had been raging for more than a year, and Pearl Harbor was a year away. She entered Germany, "the last American woman to do so," she once boasted, to convince the owner of a top bitch, Assy v Illerblick, that she would be safer with her in the United States. The owner hesitatingly sold the bitch to Carpenter. She then traveled home through Italy, catching the last ship to the United States before Italy joined the war. While she was traveling through Italy, Carpenter negotiated to buy Jessy vd Sonnen-hoehe's sire, Cherloc v Raufelsen, who had been

Ch. Dictator v. Glenhugel at six years old in 1947. Dictator was one of the Seven Sires, the group that founded the American Doberman in the 1940s.

THE AMERICAN DOBERMAN COMES OF AGE

The first phase of separation between the German and American dogs began in 1935 with the publication of the first all-American breed standard. The second stage of separation was World War II. The Americans had scooped up most of the best German dogs, and during and after the war they consolidated and shaped the Doberman the way they thought it should be shaped.

During World War II, Dobermans served their country on both sides of the conflict. The American dogs served at home and in the Pacific as the official war dog of the United States Marine

sold to Italy as a safety measure at the beginning of the war. Cherloc was also the grandsire of the bitch Carpenter had purchased days before in Germany.

It was a dangerous but exciting end to the golden age of imports. The Americans now had most of the best dogs from Europe, the best in the world, and the golden age of American-bred Dobermans was about to begin.

Corps—"Devil Dogs," the Marines called them. Close to 900 Dobermans, which was about 90 percent of the Marine Corps war dog contingent, served in Marine War Dog Platoons as scouts, messengers, guards and bomb-sniffing dogs. The dogs were recruited around the United States, with Dictator serving as a poster dog in the recruitment drive. They spent 14 weeks in boot camp, working with their Marine handlers and learning how to

Jack was donated for war service by his owner, and was commended for "outstanding performance of duty against the enemy on Bougainville Island" during World War II.

ignore bomb blasts, rifle fire and all the other sounds and smells of war. Others were trained as mine- and bomb-sniffing dogs.

After the war, many of the dogs were returned to their owners, while many had so bonded with their handlers that they remained with them for life. Only a handful had become too sharp to make it back into society after the horrors of war.

The campaign to recruit the Marine Devil Dogs was led by the Doberman Pinscher Club of America and was handled nationwide by Richard Webster of the prominent Marienland kennel in Baltimore, Maryland. Webster not only did a marvelous job in the war effort, but his breeding

program at home was also doing wonderful things for the American Doberman. He produced two of the illustrious Seven Sires of the 1940s, Domossi and Emperor. The only female of that era to rate with the Seven Sires was Ch. Dow's Illena of Marienland, also bred by Webster.

Illena was purchased for $150 by then-novice Marge Kilburn of Pottstown, Pennsylvania, from Webster. It is ironic that Kilburn, who became a long-time judge and one of the breed's most respected icons, bred Dobermans for just five years because she was deeply troubled by the heartaches and setbacks that come with breeding. But what a five years! Kilburn was able to produce more than 30 champions and make an indelible mark in Doberman history for herself, Illena, and a host of other Kilburn dogs.

AMERICA BUILDS ITS OWN DYNASTIES

Before the 1940s ended, two black dogs of lasting greatness, Delegate and Storm, were on the march. Ch. Delegate vd Elbe, born in 1947 to a Uranus son and a Domossi daughter, was a 28½-inch, 90-pound black dog that carried the genes for all four

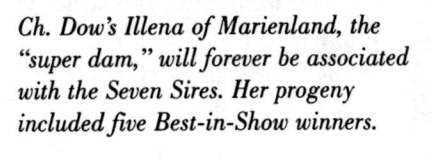

Ch. Dow's Illena of Marienland, the "super dam," will forever be associated with the Seven Sires. Her progeny included five Best-in-Show winners.

Ch. Delegate vd Elbe is fourth on the all-time champion-producing list, born in 1947. As you can see from the photo of his grandson, Ch. Steb's Top Skipper, he was dominant in passing on his handsome traits.

color combinations. But despite his large size and genetic dilution, he sired 55 champions in 60 breedings—still good enough today to rank him fourth on the all-time championship-producing list.

Delegate was a rare producer, siring the two-time (1954 and 1955) winner of the DPCA National Specialty, Ch. Dortmund Delly's Colonet Jet, who in turn was the sire of another immortal, Ch. Steb's Top Skipper, himself the sire of almost 50 champions. Delegate was also the grandsire of two-time National Specialty winner (1962 and 1963) Ch. Singenwald's Prince Kuhio, who was in turn the grandsire of Ch. Highland's Satan's Image, the black sire of the 1960s and 1970s who is sixth on the all-time producing list with 53 champions.

Delegate was also the prime factor in launching the historic Ahrtal kennel of German-born Tess Henseler in Pennsylvania. Henseler migrated from Germany and managed a horse farm in Pennsylvania before turning to Dobermans after a serious riding injury in the 1940s. She began in 1947 with Meadowmist Isis of Ahrtal, a black bitch sired by Emperor who proved a sensational mate for Delegate. Both dogs carried the genes for several colors, which helped make Tess a powerful force in the consolidation of the American Doberman. She won a long string of Breeder of

Ch. Steb's Top Skipper, a Delegate grandson, produced almost 50 champions.

the Year awards and gave the fancy two great sires: the blue Felix v Ahrtal, a grandson of Storm and a great grandson of Delegate, born in 1958; and Cassio v Ahrtal, a black dog very much linebred on Delegate, born in 1964.

Dogs of dilution were not exactly the most sought-after animals in those times (and not even today) because of their widespread inherent coat problems. It is great testimony to Felix that he was given the chance to sire 28 American champions. Cassio sired 37 champions in his illustrious career.

Ch. Rancho Dobes Storm, born in 1949, an Alcor grandson and a great-grandson of Ferry and Muck, was a meteor who streaked across the canine world in spectacular fashion. He was in and out of the ring in 25 shows with 25 breed wins, 22 Group wins and 17 Bests in Show, including back-to-back successes at Westminster in 1952 and 1953. Dobermans have four victories at that prestigious show, and Storm owns two of them. (The other two were Ferry and the red bitch Ch. Royal Tudors Wild as the Wind in 1989.)

Fleitmann, no doubt proud of the Westphalia heritage in Storm, wrote, "The Germans have not yet produced a dog to beat Storm. But then, there is quite a difference between Storm and the next best American dog." Adamson was the first to breed to Storm, taking a daughter of Dictator, Damasyn Sikhandi, to him.

One of the top dogs in the 1950s and 1960s was Ch. Borong the Warlock, CD, heavy in Damasyn and Dictator on the dam's side. He was bred, owned and handled by Henry Frampton, who had a wonderful partnership with Warlock until he was retired at the grand old age of 11. He won the National Specialty show in 1956, 1957 and 1960—a feat matched only by the all-time winning Doberman, Ch. Brunswig Cryptonite in the 1990s. Warlock had a trophy case that included 234 breed wins, 61 specialty show wins and seven all-breed Best-in-Show victories. Frampton took Warlock to Germany when he was just two years of age, and gained an "excellent" rating at the national Sieger show.

Warlock, a dominant black dog, sired 39 champions, including the 1964 National Specialty

Tess Hensler of von Ahrtal Kennels in Pennsylvania with two of her puppies.

Ch. Rancho Dobes Storm has a spectacular show career. Only three Dobermans have won Westminster, and Storm won it twice. This is his first win in 1952.

winner, Ch. Jem's Amythest v Warlock, CD. Frampton died suddenly of a heart attack when showing Amythest at a show in South Carolina in 1966. Warlock died three days later.

One of the great curiosities of the breed is that the name Warlock is still misrepresented many times over in newspaper advertisements for Doberman puppies. Newspaper advertisements,

predominantly in the South, often announce "Warlock bloodline pups" that have nothing to do with the original Borong the Warlock. It appears that the unknowing advertisers, anxious to sell pups, merely follow the popular trend of the day and announce they have "Warlock bloodlines." Maybe there was some old dog in Louisiana named Warlock, but it sure isn't the original who died more than 30 years ago!

The great Dictator spread his influence across the United States, making him the basis for a number of major kennels. The most significant was the Midwest connection of Browns kennel, owned by Jack and Eleanor Brown in St. Louis, and Marks-Tey, owned by Joanna and Keith Walker of nearby

Ch. Borong the Warlock, CD, a standout of the 1950s, was often used as an example of near perfection when illustrating the breed standard.

Centralia, Illinois. The Browns began with a Dictator daughter, Ch. Dow's Dame of Kilburn, and bred her back to Dictator to produce a red male many thought was Dictator's best son, Ch. Brown's Eric, the sire of 28 champions. One of Eric's daughters, Ch. Brown's Bridget, gave the Browns their first of four DPCA National Specialty wins in 1961. Bridget was later bred to her litter brother, the black Ch. Brown's Dion, in another spectacular inbreeding experiment. One of the offspring, the red Ch. Brown's Gi-Gi of Arbel, became the mother of two more DPCA National Specialty winners: the red Ch. Brown's A-Amanda in 1971, and the two-time winner, another red, Ch. Brown's B-Brian, who was successful in 1973 and 1975.

Keith and Joanna Walker met while Keith was an American serviceman in England during World War II. They began with a double Dictator granddaughter they bought from Peggy Adamson: the very dark red bitch, Ch. Damasyn the Waltzing Brook, CD, or Mitzi as she was called. Mitzi was bred to Ch. Brown's Eric to give the Walkers a bloodline concentrated heavily on Dictator.

Marks-Tey became a major force in the breed behind Ch. Derek of Marks-Tey, a red male who carried the color dilution factor but had the opportunity to produce 10 American champions and helped in the foundation of the all-time top-producing kennel, Marienburg, owned by Mary Rodgers.

In their prime, the Walkers had a profound effect with an outstanding breeding program that included some of the greats of American Doberman lore, including Derek, Ch. Marks-Tey Melanie and their offspring, Ch. Marks-Tey Shawn, CD (sire of 16 champions), and the top-winning and producing Ch. Marks-Tey Shay.

While the Walkers, who now live in retirement in North Carolina, might breed only an occasional litter today, they have made a monumental contribution to the breed and the blind of America with a passionate involvement in producing, selecting and training pilot dogs and raising many thousands of dollars for Pilot Dogs, Inc., of Columbus, Ohio. The Walkers have contributed countless dogs, including rescue dogs, puppies donated by other kennels and an occasional litter of their own.

The general Marks-Tey breeding program, based on the same type of dog and the same

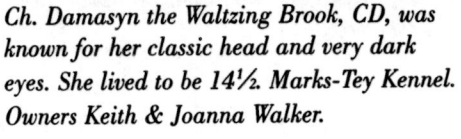
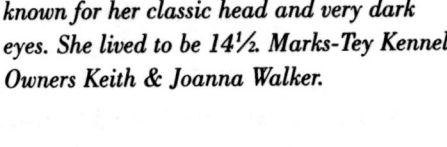

Ch. Damasyn the Waltzing Brook, CD, was known for her classic head and very dark eyes. She lived to be 14½. Marks-Tey Kennel. Owners Keith & Joanna Walker.

Ch. Brown's B-Brian sired almost 30 champions and won the National Specialty twice. (Marjorie Brooks)

principles and ethics of the Walkers, is now under the care of Joanna's coauthor for this book, Rod—an Australian living in Texas. He also breeds under his own prefix, Bikila. In recent times there has been success through a number of prominent champions and the 1996 Top Producing Dam, Bikila's Katarina of Marks-Tey; plus her grandson, Ch. Bikila's Qanah of Marks-Tey, a Superior Specimen Award winner at only 16 months at the 1996 DPCA National Specialty.

Dictator was also the influence in America's longest and currently producing kennel, Mikadobe, owned by the indomitable Mae Downing of Atlanta, Georgia. Downing began in 1946 with Damasyn the Bat, who was sired by Dictator out of the Domossi-Illena daughter, Kilburn Beeline. After producing such important sires as Ch. Mikadobe's Cupid, Ch. Mikadobe's Paris and Ch. Mikadobe's Ninja Warrior, she is still breeding an occasional litter today in her 80s.

Jane Kay of the important Kay Hills kennel in the Northeast was another major contributor who

Ch. Derek of Marks-Tey, a red male, descended from Dictator's line. He sired 10 champions. Owned and handled by Keith Walker. (Robert Hickey)

Ch. Bikila's Qanah of Marks-Tey, a DPCA Superior Specimen, carries on two great kennel names. (Wayne Cott)

Also, it is so much easier for breeders today to fly a brood bitch to any corner of the country or to use frozen semen to gain access to quality studs and improve breeding programs. That is what makes Delegate's 55 champion offspring and Dictator's 52 so meaningful. They are among the top-seven-producing sires of all-time, and they did it in the more leisurely era of the 1940s and 1950s.

TODAY'S STANDOUTS

Ch. Brunswig's Cryptonite has more than 100 Bests in Show and 100 championship offspring, making him the winningest and most productive Doberman in American, and most certainly world history. (Cryptonite is the handsome dog in the photo at the beginning of Chapter 15.) This three-time winner of the National Specialty (1990, 1991 and 1994) is the epitome of the modern high-profile show dog. He flew almost every weekend to different shows around the country, sometimes city-hopping on a single weekend, in a relentless quest for the record. His owners were Sam and Marion Lawrence, who poured hundreds of thousands of dollars into the dog and achieved it all.

But the red dog with the color dilution factor was not all about money. He was a true producer, and his undoubted quality, smooth lines and easy-to-get-along-with disposition were prime factors in his success as a stud. To be red and diluted are not easy mountains to climb in the Doberman breeding world, where black is the popular color for a stud dog. And his success continues after his death. Frozen semen taken from the dog has already produced countless animals.

will be remembered for the great brood bitches Ch. Kay Hills Paint the Town Red, Ch. Kay Hills Witch Soubretta, and Ch. Kay Hills Red Letter Day. Kay bred only 22 litters and produced 30 champions.

The incredible growth of the dog show industry and the ease of travel for dog owners, some even using private planes, has allowed modern breeders and dogs to shatter all the old records.

Ch. Electra's the Windwalker sired 94 champions. His daughter won Westminster, and his grandson was the top Working Dog of all time. (Judith Bingham)

Cryptonite's grandfather, the red Ch. Electra's the Windwalker, bred and owned by Judith Bingham in California, sired 94 champions from only 41 dams, and will be remembered for his incredible influence. He was a good show dog but a better producer. His red daughter, Ch. Royal Tudor's Wild as the Wind (or Indy, as she was affectionately called) amassed a great show record, including 46 Bests in Show topped by the biggest one of all: Westminster in 1989. Indy was bred and owned by Sue Korp in California.

Indy was one of the breed's greatest representatives. Apart from all her show records, she became the first Doberman champion to obtain her UD

and TDX titles in obedience competition. (There's a photo of her in Appendix D.)

All Indy's show records are being broken by another of the modern jet-set show dogs, the red Ch. Toledobes Serenghetti, winner of the 1996 DPCA National Specialty. (There's a photograph of her at the very beginning of this chapter.) She carries the prefix Toledobes of Judy and Pat Doniere, of Toledo, Ohio, breeder-judges who have dedicated much of their lives to the Doberman breed.

The other top studs on the all-time list are Ch. Gra-Lemor's Demetrius vd Victor, a dog produced and owned by Grace Moore of Pennsylvania, and Ch. Marienburg's Sun Hawk, CD, bred and owned by Mary Rodgers of California. Demetrius, born in 1966, was the epitome of Damasyn breeding, sired by Ch. Damasyn Derringer. A black dog capable of producing all four colors, Demetrius was the number five producing sire of all time, with 54 champions.

This 29-inch male with a tough attitude, especially to other dogs, overcame the dilution prejudice to achieve his greatness. It is very interesting that the number one producer of all time, Cryptonite, is a red with the dilution factor, and Delegate and Demetrius also carried dilution.

The number three champion producer of all time, Sun Hawk (born in 1973), ironically made it three reds at the top of the list, behind Cryptonite and Windwalker. Sun Hawk, who had 85 champions from 42 breedings, also had his roots in Dictator through the Browns and Marks-Tey kennels. He is the vanguard of the incredibly successful Marienburg kennel of Mary Rodgers, who has

Ch. Marienburg's Sun Hawk, CD, sired 85 champions and is definitely one of the greats.

amassed all the major records as a breeder in the United States. Rodgers, who began in the 1960s, has produced more than 120 champion Dobermans and will no doubt keep adding to her record despite spending more time on the judging circuit.

Her success at the DPCA National Specialty, where she has owned and bred no less than six winners, is legendary. She purchased the 1967 and 1968 winner, Ch. Sultana v Marienburg, a granddaughter of Top Skipper; and she bred Sun Hawk, who won in 1976 and 1978, and Sun Hawk's black daughter, Ch. Marienburg's Marty Hartman, who won in 1979 and 1983.

There are many dedicated breeders and many animals who are not mentioned here who have played a role in the development of the American Doberman. Space does not permit a list, but it's safe to say that the breed is in many good hands as we begin the next one hundred years.

(JoAnn James)

CHAPTER 12

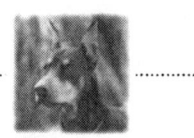

What You Should Know About Breeding Dobermans

Breeding a litter of Dobermans, or dogs of any breed, is a huge responsibility to the individual dogs and to the breed, and anyone who takes it on should have a high level of learning and experience. That includes a complete understanding of the breed standard and a "mind's eye" view of breed type, the breed's strengths and weaknesses (including health considerations) and a working knowledge of genetics. And it sure would help to have some knowledge of linebreeding, inbreeding and outcrossing, as well as all the physical aspects involved in breeding, including the mating, care of the brood bitch, the birth process and the inherent dangers therein, rearing and feeding puppies and how to handle tail docking and ear cropping. In other words, a Doberman owner had best spend a lot of time in the breed listening, learning and helping out others before even thinking about that first litter.

THE MYTHS OF BREEDING

Breeding is not, as many people believe, as simple as throwing two animals together to breed in a room or the backyard, waiting nine weeks for the puppies to arrive, and then having the mother feed them until they go to their new homes.

It is truly disconcerting to hear somebody who has been in the breed for about five minutes declare that they are going to breed a litter. It is also worrisome when a well-meaning but unprepared family decides to breed little Annie the Doberman because they think she needs to have one litter, or because the kids should be exposed to the miracle of birth. But all these things are happening somewhere as you read this.

No reputable breeder gets into it for the money. Taking proper care of Doberman puppies is likely to cost far more than you make from selling them. (Rod Humphries)

It is equally disconcerting to hear a prospective puppy-buyer, when told the price of a top-quality Doberman pup, say, "Gee, that's a lot of money. I ought to get myself some bitches and get into breeding." Such a person is not likely to produce pups of any quality. In fact, no responsible breeder makes money on purebred litters. If the breeder does all the right things and doesn't cut corners, the expenses almost always outweigh the income. If somebody tells you they are making good money breeding Doberman pups, they are probably doing a disservice to the breed and representing their pups as much better than they really are. In the 1970s and early 1980s, quick-money people got into Dobermans because they were popular as guard dogs; after breed registrations ran to incredible numbers, the bust came because their indiscriminate breeding created health and temperament problems.

THE JOYS OF BREEDING

Anybody contemplating a litter should ask himself five basic questions:

1. Do I really know what I am doing if I breed a litter of Dobermans?

2. Will the particular mating I am considering improve the Doberman breed?

3. Do I have the time, dedication, patience and financial resources to spend months preparing for and raising a litter?

4. Do I have the stomach for the blood, diarrhea and mess, and the heartache of possible stillborn pups and pups fading to death?

5. Do I have a market for the pups, or will I be forced to keep some or give them away without any financial return?

If you can answer a resounding "yes" to all five questions, then breeding can be a highly rewarding experience. It is a truly amazing process in which you get to share the most intimate moments of your dog's life. The bond between owner and brood bitch becomes stronger, and the breeder gets to share in the joy of the offspring with her. The breeder plans the litter genetically and physically, and then has the heartwarming task of helping the mother to shape their personalities and their lives.

Breeding is a creative art form. It is a joust with Mother Nature. It can be tough and cruel when things go wrong, and it requires hard work, dedication and often frustration. But it can become a passion. It gets in the blood. And the next thing you know, it is 30 or 40 years later and you are still losing money—and loving every minute of it.

START WITH A GOOD PUPPY BITCH

The breeders are the owners of the bitch. It is they who plan and raise the litter. If prospective puppy owners have any thoughts

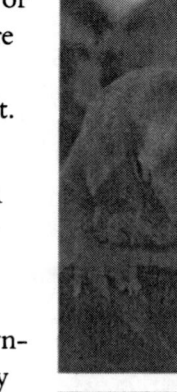

If you are ready for the demands of breeding wisely and well, it can be an amazing experience. (JoAnn James)

at all of breeding, they should buy a puppy bitch. A puppy bitch may not turn out to be a Champion, or even a show dog, but it may have sufficient quality and excellent prospects as a brood bitch. In that case, the owner has the opportunity to choose a top stud dog and upgrade the quality in the bitch's first litter.

Male puppies are of little use for a breeding program unless they are so special that one day they could be used as a stud dog. The chances of that happening are extremely slim, because only a very limited number of males nationwide are good enough and campaigned enough to have even a limited number of bitches brought to them for service. Good breeders only go to the best studs, even if that means driving a thousand or more miles or shipping the bitch by plane. They are not going to use a local dog just because it is a Doberman and it is convenient. So if you eventually want to breed, think bitch, not dog.

The next step is to get the best quality bitch puppy available, a subject we covered in Chapter 5. The more quality and the fewest faults in your foundation bitch, combined with the stud dog that best complements her, means you will be more likely to end up with high-quality puppies in the first generation. However, it is not easy to pry top-quality bitches away from breeders, so a co-ownership with the breeder may be a route worth investigating.

Incidentally, we said start with a puppy, but you should not breed a bitch until she is at least two years of age. Why not? It takes that long for certain inherited flaws to show up. Your bitch must also be mature enough to handle a litter and be a good mother.

Is This Bitch a Good Prospect?

In other words, will breeding this bitch improve the Doberman breed as a whole? The United States is overpopulated with dogs, and shelters and rescue groups all over the country are picking up unwanted Dobermans. Is the bitch *so good* that she needs to be bred? Should her temperament be perpetuated?

A thorough knowledge of breed type and the standard are imperative in answering these questions, and a good dose of honesty and common sense must be added to the mix. It's wise to talk to the bitch's breeder and to other people knowledgeable in Dobermans, and to make a calculated decision and not an emotional one.

If the bitch passes the first test of conformation and temperament, the next questions are about physical and genetic health. The Doberman has its share of inherited health problems, primarily the Killer C's: cancer, cardiomyopathy and cervical vertebral instability (described in Chapter 8), and a breeder has an obligation to the puppy itself, to the breed in general and to the people who receive that

A top breeding program is based on a high-quality foundation bitch. Ch. Moraga Hills High Fashion was the dam of 19 champions. (Rich Bergman Photos)

puppy to avoid breeding certain dogs or a family of dogs that have these problems. This is no guarantee that a particular puppy will have a disease-free life, but it is an enormous step in the right direction.

Making the Tough Choices

Sometimes excluding a dog from a breeding program can be a most difficult decision, as the dog or dogs involved may be great show winners or wonderful working dogs who otherwise have all the important traits a breeder is looking for. One of the hardest things Rod Humphries had to do was to eliminate one of his most outstanding males from his breeding program in the early 1990s. The dog, Ch. Bikila's Jet Setter of Marks-Tey, an outstanding show animal and a promising stud, died suddenly of cardiomyopathy just before his seventh birthday.

It was the first time Rod had encountered the disease in his program. He informed all those who had used the dog at stud, and those who had puppies, of the dog's death and recommended that none of the offspring be used in any breeding program. The next step was to eliminate Jet Setter from his own program and pedigrees. A dozen litters later, there has been no further instance of cardiomyopathy at his kennel.

Many people suggested to Rod that he not eliminate all of Jet Setter's offspring from the breeding program, "because you can breed away from the disease." By "breeding away," they meant that Rod could breed Jet Setter's offspring to "clear" dogs and slowly eliminate the disease that way. But there is no genetic test for cardiomyopathy and it can strike at any age, so who is "clear"? The point is that the breeder has the responsibility to do all he or she can to eliminate such problems.

The breeder needs to do homework on the health background of the bitch and prospective stud dogs, and make decisions that are beneficial to the breed. If there are nagging questions as to whether either dog or bitch may be a carrier of

Sometimes breeders have to make very difficult choices. When this Group winner, Ch. Bikila Jet Setter of Marks-Tey, died of cardiomyopathy at age six, all his offspring were eliminated from the breeding program. (K. Booth)

some debilitating genetic disease, then perhaps things need to be reevaluated.

Stud dog owners have a stake in this decision-making, and while some uncaring owners will breed their dog to any bitch, for most the reputation of the dog and the quality of the pups he produces are important to the stud's future. So many bitches get turned down by caring stud owners. A good stud owner will also ask for copies of tests done to ensure the health of the bitch before making a final decision on whether the stud will breed a bitch.

INBREEDING, LINEBREEDING AND OUTCROSSING

Inbreeding, linebreeding and outcrossing are the three methods of breeding animals of the same breed. Crossbreeding is the term used when dogs of different breeds are mated—a method used to develop new breeds such as the Doberman Pinscher in the 19th century.

Inbreeding

Inbreeding means mating closely related dogs: father and daughter, mother and son, or brother and sister. Some geneticists also call half-brother to half-sister matings inbreeding. By breeding a daughter to her father, the qualities of the sire are perpetuated because the resulting offspring will have three-quarters of the bloodline of the sire. If a breeder wants to perpetuate the dam, then breeding a son back to his mother is the best course. Brother-to-sister mating preserves the "blood" of both parents in equal amounts.

One of the great myths of our time is that inbreeding causes mental problems, lack of fertility, diminishing vigor and other serious health problems in humans, dogs and any other animal. It is important to debunk that myth, because so many novices quickly shy away from inbreeding when they hear the word or see it in canine pedigrees. Many prospective owners have lost the chance to gain outstanding pups because of their fear of inbred dogs.

If the truth be known, most great producers have been inbred, and one of the greatest gems a prospective breeder can find in the dog world is an inbred bitch from a breeding program that has eradicated many of the health problems of Dobermans and refined the type.

If done correctly, inbreeding is the greatest tool in the hands of any person involved in animal husbandry. The key phrase here is "if done correctly." If two closely related, superior members of any species who have a history of good body, mind, health and fertility are mated together, they can be expected with some certainty to produce superior offspring. If a breeder mates two closely related animals who have a poor history and a load of problems, particularly if each has the same problem, the results will be disastrous. To use the old computer adage, garbage in, garbage out! Inbreeding in and of itself will not produce mental midgets or diminished health. It is the individual animals and their traits that will determine whether inbreeding is successful.

In a nontechnical sense, every time a Doberman is bred to another Doberman, it is inbreeding. The breed could not have been established without inbreeding—locking in traits by breeding close relatives. The original characteristics that make a Doberman a Doberman and not a German Shepherd have been inbred since the beginning. In the wild, every pride, pack, colony and flock is almost totally incestuous. Survival of the fittest eliminates the weaklings, and the group just keeps moving forward with more inbreeding than one could ever imagine. One of the reasons that results are not always as robust is that we keep the weak members of a species alive using medical technology.

If done correctly, inbreeding can produce outstanding dogs. Bikila's Katarina of Marks-Tey, an inbred bitch, was the DPCA top-producing dam in 1996. (Rod Humphries)

You can liken inbreeding to playing a "fixed" slot machine at Las Vegas. On a machine with five rollers, outcrossing means the breeder has all five in play and the combinations are practically endless, making winning very difficult. In linebreeding, there are two aces locked in and the breeder is playing with three rollers. With inbreeding, four of the rollers are locked on aces and the breeder is playing with only one roller.

Inbreeding—and to a lesser extent, linebreeding—reduces the number of unpredictable factors in a mating because you are using dogs with very similar genetic makeups. Inbred dogs become dominant for certain traits, because they both carry the gene for that trait. Therefore, phenotype (what the dog looks like) and the genotype (what the dog carries genetically) become the same in many, many instances: What you see is what you get.

The two most important advantages of inbreeding are that it enables a breeder to genetically lock in the traits and the "look" they wish to perpetuate; and it acts like a genetic filter to quickly flush unwanted genes to the surface. If two breeding animals are closely related, they are very likely carrying the same recessive, or hidden, copies of problem genes. The breeder obtains instant knowledge of any problems in his or her stock and can then do the right thing and eliminate affected animals from the program.

Having made a case for inbreeding, we must warn any potential breeder that inbreeding is a loaded gun in the wrong hands. The novice may be out of his or her depth with inbreeding, because it relies on a very deep knowledge of the ancestry of each breeding animal and the breed in general. And novices are not always likely to have superior breeding stock at their disposal. But understanding inbreeding and not being afraid of it is a most important part of the education of a new breeder.

Linebreeding

Mating animals that are closely related in line to the same ancestor is called linebreeding. If done correctly, linebreeding perpetuates the qualities of that ancestor. When a stud dog is advertised as having a top-producing dog that appears several times in several generations of his pedigree, that is good linebreeding. However, there are people with insufficient knowledge of the subject who advertise that they have a linebred dog when they most

With inbreeding and linebreeding, a breeder is often able to lock in desirable traits and produce more consistent quality. These two pups are sisters. They both became Pilot Dogs. Breeder, Joanna Walker (John & Pat Gray)

definitely do not. Most of the time, the owner will quote a certain dog who merely appears on both sides of the pedigree, often too far back to have any genetic significance. That is not linebreeding.

Linebreeding is the breeding method of choice for many accomplished breeders. They believe they can edge toward perfection by linebreeding on a particular dog without throwing all their eggs into one basket by inbreeding.

Outcrossing

Outcrossing means mating dogs of the same breed that are not immediately related. Even if the sire and dam have a mutual ancestor in say, the third, fourth or fifth generation, that is still considered outcrossing. Although it is not scientifically precise,

to better understand outcrossing one must consider that each parent provides 50 percent of the hereditary factors in the offspring, the grandparents 25 percent, the third generation 12.5 percent, the fourth generation 6.25 percent, the fifth generation only 3.125 percent and so on.

Outcrossing is normally not a recommended form of breeding, unless a breeder has a strong need to go outside of a family line to obtain a certain characteristic that is lacking in an inbred or linebred program. Outcrossing will produce some outstanding animals, often in the first generation, but the variations in type and size are enormous, and it is difficult for a breeder to obtain any continuity of type.

If an inbreeder runs into trouble in his or her program, he or she can bring the inbreeding to zero with one outcross. On the other hand, an outcross breeder who runs into trouble has absolutely no logical path to follow.

The Mating

The stud-dog owner has complete charge of the mating process. The stud-dog owner will request certain health tests, certainly including canine brucellosis (a sexually transmitted disease that can cause infertility) and a veterinary check for any obstruction that may cause physical problems in the mating. The bitch owner should most definitely get the bitch a complete checkup, including tests for internal parasites, before breeding. Be sure

Linebreeding is the method of choice for many breeders who do not want to throw all their eggs into one basket by inbreeding. (Alan & Jacquie Wendt)

all vaccination shots are current *before* the mating, not after, so that the mother can pass the antibodies on to her offspring.

The progesterone level in the blood gives an almost infallible indication of when a bitch is about to ovulate. Several progesterone level tests should be done after the heat cycle begins to determine the best time for breeding. Many breeders today use artificial insemination with recently chilled or frozen semen, and it is imperative in that case to have the timing right. Also, if the bitch owner has to drive a long distance for the mating or is sending the bitch thousands of miles by air, it is simply common sense to have the ovulation time pinpointed by testing.

Some bitches are receptive to the stud dog when they are not truly ready to breed, and some excited studs—often the young ones—will misread signals. That's why in the old days there were a lot of breedings that did not produce litters. The heat cycle lasts three weeks, and the rule of thumb is that a bitch is ready to breed from the 12th to the 14th day. But in a long history of breeding, the authors have had successful matings from the 7th to the 21st day. The progesterone tests have taken so much of the guesswork out of breeding.

The stud owner will orchestrate all the proceedings during the mating, because he or she knows the stud dog and his idiosyncrasies. The bitch will probably be muzzled the first time, and the stud owner may or may not want the bitch owner to handle the bitch during the mating.

Just like *canis lupus* in the wild, *canis familiaris* has a rather unique physical phenomenon at mating called the tie. During intercourse, the bulbis glandis (a knot at the base of the penis) swells, and the male is then held in place by the muscles of the vagina. The tie can last from a few minutes to 45 minutes or more, with the male either resting on top of the bitch or turning a leg over her back so that the animals are back to back. Never try to separate two tied animals, as it could cause injury. To quash another myth, the length of the tie has no bearing on the size of a litter.

COAT COLOR INHERITANCE

The Doberman comes in four accepted colors: black, red, blue and fawn. However, when you consider all the possible combinations of dominant and recessive genes, plus the non-dilution and dilution factors, there are nine genetic color profiles. In referring to these combinations, uppercase B represents the dominant color black and lowercase b represents red, which is recessive to black. Uppercase D is the non-dilution factor, which is dominant over the dilution factor d. Blue is a dilution of black, and fawn is a dilution of red.

1. BBDD: A black dog with no recessive and no dilution. It will produce only black offspring, no matter what the coat color of the dog is to which it is mated.

2. BBDd: A black dog with dilution for blue. This dog can produce only black and blue offspring.

3. BdDD: A black dog with red recessive and no dilution. This dog can produce only black and red offspring.

4. BbDd: A black dog with red recessive and dilution. This dog can produce offspring of all four colors.

5. BBdd: A blue dog that can produce only black and blue offspring.

6. Bbdd: A blue dog with red recessive and dilution. This dog can produce offspring of all four colors.

7. bbDD: A red dog with no dilution. This dog can produce only red and black offspring.

8. bbDd: A red coated dog with dilution. This dog can produce offspring of all four colors.

9. bbdd: A fawn dog that can produce offspring of all four colors.

Determining the genetic number of a brood bitch or a stud dog is obviously not easy. There are some combinations that are simple to trace if the parents of the bitch are known. For example, if a dominant black dog (1) had

CARE OF THE PREGNANT BITCH

Gestation is 63 days, or nine weeks, from the first mating. It is not unusual for pups to be born a couple of days early or late, but a swing of five or six days does not augur well for survival. A vet should be able to palpate the bitch in search of puppies at 26 days. Some breeders, anxious to know, will have an ultrasound done.

The bitch must be kept in tip-top shape because she will need to be healthy and strong for her labor. She should receive normal exercise and food in the early weeks of pregnancy, and then at about the fifth week she should get an been bred to a red bitch with no dilution (7), then every one of the offspring would be black with a recessive gene for red (3).

Some people will do test breedings to try to determine a dog's genetic color makeup. For example, if the owner of a promising new stud dog is wondering if his black male carries dilution, a simple test breeding to a fawn bitch would be enlightening. If all the pups were black, the owner could expect that his dog is a dominant black (1); if only black and blue dogs were produced, chances are his stud is a black (2); if there were only black and red dogs in the litter, it would almost certainly tag the stud as a black (3); and if the offspring were all four colors, there would be absolutely no doubt he was a black (4).

A Coat Color Inheritance Chart, which lists all the possible combinations and the expected percentages of breeding any combination over a significant number of litters, is available through the Doberman Pinscher Club of America.

increase in food rations and a change to higher-protein food especially formulated for lactating bitches and puppies. The food increase is normally a trial-and-error situation, as each bitch is different. Weight must be watched carefully, as novice owners are inclined to overfeed because they feel the bitch may not be getting enough.

Overfed bitches lead to fat puppies and difficult births.

Supplements for vitamins C and E should be increased at this time. Rod increases vitamin C to his bitches from the normal 6,000 mg to 8,000 mg, and vitamin E from the normal 400 IUs to 600 IUs a day. There is no doubt that this helps strengthen the uterine muscles and aids the bitch in long labor.

Some bitches have morning sickness around the third or fourth week of pregnancy and might need to be fed smaller meals throughout the day. The same procedure may be needed if the bitch gets so big that she is uncomfortable, sometimes going off her food.

Many flea and tick applications and other drugs, including certain antibiotics, are harmful if used during pregnancy. The breeder should check with the veterinarian before using any medication.

FINAL PREPARATIONS

The breeder should also talk with the veterinarian about 10 days before the delivery to make final preparations and arrange for veterinary help should there be a crisis, particularly in the middle of the night.

The whelping box and all the necessary materials should be in place a week in advance. Whelping boxes come in all shapes, sizes and materials, and the newcomer should talk to experienced breeders about what works and how to go about either buying one or making one. Rod has an 8-foot-square box that consists of 4-foot-high wooden walls bolted together with no base. The box can be quickly assembled and is easily cleaned and stored away. Each of the walls has a small shelf, which prevents the bitch from rolling on pups that are lying against the wall.

To make the base, Rod begins at a hunting or camping store by purchasing large ½-inch or inch-thick pads of sponge rubber and several inexpensive, tearproof and waterproof tarps. He lays the sponge on the linoleum floor and then places the tarp over the sponge. Finally, the bolted box is laid over both. To prevent the tarp from moving when the bitch is vigorously nesting, Rod will sometimes tape it to the linoleum floor, or use the small pieces of rope that come with the tarp and tie it to the bolts of the whelping box wall, holding everything securely in place. The brood bitch then has a soft, easy-to-clean bed.

There is a lot of blood, fluid and afterbirth material during and after the delivery, and it can be quickly cleaned off the tarp. Rod uses some newspapers during the whelping and later uses old blankets, but at whelping time he primarily wants a soft, easy-to-clean surface that reduces the risk of infection. Joanna Walker uses washable indoor-outdoor

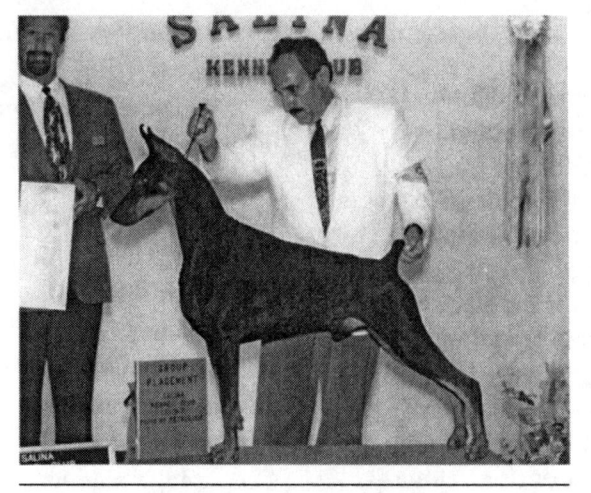

The stud dog owner controls the mating. Owners of both stud and bitch should make sure the dogs have had complete health checks before they meet. (Don Petrulis Photography)

carpeting as the base for her whelping box. Joanna hates to see newborn pups trying to negotiate slippery newspaper to reach their mother, and prefers to use a washable, double-bed-size quilted mattress cover.

In case supplementation is needed to give a pup a good start, you'll need to have some puppy milk formula on hand (not regular cow's milk or formula for human babies). Many people use commercial milk replacers made especially for puppies. Joanna's formula is one can of condensed milk with an equal amount of water, blended with two egg yolks and a tablespoon of honey. Keep the mixture refrigerated until needed.

It is absolutely vital to ensure that the newborn pups don't have temperature shock and become chilled—a regular killer of newborns. They need an atmospheric temperature of 82° to 90° to maintain good body heat. A pup's nervous system is not developed, and because puppies have no shivering reflex, they are very vulnerable to changes in the outside temperature for the first few days of their lives. Some breeders keep the room temperature at 82° or more, while others will install heat lamps or pads. The breeder must also make sure that the pups can get away from the heat if they are overheated.

A pregnant bitch can become very large. The sleekness of her back shows that Sufi is big but not overfed. (Marsha Sheppard)

The brood bitch should be introduced to the whelping box several days before the birth. She may not be interested at first, believing in her own mind that the whelping will take place somewhere outside where she has probably been digging for a number of days—or up on your bed, where she likes to sleep. The owner should take her to the

WHELPING SUPPLIES

In addition to the whelping box and good flooring and bedding materials, you'll need plenty of other supplies. Here is a quick list, but do talk to an experienced breeder about what you should have on hand.

A lot of newspapers, which can be shredded for use in the box.

Gallons of antibacterial disinfectant, sponges and paper towels to continually clean the box. (Unprinted newspaper is good.)

Regular towels to clean the newborn pups.

A thermometer to check the bitch's temperature.

Sterilized scissors in case umbilical cords need to be cut.

Iodine to clean severed umbilical cords.

Baby bottles with easy-flow nipples and the correct pet milk formula.

Supplemental heating for the whelping box.

Experienced breeders may keep tubes ready for feeding straight into the pup's stomach, but that is not something we recommend for novices; the tube being pushed down the throat may be diverted to the lungs, and a puppy can quickly drown.

box and let her rest there. She will eventually get the message.

THE WHELPING

In the final stages before delivery, the brood bitch will become increasingly restless. She may seem distressed and want to dig in dirt outside or maybe even in a part of the house. Bitches will not normally eat on the day of the whelping, although some will take food. The body temperature should be checked regularly with a rectal thermometer. When the normal temperature of about 101° dips to below 100° (sometimes to 98°), she is then within 8 to 12 hours of the delivery. The breeder should not be fooled by some bitches whose temperature remains normal until only a short time before delivery. And it is important to remember that any time a dog's body temperature is over 102.5°, there is infection that should be treated by a veterinarian.

When her temperature dips, get the bitch to the whelping box. If she wants to go outside, make sure you watch her carefully. Many a puppy has been unknowingly born in a breeder's backyard, sometimes detected after it is too late.

If there is a word of advice that we can give a novice breeder, it is: Leave the bitch alone. Mother Nature has given her instincts and she is better equipped to handle the delivery than you are. Most novices worry and fuss too much and get in the way. Even breach births, where the feet come first, are fairly normal in dogs. The bitch will, by instinct remove the fetal membrane, shred the umbilical cord with her teeth and clean the pups by licking,

thus stimulating the newborns to breathe. The authors have had bitches who handle large litters by rotating little groups onto the teats. Mother knows best.

The only time the breeder really needs to help is when the pups are coming thick and fast and the bitch cannot work on all of them at once, or when there is a difficult birth or a pup is born motionless. In the first instance, the breeder may need to pull the membrane away from a pup's mouth to get it breathing. The breeder may also need to cut the umbilical cord, but be sure not to cut it too close to the body and to dab it with iodine, because this place is ripe for infection—which can spread quickly to other parts of the small body. The cord may need to be pinched momentarily to stop the bleeding.

The breeder should give each pup a good start by placing it on a nipple. Puppies can go without food for a number of hours before it becomes a problem, but starting them immediately on a nipple, or supplementing if there are a lot of pups, is good advice.

If a new pup is not moving, do not panic. Pick up the pup in a towel and, supporting the head, face the pup downward and work the hands vigorously to help remove the fluid in the lungs. Don't give up easily on a motionless pup, as it might surprise you with a sudden cough and a squirm when you think all is lost.

The breeder must step in quickly if a bitch, losing strength, has difficulty pushing out a pup, and the pup, still in the membrane, is easing back and forth at the vulva. The breeder has to work quickly because once the whelp leaves the uterus and moves to the vaginal canal, the mother is no longer supplying oxygen. The membrane is slippery, so cloth should be used to grasp the pup, preferably along the back or rib cage. The breeder should try to avoid using any force on the head, neck or legs, as it may cause later joint problems.

Whenever you're in doubt, call the veterinarian. The vet would rather get to an obstruction problem early, when a labor-inducing drug or manual manipulation can be effective, rather than waiting until emergency surgery is necessary and lives are at stake.

Here are two general rules about when to call the vet:

1. When a bitch has been straining in heavy labor and no pup has arrived within two hours of the beginning of that labor

2. When the breeder is sure there are still pups to be delivered and it has been three hours since the last birth

Most bitches will stay glued to their pups, but some experienced ones will want to go outside and relieve themselves. Sometimes bitches will take water during the delivery process. Water and some food can be offered to the brood bitch after the whelping is complete, although it is unlikely she will take food until after she has settled down with the pups.

The veterinarian should check the bitch within a few hours after the birth and give her an injection to eliminate any lingering placentas or other material from her body. This reduces the risk of infection.

THE PUPS

If the mother has good milk production, the breeder will have very little to do for the next 10 days or so, as the mother will generally handle everything with the instincts of a professional. Keep a close eye on proceedings, though, and make sure all the pups are getting a fair share of the breast time.

Check the milk to make sure it is not discolored, which means it could be infected. Mastitis, an infection of the mammary glands, can strike in an instant and cause enormous problems. If there is any doubt, use the thermometer to take the bitch's temperature, and report any variations to the veterinarian. Years ago Rod had a brood bitch that began growling throatily at her pups two or three days after the delivery. Within a short time, the bitch collapsed in shock and had to be rushed to the veterinary hospital. The bitch's body had formed a sterile pocket trying to contain the toxins of acute mastitis, but it could not hold and suddenly the toxins ran through her system like a torrent, causing her to collapse. Rod had not understood that the growling meant the bitch was hurting when the pups were sucking on the nipples. The bitch survived, but gangrene caused her to lose an entire breast. Even more disturbing was the fact that the pups had consumed the infected milk and the infection went quickly to their eyes. All the pups had to be rushed to the vet, where puss-filled eyes were opened prematurely and cleaned, and the pups were placed on antibiotics. Two puppies lost sight in one eye due to the infection.

Tail docking is done at two to three days, and it is best done without the mother in attendance so that she cannot hear the yelps of her youngsters. Some experienced breeders prefer to keep the bitch at home, while others will take the bitch to accompany the pups in the car to the vet, but not allow the mother in or near the operating room.

The new breeder should check with knowledgeable Doberman people who are familiar with the work of local veterinarians. The owner should not be afraid to show the vet where the cut is to be made, preferably at the second joint; otherwise anything could happen, and often does. The vet should fold back the skin so that when the cut is made on the bone, there is enough skin to stitch underneath the tail, thereby avoiding the unsightly calluses that appear on some docked tails.

The pups will open their eyes at about 10 days, and by the second week solid food can be offered in what is the beginning of the weaning process. The type of food offered at this time varies drastically from breeder to breeder.

Joanna begins by making small individual meatballs for each pup in the litter and feeds them in small pieces as the pups sit in her lap. The size of the meatball increases with the growth of the pups. At three weeks, she starts them lapping with a mixture of the pet milk formula and chunks of wheat or oatmeal bread blended into a thick gruel. At three-and-a-half weeks Joanna starts her pups on cottage cheese and poached eggs, and at four

Puppies can eat dry puppy food or special formulas you mix up yourself. (Alan & Jacquie Wendt)

weeks she begins adding dry dog food to the meat. The dog food slowly becomes the main diet, while the meat is slowly diminished until it is completely eliminated.

Rod uses the same pet milk formula, minus the eggs, and normal dry baby cereal of rice or oats with banana or apple ingredients, mixed with the pet milk formula. When the pups are heartily consuming the cereal mix, he slowly introduces the dry puppy food, at first in a soft mix with the pet milk formula. Rod then slowly eliminates the milk formula and replaces it with water. In the old days, pups got very messy with sticky cereal, but that has been improved enormously with the invention of what Rod calls the "sombrero" feed dish. The dish has an elevated center, which pushes the food to the outside and deters the pups from getting into the food dish.

Rod also begins vitamin C supplementation in liquid drops from day one, and then slowly increases the vitamin C and adds vitamins E, A and D as per the schedule in Chapter 7.

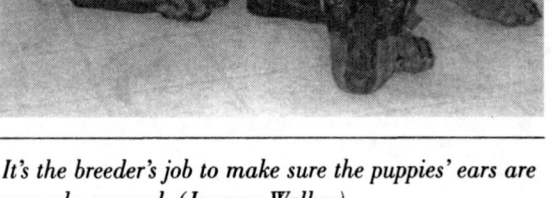

It's the breeder's job to make sure the puppies' ears are properly cropped. (Joanna Walker)

Both authors agree that pups should be weaned from their mother by four and a half weeks, and should be fed four times a day until they are three months old; then feed them three times a day until about five or six months, and then twice a day for life.

The razor-sharp teeth and nails of puppies are brutal on the mother's breasts, and she is less and less inclined to feed the pups after four weeks. Weaning at four and a half weeks also allows the bitch to start drying up her milk and getting back into shape. Bitches who nurse for six or eight weeks invariably do not come back into shape as well as those who have their pups weaned at four and a half weeks.

The last task for the breeder, which is probably the most difficult, is ear cropping. This is covered Chapter 8. Prospective breeders should also see Chapter 6 on socializing and training puppies.

THE FIRST IMMUNIZATIONS

The breeder must ensure that the puppy is given a head start in life with a healthy mother who passes on good colostrum to the offspring. Colostrum is the first milk secreted by the mother, and it contains antibodies that protect puppies against all kinds of diseases during the first weeks of their lives. Bitches which have not been vaccinated for a year should be given a broad-spectrum shot before being mated. The breeder must also strive for a bacteria-free environment.

No puppy should be exposed to the outside world before it has been given at least temporary vaccinations by a veterinarian. Any vaccinations given before pups are nine weeks old are considered temporary. These can include distemper, infectious hepatitis, leptospirosis, parvovirus and parainfluenza in one shot (commonly referred to as DHLPP), plus a coronavirus vaccination.

Many breeders will give precautionary parvo shots at four weeks. At six to seven weeks of age, the pup can receive the first broad temporary vaccination of DHLPP plus corona. This is followed by the first adult shot two weeks later, which is also DHLPP plus corona. Four to five weeks later is the second adult DHLPP vaccination. There is a vaccination for kennel cough that can be administered at 16 weeks. Rabies is prevalent in the United States, particularly in the southern regions, and vaccinations should begin at three months and continue each year throughout life.

No puppy should be exposed to the world beyond its own yard until it has been protected by a full round of vaccinations. (JoAnn James)

Breeders should also guard against worms and should have the pups' feces checked under a microscope. Good breeders will often do precautionary worming even if there is no obvious sign of worms.

Puppies are protected from heartworm by their mother's medication for the early days of life, but heartworm medication for the individual pup should begin at three months, especially in areas with large mosquito populations.

(Barbara Eastwood)

CHAPTER 13

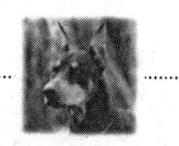

Special Care for the Older Doberman

Life moves so fast for humans. Thirty doesn't seem that long ago, then forty, and suddenly the years slip by at an amazing pace. Unfortunately, life moves even faster for our dogs, most of whom live only about 10 years. In fact, there have been studies done that show a mere 10 percent of the American canine population, which includes all breeds and crossbreds, is over 10 years of age.

LONGEVITY IN DOBERMANS

On average, the Doberman has never been an exceedingly long-lived breed—certainly not one that consistently lives into the teens. To our knowledge, there have been three somewhat unscientific studies done over the years that show the average life expectancy ranges from 8½ years to 9½ years. There are, of course, many animals, mostly bitches, that live heartily into their teens. Males do not do so well, especially considering the ravages of cardiomyopathy, and one that lives over 10 years is a gem.

These life expectancies have been criticized in some quarters, because they can become a self-fulfilling prophecy with breeders setting no goals for longevity. To that end, the Doberman Pinscher Club of America has introduced a certification program that rewards any dog that lives to 10 years. The title,

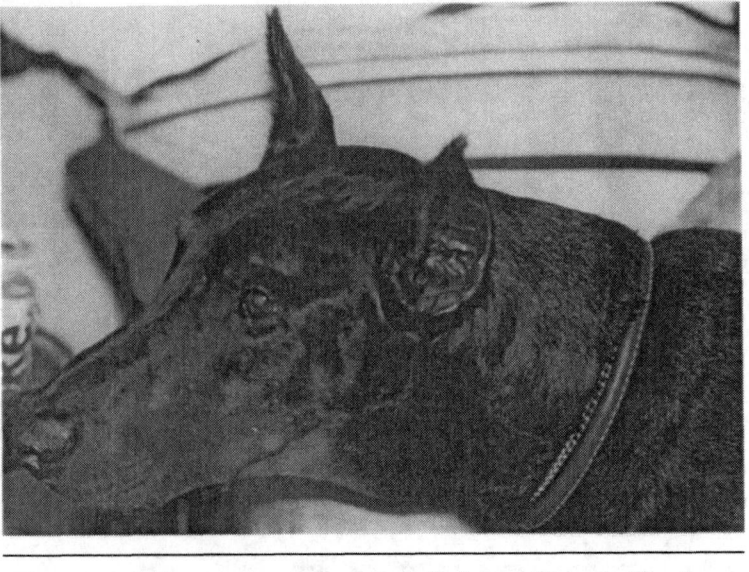

This sweet old boy was rescued at age 8. He is now 13 and still going strong. (Archie Watson)

LC (Longevity Certification), is supplemented by the BFL (Bred for Longevity Certification), which is awarded to dogs whose parents hold the LC.

The longevity program is commendable in that it builds a database of long-lived dogs, but it would be more meaningful if it went hand-in-hand with databases on dogs that have died of the Killer Cs: cardiomyopathy, cancer and cervical vertebral instability (read more about these problems in Chapter 8). That would really be a monumental task, but then, nothing great is easy.

THE AGING PROCESS

It is no secret that the internal organs take a beating throughout life and that degeneration of the liver, kidneys, pancreas, bladder and heart plays a major role in the aging process. At the same time, arthritis and spinal problems make it extremely difficult for the older being, human or dog, to see out his or her later years in comfort. Years of filtering impurities particularly hurts the kidneys and liver, and according to veterinarian and author Dr. Wendell Belfield, "About 80 percent of dogs eight years and over have chronic interstitial nephritis, a degenerative kidney condition caused in large part by the excess protein and impurities in commercial diets."

Belfield gives a colorful description of the process: "Down at the microscopic level of the cells, life is a battlefield. Enemies abound: viruses, bacteria, toxic chemical molecules. If nutrition is good, the cells are strong. If nutrition is poor, the cells are weak. Cells are continually challenged. Strong ones can fight off the invaders. Weaker ones cannot meet the challenge. The toll of dead and wounded cells mounts over the years."

Vitamins Can Help

Belfield maintains that all the nutrients on the vitamin and mineral team are needed to promote rejuvenation: "Vitamins C and E, however, seem to stand out. To see changes in an old dog, it is vital to supply these two versatile vitamins in abundance, but in the process do not neglect the other members of the team."

Scientists have concluded that vitamin E, in particular, is needed to provide protection against peroxidation, the process that damages and eventually kills cells. Vitamin C is another strong antioxidant that works with vitamin E to fight the aging process. However, vitamin C can cause a natural high, and Belfield does not recommend high-dose supplementation for an older dog, which might get hurt doing things it should not be doing.

For the aging medium or large dog, Belfield recommends increasing the dosage of vitamin E to 400 IUs per day but reducing the vitamin C to 750 to 1,500 mg for a medium dog, and to 1,500 to 3,000 mg for a large dog.

Rod, who has extremely active country dogs who still run hard when they are from 8 to 10 years, maintains them on 6,000 mg of vitamin C a day, sometimes even increasing it to work better as an analgesic and anti-inflammatory for injuries. Vitamin E is increased from 400 to 600 IUs a day. Other antioxidants, including vitamin A and selenium, are also given in abundance.

Joanna's dogs receive 1000 units of vitamin C each day, less for puppies, and 400 units of E plus Selenium for all grown dogs. In recent years, she has found that Solid Gold Seameal is of great benefit. This is given twice a day since it only stays in the system twelve hours.

All of her dogs and puppies are given LoveLand conditioner, an all natural product that has also proven to be great protection against fleas. She has not seen a flea in more than seven years.

Joanna is also a believer in good doses of vitamins C and E and selenium for older Dobermans. When the dogs get a little stiff, she also administers glucosamine and chrondroiton complex. This neutraceutical helps lubricate and restore cartilage at the joints.

Jymm Russell with Ebony, a Pilot Dog who had a very long career.

FOOD AND EXERCISE

Most older dogs do not exercise with the vigor of yesteryear, so they do not require the calories or the protein that they needed in youth and middle age. Weak kidneys in older dogs cannot handle large amounts of protein. You should choose a dog food that is geared to the senior dog.

There is a tendency for dog owners to slip the aging family pet a few more treats and scraps, but it can be dangerous because the calorie count far exceeds the dog's activity level. Obesity in older animals can be debilitating and can put a strain on the heart and joints.

Joanna increases the intake of vegetables, such as carrots and green beans, to help keep an older dog's weight down.

If possible, the older Doberman should maintain an exercise regimen that meets its physical capabilities. Remember the old saying, "Use it or lose it." This is very appropriate when it comes to exercise for both dogs and humans. If the dog is capable, keep it moving every day as much as is physically possible.

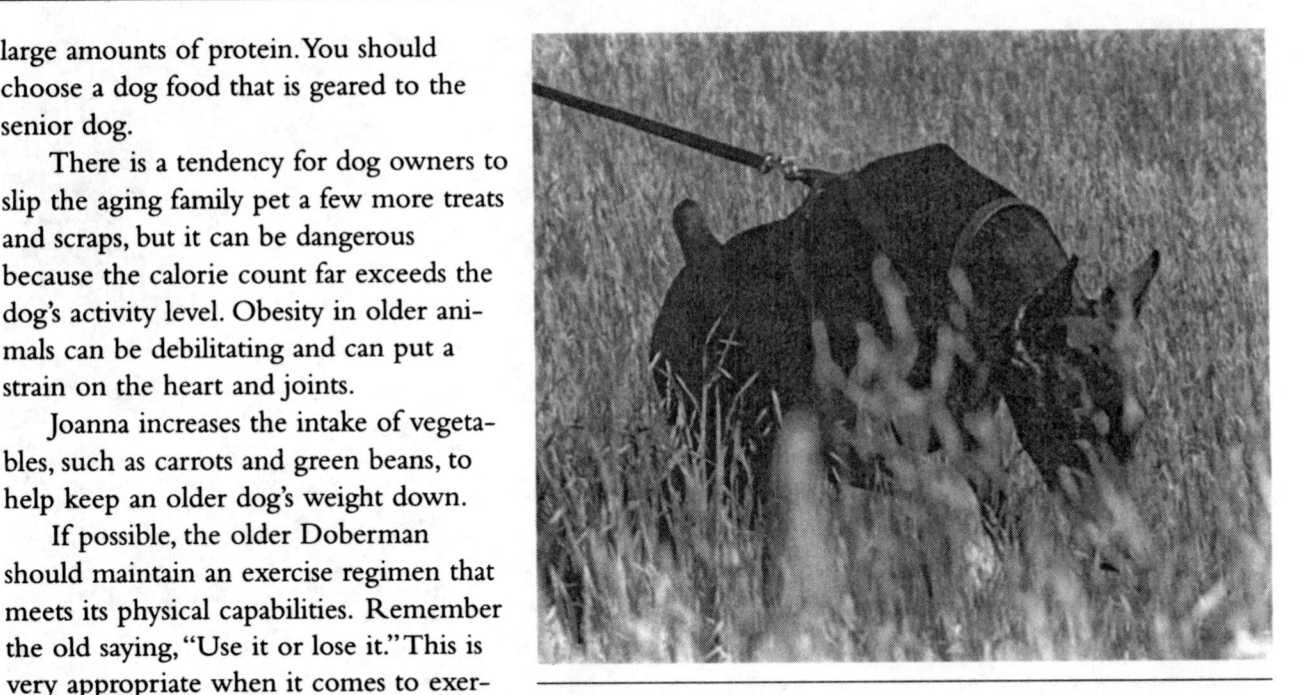

An older dog should stay as active as it is able. This is Ch. Royal Tudor's Wold as the Wind, UDTX, still tracking with the best of them at age 11. (Sue Korp)

VETERINARY CHECKS

Regular veterinary checks are probably more important as the dog gets older. In fact, it is smart to get a full battery of tests—including liver and kidney function, thyroid levels, electrocardiogram, and urinalysis—every year for an older dog. Groom your senior regularly and check the body for lumps or growths, which must be analyzed by the veterinarian. Older dogs can often be more quickly stressed by trips to the veterinarian or a hospital stay, so prevention is better all around than the alternative.

If an old Doberman does need to have surgery or a prolonged stay at the hospital, the dog's bed and other items from home should be provided to lessen the stress. That includes you; spend as much visiting time as is allowed with your old dog.

Tartar buildup and gum disease are prevalent in old dogs, and it is wise to clean the tartar regularly using a dental tool. Otherwise, the alternative is surgery to remove problem teeth. Rod has some older dogs who have worn down parts of their teeth over the years, and when they graze on grass (all Dobermans graze) it gets caught in the teeth. Rod uses a toothpick each night to remove the grass, which, if left unattended, rots and causes gum problems.

BRINGING IN A PUPPY

Owners who wish to plan for the inevitable day when the old Doberman is gone should not be reluctant to bring in a puppy when the old dog is still alive. Some people fear that the old dog will be upset and get its nose out of joint, so to speak. Mostly, the opposite is true. The puppy is normally totally respectful of an older animal, and the old-timer more often than not gets a new lease on life.

Joanna's Ch. Damasyn the Waltzing Brook, CD, was 12 when Joanna kept her grandson, Shawn. She controlled Shawn as if he were her puppy, and fussed and corrected him when necessary, but she loved him deeply. Shawn would follow his grandmother around and would lie in the sun with his head on her paws. Joanna believes that this gave the old dog a new interest in life, and she lived to be 14½ years old.

QUALITY OF LIFE

The quality of life is the most important thing for older dogs. Quality of life means a relatively

Older Dobermans can have lots of fun with new puppies, and the interaction helps keep them young. (Rod Humphries)

pain-free existence and the ability to do things that continue to make life interesting, even if there is a noticeable creak in the joints. Some dogs, like people who are still running miles a day in their 70s, can be very active, and owners should not shut off the exercise time just because their beloved pet is old and may get hurt. Older, retired dogs need just as much mental stimulation as retired humans. Some dogs lived action-filled lives as show or working champions, and they do miss the roar of the crowd, so to speak, and the fussing that comes with being a winner.

Quality of life means spending time with your dog on walks and taking it to places where people will still stop and stroke the dog and tell it how beautiful it is.

One of the most moving moments at some dog shows is when the veterans compete in their own special class, or when they appear in the Stud Dog or Brood Bitch class with a silver muzzle and a sprightly gait. Some are still hams, eating up the applause and putting on a lump-in-the-throat performance.

Quality of life is peace of mind for the animal, an afternoon nap in the sun, a good meal and a leisurely walk with the boss. It is not pain that makes it almost impossible to get up and walk, nor

With a little extra care, your Doberman can have a great life even as a senior. (Cheryl Snyder)

the loss of dignity that comes with an uncontrollable bladder or bowel. It is not increasing seizures or a body sling with wheels so that the dog can be wheeled outside to eliminate. It may not even be chemotherapy for a cancerous tumor or another surgery to attempt to fix the bulging lumbar disc.

Euthanasia: The Hardest Choice

Quality of life may mean different things to different dogs and their owners, but whatever it means, when it is gone the decision to euthanize should be made quickly so that there is no unnecessary pain and suffering. The authors have done it many times—too many times—and it never gets any easier. But both have always been there when the injection is administered, holding their dogs

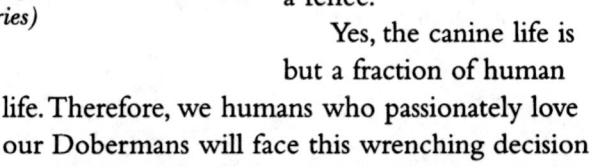

The circle of life is never ending, in the canine world as it is in ours. (Rod Humphries)

and comforting them to the end.

At Joanna's country home in North Carolina is a gravestone walk of fame in the woods. At Rod's property in Texas, a live oak springs from the ground where each of his beloved Champions and equally beloved pets is buried. Rod says he knows the spirits are there, so he has buried the antagonistic males on opposite sides of a fence.

Yes, the canine life is but a fraction of human life. Therefore, we humans who passionately love our Dobermans will face this wrenching decision over and over, and maybe over again. Sometimes it seems unfair that we outlive so many of our canine friends. But we keep coming back, finding new friends, new family, and anybody who has lost a dog should never hesitate to do just that.

(Ray Hill)

CHAPTER 14

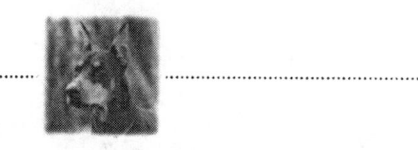

The Doberman as a Service Dog

From the beginning, the Doberman has been stereotyped as a protection dog. Herr Dobermann set the tone for the breed and Otto Goeller, a master promoter who truly popularized the breed, made a good living by selling multitudes of dogs to protect the home and family.

America, with different laws, culture and philosophies, has charted a separate course for the Doberman. Today the American breeders point proudly to the Doberman's service in areas other than protection work: eyes for the blind; therapy work in hospitals and in senior citizens homes; ears for the deaf; and search-and-rescue operations. Hunters will also vouch for the incredible abilities of the Doberman in the woods and open field.

PATH FINDER

Thousands of Dobermans have become eyes for the blind, beginning with Glenn Staines' Path Finder organization, which produced more than 1,000 trained dogs for blind owners between 1936 and his death in 1951.

Staines was a pioneer of great magnitude, developing the Doberman as a show and breeding animal in his Ponchartrain kennel and training guide dogs in his Path Finder organization. Staines bred numerous champions and imported two important studs of that era: the Sieger Lux vd Blankenburg, and his grandson, Figaro v Sigalsburg. It is interesting that Staines imported these two dogs, which were well-known for their sharp and fiery temperaments, yet he was a leader in toning down the Doberman temperament to make dogs suitable for the steady life of a Path Finder.

Staines poured most of his personal earnings into a dog training school, which at times had 100 dogs in training for all kinds of services. In 1936 he was introduced to a blind man named T.W. Pritchett, who had been turned down by a guide dog school as being too old to handle a guide dog. Staines put the man up at his home and, without any recompense for the dog or the training, he produced the first Path Finder Doberman. Staines dedicated the rest of his life to training these dogs for the blind.

Path Finder grew so big that Staines had to separate his organization into two homes: the Ponchartrain show and obedience dogs remained in Royal Oak, Michigan, while the Path Finder group, including paid trainers and staff, moved to a large house in Detroit. The trainers were some of the best in the land, including the famous Willie Necker and Roy Lewellen—a veteran of the Barnum and Bailey Circus. Other staff at Path

World Heavyweight Champion Jack Dempsey was the proud owner of two Pontchartrain Dobermans from Glenn Staines. He is shown here visiting with Leonard Leon, a blind man learning how to use his Path Finder dog—in this case a German Shepherd. (Detroit Times)

Finder included handicapped and blind workers, including one young farm boy, Stanley Doran, who would eventually continue Staines' work in the Pilot Dog organization of today.

Staines was a very generous man who often waived the $200 fee to blind owners who did not have the money for the dog, training and accommodation at the Detroit headquarters. During the Depression years, his kennels were filled with stray Dobermans and dogs unwanted by their owners or those left by owners who could not pay the boarding fees. He was most definitely the forefather of today's Doberman Rescue operations. And after

World War II ended, Staines offered blind veterans his Path Finder Dobermans free of charge.

Staines' obituary from the annual Doberman issue of *Dog News* in 1951 read: "Had you been at Glenn's funeral, the wealth of floral offerings would have mutely told you of the affection and respect with which thousands of people throughout the country regarded him, but it would have been the many, many blind people with their Doberman guide dogs which walked down the aisle of the Chapel at the funeral that would have made you realize that as great as Glenn's contributions were to every phase of Dobermans, it was the Path Finder project which will serve as an everlasting tribute to his memory."

What was also truly significant was the new acceptance of the Doberman as a service dog. The dog that once struck fear into the hearts of many was now being slowly accepted as a true working dog, leading blind owners through the maze of life.

PILOT DOGS TODAY

Stanley Doran was legally blind when he helped Staines at Path Finder from 1942 to 1947. When he returned home to the Columbus, Ohio, area in 1947, he was able to acquire some of the Dobermans from Path Finder and, with his brother Walter, who was head trainer, started a school called Pilot Dogs, Inc.

With the financial backing of Dr. Charlie Meric and Everett R. Steece, the Dorans were able to build the Pilot Dog school building, which is still at the same location on West Town Street in Columbus. Pilot Dogs received its charter in 1950.

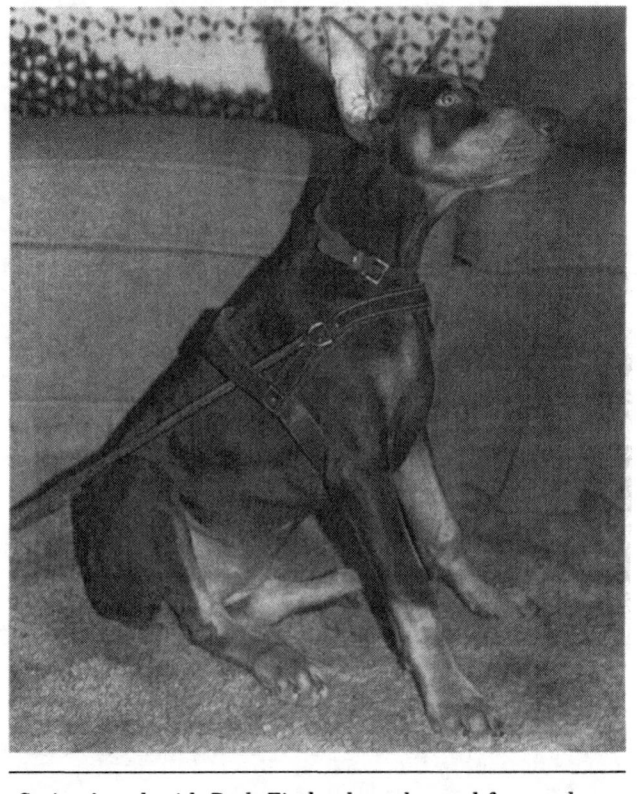

Staines' work with Path Finder dogs changed forever the way the general public views Doberman Pinschers. Pilot Dog "Star," shown here at four months, wears a Path Finder harness. (Joanna Walker)

When Doran started Pilot Dogs he had to charge clients for their dogs because he just did not have sufficient funds. But as donations grew, Pilot Dogs was eventually able to fully finance every phase of a client's quest for a dog, including airfare to and from Columbus and accommodations while training at the school. The cost today is $5,500, all-inclusive, to graduate a blind person and their dog. The Doberman is still one of the key

The Doberman is still one of the key breeds used at Pilot Dogs. (Joanna Walker)

breeds training at Pilot Dogs, Inc., but other breeds have been added to keep up the numbers.

Under the executive directorship of John, Pat and Jay Gray, the school has grown into an operation that would surely draw a warm smile from Staines. It now includes a separate puppy-raising and training area. Brood bitches of several different breeds are placed in appropriate family homes in the area, and a structured breeding program is used to supply the best pups available to work with the blind.

The school celebrated its 5000th Pilot Dog in 1998, and records show that between 1970 and 1998, some 460 Dobermans graduated to work with a blind owner. Most of those can be directly attributed to Joanna Walker, who began her crusade for Doberman Pilot Dogs in 1981. Joanna had an ambition to be a guide dog trainer when she was a youngster in England, and came into direct contact with guide dogs when she convinced a blind friend to obtain a trained dog. Joanna spent a great deal of time with her friend when she visited the British Guide Dog School.

Like Staines, Joanna began with show and obedience Dobermans with her husband, Keith, in the Marks-Tey kennel. Also like Staines, she was very successful as one of the icons of the breed. Then in 1981, Joanna rescued a little five-month-old red bitch she named Little Red and trained her to become her first donation to Pilot Dogs. A fire was kindled, and Joanna made it her life's work to secure eyes for the blind through the breed she loved so much.

Joanna was not enamored with the quality of the Doberman specimens being used for Pilot Dogs when she first became involved. At that time, the dogs had to be under 25 inches at the shoulder, which eliminated most of the quality conformation dogs. But in time Joanna pressed for a slightly taller animal and eventually the restriction was lifted. This allowed her to tap into the breeding stock of leading kennels across the country. Joanna produced some of her own Pilot Dogs at home, but also relied on donations of animals from many enthusiasts.

In the beginning, Joanna rescued Dobermans chained in squalid conditions in backyards and factories, and lovingly rehabilitated them for a life of service. She has since widened the scope to include dogs of great heritage in her operation, obtaining puppies and brood bitches for the program and free studs from champion producers. She also has set up a network of foster homes for puppy training and homes for brood bitches and puppy rearing. She has even co-opted a group of retired pilots, called Angel Flight, to help in picking up Dobermans unable to be transported by normal means when the weather is bad.

After the Doberman pups are reared for a year in foster homes, they go back to Joanna for harness and on-site training. So if you see a bespectacled English lady with a Doberman in harness wearing a blanket that reads "Pilot Dog In Training" on the street, in a department store, in a restaurant or on a plane somewhere over America, that's Joanna Walker.

VERSATILITY OF SERVICE

There are countless Dobermans in other service activities across America. Therapy dogs are certified to attend hospitals, rest homes and retirement homes, schools and other places where people get joy and comfort from the presence of a dog. Many Doberman owners involve their dogs in this worthwhile activity, which helps to make life a little happier for sick children and adults, and the elderly retired. The fact that the once-feared Doberman can be seen as such a gentle dog has been of great benefit for public understanding of the breed.

Pet Therapy, Inc., the Delta Society and Pet Therapy International are organizations that certify and use therapy Dobermans. All organizations

Top-quality Dobermans are a hallmark of Pilot Dogs. Becky Floyd and her guide dog Heather placed third in their Obedience class to earn Heather's Companion Dog title. (Luis Sosa)

require a dog to be tested and certified first. The Doberman is tested around other dogs, as well as wheelchairs and walkers and the people who use them as aids. Most organizations require the dog to

A gentle therapy dog brings joy wherever it goes. (Carol Watson)

Tino, a disaster search-and-rescue dog, is learning to rappell. (Irene Korotev)

Sandra Anderson and Eagle search a lake for a missing person. From the surface, Eagle can catch the scent of a body on the bottom of the lake. (Sandra Anderson)

be at least a year old. It must be outgoing but under control, because behavior is obviously of major importance around frail people.

Therapy work with Dobermans has produced many touching stories. Joanna has one such experience with a Pilot Dog in training, a bitch named Extra who gave new meaning to life for an old man in a retirement home. The man had been sitting silent in his wheelchair with his head slumped to his chest for months, and nobody could elicit from him any words or emotions. When Joanna walked up to him with Extra, the man lifted his head, held out his hands and called to the dog. He began to cry and said, "I have owned 16 beautiful Dobermans in my lifetime." He hugged Extra as she covered his face and tears with wet kisses.

Dobermans have saved people in other ways, too. A red Doberman named Cinnamon was prominent on American television news reports from Mexico City several years ago for her work in searching for victims of the massive earthquake there. Cinnamon, owned by Shirley Hammond of Palo Alto, California, is a stark reminder of the tireless work that Dobermans and their owners do in certified search-and-rescue operations.

There are many different kinds of search-and-rescue dogs, and the various disciplines include area search, avalanche search, cadaver search (which can be on land or in water), disaster search, evidence search and drug search. Search-and-rescue requires a dedication that only a few people are prepared to go through with their Doberman, but the personal satisfaction and rewards are enormous.

Dobermans also are used as hearing dogs for the deaf and as seizure alert dogs, which warn owners of a pending seizure—all of which illustrate the working abilities of this breed. The Doberman has come a long way.

(Mikron Photography)

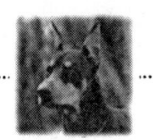

CHAPTER 15

The National Breed Club

Above all else, the Doberman Pinscher Club of America (DPCA) is the keeper of the breed standard, and therefore the keeper of the Doberman in the United States. The DPCA, which was formed in 1921, first used the German standard, but has written its own breed standard since 1935.

The DPCA has tinkered with the breed standard ever since, but the refinements have been, for the most part, positive. The club spurned the German ideal of a sharper dog and has been rightfully conservative in holding the height to a maximum of 28 inches for males—compared to the German standard which, with accepted margins, now reaches over 29 inches.

In 1948, the DPCA led the way in this country when it forced the American Kennel Club to excuse vicious and shy Dobermans from the show ring—the first breed club to institute such a rule.

The DPCA leadership in the late 1960s gave in to the will of the members and legalized the fawn, or Isabella, color in Dobermans. This is much to the chagrin of the Germans, who have eliminated both blue and fawn. The DPCA more recently has fought a successful battle called Operation White Out against the albino white Doberman, maintaining the ban in the show ring and forcing the American Kennel Club to tag the breed with special "Z" registration that allows the fancy at large to avoid this dangerous genetic mutation. There has also been the passionate defense of ear cropping and tail docking and the successful mustering of all the affected breeds into an alliance to maintain the breed club's right of choice.

The American Kennel Club approves the breed standard for use at its sanctioned shows and trials, but it does not write it. That is in the hands of the DPCA and, ultimately, in the hands of the rank-and-file membership. They have been excellent stewards.

First and foremost, the Doberman Pinscher Club of America is the guardian of the breed standard. (Alan & Jacquie Wendt)

The title of Keeper of the Breed Standard is only one aspect of the activities of the Doberman Pinscher Club of America, a club that has more than 2,000 individual members and 58 chapter clubs.

THE NATIONAL SPECIALTY

The DPCA National Specialty and Convention is the annual October meeting of the clan. (A specialty show is one held for a single breed.) It draws 500-plus dogs and many more people. Its first three years, the National (which began in 1924) was held at the Germantown Cricket Club in Philadelphia. From 1927 until 1955, the National was exclusively held in Chicago, but since 1956 the site rotates from the East Coast to the West Coast and central states.

The National, which is still exhilarating for the experienced Doberman owner, is an absolute wonder to the novice. Dobermans in elevators, in the lobby, on walkways and parading competitively in large hotel ballrooms are quite a sight for the uninitiated, especially unknowing hotel guests who are also not quite sure about all that barking from behind hotel room doors!

The National begins with the annual Top 20, a competitive event that showcases the top point-getters in breed competition throughout the year. The judging is unique in that a three-judge panel, all in formal attire, evaluates each dog using the old point scale that has now been abandoned in the breed standard. The winner is announced at the annual awards banquet at the end of the week.

The Obedience Top 20 is also a black-tie affair and is followed by the National Futurity for pups ranging from 6 months to 18 months; the breed and obedience classes held over two days; the Veterans classes, Stud Dog and Brood Bitch competitions; temperament testing; agility; and finally the Best of Breed class, with sometimes up to 150 of Americas top champions, plus some competitors from Canada, Mexico and South America who have achieved their American Championships.

The convention side of the National includes fund-raisers for health research, education research, and breed rescue efforts; the chance to view DPCA

Archives material; Pilot Dog demonstrations; an exchange of information and ideas at an International Doberman meeting; plus numerous seminars, which can include everything from the intricacies of breeding the Doberman to updated studies on genetic health. The week ends on a Saturday night with a black-tie awards banquet where the Top 20 winner, top-producing Stud Dog, Brood Bitch, obedience titleholders and recipients of many other awards are announced.

The Top 20 is a formal affair in both conformation and obedience. This is Elite Dobe's First Edition, CDX, TDI, CGC, an obedience winner. (Mikron Photography)

AFFILIATED FOUNDATIONS

The DPCA has spawned two very worthwhile nonprofit foundations: the Doberman Pinscher Foundation of America and the American Doberman Pinscher Educational Foundation. The first is health-related and raises many thousands of dollars a year that are allocated to various health studies on diseases that affect the Doberman, including cardiomyopathy. The focal fund-raiser is a benefit bash at each National Specialty.

The American Doberman Pinscher Educational Foundation offers educational materials such as the booklet *Learning to Judge the Doberman Pinscher By Applying the Official Standard of the Breed*, originally written by scions of the breed Frank Grover, the late Peggy Adamson, Marge Kilburn, Pat Doniere, Jane Kay and Nancy Heitzman, the longtime keeper of the DPCA Archives.

THE FUTURITY

The annual Futurity is a special event that offers a cash award to the breeder, owner and stud dog owner of a winning pup. It's also something of a gambling event, because to be part of the Futurity, DPCA members must nominate a brood bitch for Futurity judging *before* the birth of her pups, and then must nominate each individual pup before it is four months of age. Each step requires a fee, and the stakes money is then allocated to class and other advanced winners of the Futurity. The classes are 6–9 Month, 9–12 Month, 12–15 Month, and 15-plus Months, with each broken down by sex and color.

Supporting research into the health of the breed is an important priority for the Doberman fancy. (Evelyn Stackpoles)

CLUB TITLES

The Working Aptitude Certificate (WAC) and the Register of Merit (ROM) have been part of the DPCA since 1976. The WAC recognizes a Doberman's steady temperament and basic aptitude for the work it was intended to do. The ROM recognizes outstanding dogs with all-around ability.

The DPCA has a panel of evaluators who hold WAC tests for chapter clubs throughout the country during the year and at the DPCA National Specialty. The WAC is open to Dobermans over 18 months, and is a series of fairly simple tests that evaluate a Doberman's reactions to people, gunshots, an umbrella opened quickly in close proximity to the animal, uneven footing and an agitator.

The WAC can be converted to a ROM if the Doberman is also a Conformation Champion and has achieved at least a Companion Dog obedience title.

BREED RESCUE

The incredible boom in the number of Dobermans in the 1970s, and the subsequent bust that left many homeless, was behind the formation of the Committee on Population (Cope) and a similar group, the National Rescue Committee. In 1977, these two groups merged to form Cope/Rescue.

Because the number of Doberman registrations has dropped from a staggering 81,964 in 1978 to around 15,000 at the end of the century, the number of Dobermans being discarded is much lower. But it's still a problem. And the national club, the guardian of the breed in so many ways, is also the guardian of the less fortunate dogs in it.

Rescue organizations find Doberman Pinschers in trouble and in need of homes, take them in, evaluate and rehabilitate them and find them good, permanent homes. If you are interested in getting involved in rescue, the AKC can put you in touch with the DPCA national rescue coordinator, who will direct you to a group in your area.

One of the main thrusts of the committee today is education of prospective breeders, helping them to understand that they must take responsibility for every puppy they breed, for the life of the dog. Its efforts include an award-winning booklet, *The Beginner's Doberman Pinscher*.

This little angel, Ch. Bikila's Isilya of Marks-Tey, CD, ROM, SchBH, collected donations for Cope/Rescue at the National Specialty. (Mikron Photography)

DPCA PUBLICATIONS

Apart from those booklets already mentioned, the DPCA publishes:

The semi-annual magazine *Pipeline*

A 40-page booklet, *The Doberman Pinscher Illustrated*

An in-depth, 24-set series of articles approved by the DPCA that covers all aspects of owning, breeding, showing and working the Doberman

The DPCA Yearbook and Directory of Breeders

The DPCA Membership List Booklet

Selected videotapes and slides of shows and historic animals are also available to chapter clubs for special presentations and lectures

Local dog clubs sponsor all kind of events and are a great way to get more involved in Dobermans and in the sport of dogs. (Cheryl Snyder)

JOINING THE CLUB

Membership in the DPCA is open to anyone over 18 years of age who is endorsed in writing by two active members of the club. The DPCA recommends that prospective members visit dog shows and meet DPCA members, who then may be interested in sponsoring their membership. The DPCA also advises that newcomers obtain a copy of the *Yearbook and Directory of Breeders* and contact people in their area of the country to build friendships that would in gaining sponsorship.

Why is sponsorship required? Because DPCA members vote on what will be in the breed standard, in the club's code of ethics and in other crucial documents related to the Doberman Pinscher. This is why it is so important to make sure members of the national club are actively interested in the breed and in keeping themselves educated and informed about Dobermans and about dogs in general.

The DPCA also has 58 chapter clubs, and joining a local club can be a lot of fun. You get to know Doberman owners and their dogs, and you can become as involved in the club activities as you want. These will usually include shows, fun matches, classes, sporting events, picnics and more. It's a great way to make friends and get active in the sport of dogs.

THE UNITED DOBERMAN CLUB

The DPCA has done a remarkable job of establishing and maintaining the American Doberman. However, as we mentioned in Chapter 3, the American Doberman has a somewhat different disposition than its European cousin. In 1990, after the AKC banned Schutzhund activities in member clubs, including the DPCA, the United Doberman Club was formed. Its members believe that the breed historically is a working dog that excels in protection. They say that the DPCA does not in any way emphasize the protection aspects of the Doberman—as does its German counterpart, the Dobermann Verein. It is an argument that has raged since the 1920s and undoubtedly will still be argued at the end of the 21st century. Different countries, different cultures, different laws.

The UDC's primary interest is maintaining the working capabilities of the Doberman, particularly

The UDC's main interest is in maintaining the working capabilities of the Doberman. That includes competing in Schutzhund. (Gay Glazbrook)

in protection. It is not affiliated with the AKC, but has as its umbrella organization the American Working Dog Federation.

The UDC holds a national specialty each year and publishes a quarterly magazine, *The UDC Focus*. Apart from the Schutzhund activities, the club offers a conformation championship, obedience titles, tracking, versatility titles that are awarded on points earned in 10 different performance categories and a Therapy Dog title that requires the dog to submit proof of hours of actual therapy work.

The club also has fit-for-breeding programs based upon the German ideal (ZTP) and a modified American version (FFB) that allows two missing teeth and the colors outlawed in Germany—the blue and fawn. The fit-for-breeding programs require a number of health tests that are automatically placed in a national database. However, the only test that is mandatory in fit-for-breeding is to clear the hips for dysplasia.

Epilogue

The Doberman now stands proudly at the beginning of its second century! It was in August of 1899 that Otto Goeller, the true architect of the breed, wrote the first official standard. The Doberman's journey has been an exciting but controversial one. Breeders have molded the Doberman from a small, scruffy beast with a razor sharp temperament into a taller, elegant aristocrat, a bold and energetic family dog rather than a one-man fighting machine.

So what does the new century hold for the Doberman? Will America, which has a different official standard and different philosophies on the Doberman, eventually find the chasm so deep that it declares the Doberman Pinscher a different breed than the German Dobermann? Or will the Germans finally throw up their hands and legislate to have the American Doberman Pinscher banished from their clan?

People have been shaping and reshaping dogs for their fancy and fads since before recorded history— probably since a cave man nurtured a wild dog cub because it had mutated floppy ears and looked softer for his kids.

The Doberman standards in America and Germany have been changed countless times over the first 100 years. Have we stopped tinkering? Should we stop tinkering? Nobody owns the blueprint for this manmade breed, and 100 years is just a drop in the ocean in the evolution of any creature.

How would Herr Dobermann react if he transported back more than 100 years after his death? Would he recognize our elegant Doberman? Certainly not the colors of red, blue and fawn—and if he laid eyes on a white albino mutation he would probably retain a lawyer and sue for defaming his name!

Maybe 100 or so years from now, when the world population has reached saturation and more families live in high rises than in single level homes, some entrepreneur with the flair of Otto Goeller will breed the Doberman down to 15 or 18 inches at the shoulder to be readily accommodated in an apartment.

Many will argue that after 100 years the breed has been stabilized. That's what Herr Doberman thought—then Goeller went commercial and look where we are a century later. Goeller, who died a few years after the First World War, would be hard pressed to believe this is the same breed he mass-produced at the turn of the last century.

The Doberman, or even humans for that matter, may well look and act very differently 100 years or more from now. Everything changes. The world changes. We are all just merely passing through . . .

ROD HUMPHRIES

APPENDIX A

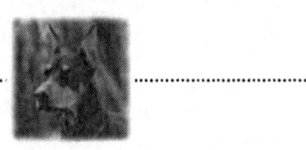

Resources

NATIONAL CLUBS

Doberman Pinscher Club of America
Janet Van Wormer, Corresponding Secretary
25551 Hunter Road
Veneta, OR 97487
www.dpca.org

United Doberman Club
3810 Paule Avenue
St. Louis, MO 63125-1718
http://members.home.net/cbx6/udc/index.htm

American Kennel Club
5580 Centerview Drive
Raleigh, NC 27606
(919) 233-9767
www.akc.org

AKC Breeder Referral Service
(900) 407-7877

United Kennel Club
100 East Kilgore
Kalamazoo, MI 49001-5598
(616) 343-9020
www.ukcdogs.com

MICROCHIPPING

Avid Microchip I.D.
(800) 336-AVID
www.avidplc.com

HomeAgain, AKC Companion Animal Recovery
5580 Centerview Drive, Suite 250
Raleigh, NC 27606-3394
(800) 252-7894
www.akc.org

HEALTH REGISTRIES

Canine Eye Registration Foundation (CERF)
South Campus Courts, Building C
Purdue University
West Lafayette, IN 47907
(317) 494-8179
www.vet.purdue.edu/~yshen/cerf.html

Orthopedic Foundation for Animals (OFA)
2300 Nifong Boulevard
Columbia, MO 65201
(573) 442-0418
www.ofa.org

PennHip/International Canine Genetics
271 Great Valley Parkway
Malvern, PA 19355
800-248-8099

VetGen Canine Genetic Services
3728 Plaza Drive, Suite One
Ann Arbor, MI 48108
(800) 483-8436
www.vetgen.com

PET OWNERS

American Dog Owners Association
1654 Columbia Turnpike
Castleton, NY 12033
(518) 477-8469
www.global2000.net/adoa/

SPORT AND ACTIVITY GROUPS

National Association for Search and Rescue
4500 Southgate Place, Suite 100
Chantilly, VA 20151-1714
(703) 222-6277
www.nasar.org

North American Dog Agility Council
HCR 2 Box 277
St. Maries, ID 83861
(208) 689-3803
www.teleport.com/~jhaglund/nadachom.htm

U.S. Dog Agility Association
P.O. Box 850955
Richardson, TX 75085-0955
(214) 231-9700
www.usdaa.com

North American Flyball Association Inc.
1400 West Devon Avenue
Box 512
Chicago, IL 60660
(309) 688-9840
muskie.fishnet.com/~flyball/flyball.htm

SERVICE DOG ORGANIZATIONS

Pilot Dogs Inc.
625 West Town Street
Columbus, OH 43215
(614) 221-6367

Therapy Dogs, Inc.
P.O. Box 2786
Cheyenne, WY 82003
(307) 638-3223
home.ptd.net/~compudog/tdi.html

Therapy Dogs International
6 Hilltop Road
Mendham, NJ 07945
(201) 543-0888

TEMPERAMENT TESTING

American Temperament Test Society
P.O. Box 397
Fenton, MO 63026
(314) 225-5346

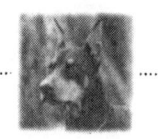

Doberman Pinscher Club of America Code of Ethics

This Code is established in accordance with the objectives of the Doberman Pinscher Club of America as set forth in Article 1, Section 2 of the Club Constitution. It is presented as a guideline for the use of DPCA members when buying, breeding, selling and exhibiting Doberman Pinschers. Violators of the DPCA Code of Ethics will be subject to prompt action under DPCA grievance and charge procedures.

1. Abide by the constitution and by-laws of the Doberman Pinscher Club of America and the rules of the American Kennel Club.

2. Keep accurate breeding records, registrations, and pedigrees. Maintain the best possible standards of canine health, cleanliness and care.

3. All services and sales arrangements shall be mutually agreed upon, stated in writing and signed by all parties involved, including all adjustments, replacement conditions, etc. Support and conduct only ethical trade practices.

4. All advertising shall be honest and not in any way misrepresentative, fraudulent or misleading.

5. Encourage and support the DPCA Health and Medical Registry Committee with specific attention to testing for health disorders directly relating to the Doberman Pinscher.

6. All dogs offered at stud shall not be bred prior to one year of age nor after 12 years of age and shall be in good health and free from communicable diseases and disqualifying genetic faults. Stud owners are responsible for puppies produced by their studs, therefore, it is recommended they verify the bitch owner is a responsible owner and breeder. Any bitch accepted for stud service must be at least 18 months of age, in good health and free from communicable diseases and disqualifying genetic faults.

7. No stud dog will be bred to any bitch whose owner is directly or indirectly involved with any puppy broker, puppy mill, pet shop, litter lot sales, or any other commercial enterprise whose business is involved in like activities.

8. No bitch shall be bred more than once a year, nor prior to one and one half years of age, nor after eight years of age and should be in good health and free from communicable diseases and disqualifying genetic faults. Breeders of litters are responsible for puppies produced by their bitches. Therefore, it is recommended that the breeders verify that the purchasers of puppies will be responsible owners who will provide proper homes and care.

9. No bitch will be bred for commercial reason. All bitches will be bred with the intention of that particular breeding improving the breed.

10. No Doberman Pinscher will be sold to commercial facilities, businesses or agents thereof.

11. Honestly evaluate the structural and mental qualities of all Doberman Pinschers sold, and fairly represent that evaluation including results of any temperament testing.

12. Prices of Doberman Pinschers shall be based on individual quality. Members maintain prices so as not to be injurious to the breed. When appropriate, some animals should be sold on limited registration or with written agreement to have the animal altered and papers withheld pending alteration.

13. At the time of sale, furnish records to each buyer of all shots and wormings, pedigree, and AKC registration or transfer documents, unless written agreement is made at time of sale that papers are being withheld.

14. All members shall conduct themselves at all times in such a manner as to reflect credit on the sport of purebred dog showing and Doberman Pinschers in particular. This includes respect for the show site, convention and overflow facilities, and all other aspects of responsible dog ownership.

First adopted by the Board of Directors in 1980 and revised in 1982 and 1993.

(4U2C Photography)

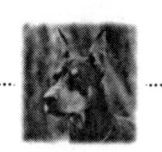

Titles a Doberman Pinscher Can Earn

AMERICAN KENNEL CLUB TITLES
Conformation and Dual Titles

Ch.	Conformation Champion	CT	Champion Tracker

Obedience

CD	Companion Dog	UDX	Utility Dog Excellent
CDX	Companion Dog Excellent	OTCh.	Obedience Trial Champion
UD	Utility Dog		

Tracking

TD	Tracking Dog	VST	Variable Surface Tracking Dog
TDX	Tracking Dog Excellent		

Agility

NA	Novice Agility	OAJ	Open Jumpers With Weaves
OA	Open Agility	AJX	Excellent Jumpers With Weaves
AX	Agility Excellent	MXJ	Master Excellent Jumpers With Weaves
MX	Master Agility Excellent		
NAJ	Novice Jumpers With Weaves		

CANINE GOOD CITIZEN

CGC   Canine Good Citizen

Although CGC is an AKC program, the title is not officially recognized. While you may put it after the dog's name, it will not appear on an AKC pedigree.

DOBERMAN PINSCHER CLUB OF AMERICA TITLES

WAC	Working Aptitude Certificate	ROM	Register of Merit

(Note: The DPCA is a member club of the AKC and recognizes all AKC titles.)

UNITED DOBERMAN CLUB TITLES

Conformation

UDC-Ch.   Conformation Champion

Obedience

D-CD	Companion Dog	D-UD	Utility Dog
D-CDX	Companion Dog Excellent		

Schutzhund

SchHI	Schutzhund I		AD	Endurance Test
SchHII	Schutzhund II		WH	Watchdog Test
SchHIII	Schutzhund III		IPO 1	International Police Certification 1
SchH A	Schutzhund Without Tracking		IPO 2	International Police Certification 2
B(BH)	Obedience/Tracking (Prerequisite to Schutzhund)		IPO 3	International Police Certification 3

Tracking

T-1	Tracking 1			Versatility
T-2	Tracking 2		VC	Versatility Companion
T-3	Tracking 3		VCX	Versatility Companion Excellent

(Note: The UDC is not affiliated with the AKC, but is a member club of the American Working Dog Federation.)

UNITED KENNEL CLUB TITLES

Conformation

U-CH	Champion

Obedience

U-CD	Companion Dog		U-UD	Utility Dog Excellent
U-CDX	Companion Dog Excellent			

Agility

U-AG1	Agility One (Novice)		U-AG111	Agility Three
U-AG11	Agility Two (Advanced)		U-ACh.	Agility Champion

NORTH AMERICAN DOG AGILITY COUNCIL TITLES

| NAC | Novice Agility Certificate | EAC | Elite Agility Certificate |
| OAC | Open Agility Certificate | NATCh. | NADAC Agility Champion |

Titles are also available for different classes, such as Gamblers and Jumpers. These would be NGC, OGC, EGC, and so on.

UNITED STATES DOG AGILITY ASSOCIATION TITLES

AD	Agility Dog	SM	Snooker Master Dog
AAD	Advanced Agility Dog	RM	Relay Master Dog
MAD	Master Agility Dog	VAD	Veteran Agility Dog
JM	Jumpers Master Dog	ADCh.	Agility Dog Champion
GN	Gamblers Master Dog		

NORTH AMERICAN FLYBALL ASSOCIATION TITLES

FD	Flyball Dog	FMX	Flyball Master Excellent
FDX	Flyball Dog Excellent	FMCh.	Flyball Master Champion
FDCh.	Flyball Dog Champion	FGDCh.	Flyball Grand Champion
FM	Flyball Master		

CANADIAN KENNEL CLUB TITLES

Most CKC titles are the same as those used by AKC, with the following exceptions:

OTCh.	The same as an AKC Utility Dog	WCI	Working Certificate Intermediate
FTCh.	Field Trial Champion	WCX	Working Certificate Excellent
AFTCh.	Amateur Field Trial Champion	ADC	Agility Dog of Canada
WC	Working Certificate	AADC	Advanced Agility Dog of Canada

COMMON ABBREVIATIONS USED AT DOG SHOWS

BIS	Best in Show		WB	Winners Bitch
BISS	Best in Specialty Show		RWD	Reserve Winners Dog
Group 1–4	Group Winner and placings 2, 3 and 4		RWB	Reserve Winners Bitch
BOB	Best of Breed		BW	Best of Winners
BOS	Best of Opposite Sex		HIT	High in Trial
WD	Winners Dog			

Ch. Royal Tudor's Wild as the Wind, UDTX, ROM. (Mikron Photography)

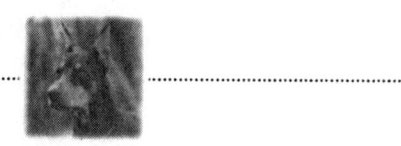

Doberman Pinscher Club of America National Specialty Winners

BEST OF BREED

1998   Ch. Foxfire's Devils N Demons
Breeder: Clarice, Tom and Michelle Santana
    and E. Kent
Owner: Michelle Santana and Clarice Tom

1997   Ch. Legend's Extravaganza v Deco
Breeder: Debbie and Mike Stiner and
    Terri Devlin
Owner: Debbie and Mike Stiner, and
    Terri Devlin and David Goldfein

1996   Ch. Toledobe's Serenghetti
Breeder: S. Brown and Judy Doniere and
    B. Randall
Owner: H. and H. Heidinger, and
    R. and S. Johnson

1995   Ch. Aquarius Damian v Ravenswood
Breeder: B. Clark and Jim Briley
Owner: Ron and Glenda Chidester and
    Jim Briley

1994   Ch. Brunswig's Cryptonite
Breeder: Robert and Phyliss Farrer
Owner: Samuel B. and Marion W. Lawrence

1993   Ch. Foxhaven Aspen Summer
Breeder: Don and Naomi Foltz
Owner: John and Joan Johnson, and
    Don and Naomi Foltz

1992   Ch. Dabney's Hot Enchilada of Le-High
Breeder: Janie Lavy
Owner: Linda and John Krukar

1991   Ch. Brunswig's Cryptonite
Breeder: Robert and Phyliss Farrer
Owner: Samuel B. and Marion W. Lawrence

1990   Ch. Brunswig's Cryptonite
Breeder: Robert and Phyliss Farrer
Owner: S.B. Lawrence, Donna Anthony and
    M. Schmid

1989   Ch. Royal Tudor's Wild as the Wind
Breeder: Beth Wilhite
Owner: Arthur and Sue Korp and
    Beth Wilhite

1988   Ch. Tolivar's Wynderwynd Ditty

1987   Ch. Royal Tudor's Wild as the Wind

1986   Ch. Cabra's Dark and Debonaire
1985   Ch. Teraden's Crystal Gayle
1984   Ch. Eagle's Devil "D"
1983   Ch. Marienburg's Mary Hartman
1982   Ch. Redyn's Touch of Class
1981   Ch. Star Dobe's Irish Fantasy
1980   Ch. Migar's Jenne
1979   Ch. Marienburg's Mart Hartman
1978   Ch. Marienburg's Sun Hawk
1977   Ch. Weichardt's A Go-Go, CD
1976   Ch. Marienburg's Sun Hawk
1975   Ch. Brown's B-Brian
1974   Ch. Loron's Aviator
1973   Ch. Brown's B-Brian
1972   Ch. Lujac's Stinger
1971   Ch. Brown's A-Amanda
1970   Ch. Checkmate's Nite Cap
1969   Ch. Rosevale's Little Nip of Loron
1968   Ch. Sultana von Marienburg
1967   Ch. Sultana von Marienburg
1966   Ch. Toledobe's Linebacker
1965   Ch. Ru Mar's Tsushima, CD
1964   Ch. Jem's Amythest v Warlock
1963   Ch. Sigenwald's Prince Kuhio
1962   Ch. Sigenwald's Prince Kuhio
1961   Ch. Brown's Bridget
1960   Ch. Borong the Warlock, CD
1959   Ch. Haydenhill's Diana

1958	Ch. El Campeon's Dioso
1957	Ch. Borong the Warlock, CD
1956	Ch. Borong the Warlock, CD
1955	Ch. Dortmund Delly's Colonel Jet
1954	Ch. Dortmund Delly's Colonel Jet
1953	Ch. Rontyelee Lady Alleyne
1952	Ch. Meadowmist Elegy
1951	Ch. Kitchawan's Cara Mia
1950	Ch. Jet vd Ravensburg
1949	Ch. Jet vd Ravensburg
1948	Ch. Alcor v Millsdod
1947	Ch. Quo Shmerk v Marienland
1946	Ch. Alcor v Millsdod
1945	No event
1944	Ch. Dictator v Glenhugel
1943	Ch. Dow's Dodie v Kienlesburg
1942	No event
1941	Cerita of Marienland
1940	Ellie v Grandzhof
1939	Ora v Sandberg-Lindenhof
1938	Ch. Rigo v Lindenhof
1937	Ch. Jesse vd Sonnenhohe
1936	Ch. Jockel v Burgund
1935	Jockel v Burgund
1934	Ch. Muck v Brunia
1933	Dash of Bardo
1932	Ch. Hamlet v Herthasse
1931	Ch. Hamlet v Herthasse

1930	Modern v Simmenau Rhinegold
1929	Alphabet of Dawn
1928	Ch. Claus v Sigalsburg
1927	Claus v Sigalsburg
1926	Hella of Ponchartrain
1925	Apollo v Scheutzeneck
1924	Red Roof Rilda

HIGH IN TRIAL

1998 Ch. OTCh. Platinum's Dangerous Liaison, UDX (Open B)
Breeder: Arthur and Sue Korp, Beth Wilhite, and C. and R. Vida
Owner: Arthur and Sue Korp

1997 OTCh. Lyndobe's Midnight Lace, UDX (Open B)
Breeder: Lynne A. Coleman
Owner: Donald C. Richardson

1996 Heron Acres Megabyte (Novice B)
Breeder: Andrew Zuckerman
Owner: Brian and Bonnie Cleveland

1995 Arca B-A-Cherri Coke (Novice B)
Breeder: Carole Watson
Owner: Carole Watson

1994 Renejade Swings on a Star, CDX (Open B)
Breeder: Nancy Christensen
Owner: Daniel Bohm and Nancy Christensen

1993 Sunray's Fire Brigade, CD (Open A)
Breeder: Lieselotte M. Hockey
Owner: Bobbie D. Becker

1992   Babak Tilla the Honey, UD (Utility B)
        Breeder: R. Dian Barker
        Owner: Audrey F. VanBeek

1991   Akela the Terminator (Novice B)
        Breeder: Lynn and Robert Robley
        Owner: Mark Stephens

1990   Ch. Suncountry's Ninja, UD (Utility B)
        Breeder: Kenneth E. and Jean Shaw
        Owner: R.H. and G. Chambers

1989   Estiny's Rampallian, CDX (Open B)
        Breeder: J. and E. Schenk
        Owner: Mariann Hein

1988   Ch. Merique's Durango

1987   Easy Does It Wind Walker

1986   Baroness von Hellvellyn, CDX

1985   Heelalong's PMG's Free Spirit, CDX

1984   Heelalong's PMG's Free Spirit, CDX

1983   Tucari's Racine Razzmatazz, CDX

1982   Acadia's Black Swan, UD

1981   Shantara's Blackbird v Shadlin

1980   Thor Warrick Englebert, UD

1979   Shantara's Blackbird v Shadlin

1978   Larwyck's Czarina, CDX

1977   Fiesta's Tushee Twister, CDX

1976   Hahn's Fawn von Hoytt, CD

1975   Frederick's Trimbrel, UD

1974   April Acres Black Magic, CDX

1973   April Acres Black Magic

1972   Schauffelein's Dilemna

1971   Ronsu's Clipper Blue Jacket, UD

1970   Ava Danica Hartmann, UD

1969   Countess Misty of Manistee, CDX

1968   Azteca's Bellona, CD

1967   Little Mist v Frederick, UDT

1966   Ch. Commando's Silver Sandal, UDT

1965   Ch. Commando's Silver Sandal, UDT

1964   Valjan's Amber

1963   Ch. Commando's Silver Sandal, UDT

1962   Rad's Friendly Jest of Summer

1961   Diablo of Rosevale

1960   Rad's Friendly Jest of Summer

1959   Titan of Ashworth

1958   No event

1957   Guiding Eyes Magdolin

1956   No event

1955   Readington's Dynamite, UD

1954   Creb's Betty Girl

1953   Beechurst's Ajax the Great

1952   Teresa v Mac, CDX

1951   No event

1950   Abbenoir

1949   Von Ritter

1948   Ch. Asault v Aleck, CDX

1947   Fritz v Darburg

1946   Ines Gozo de Feliz

1945   No event

1944   Princess D. Wilhelmina

1943   Ch. Danny v Neckerheim

1942	No event	1939	Princess D. Wilhelmina
1941	Tiger of Ponchartrain	1938	Duke of Schroth Valley
1940	King !V, CDX	1937	Ducat vd Rheinperle

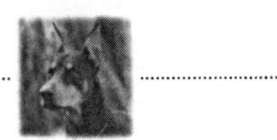

The German Standards for the Doberman Pinscher

THE CURRENT GERMAN STANDARD

GENERAL APPEARANCE: The Dobermann is of medium size, strong and muscularly built. Through the elegant lines of its body, its proud stature, and its expression of determination, it conforms to the ideal picture of a dog.

IMPORTANT PROPORTIONS: The body of the Dobermann appears to be almost square, particularly in males. The length of the body measured from the point of the shoulder to the point of the buttock shall not be more than 5 percent longer than the height from the withers to the ground in males, and 10 percent in females.

BEHAVIOR AND TEMPERAMENT: The disposition of the Dobermann is friendly and calm; very devoted to the family and fond of children. Medium temperament and medium sharpness, as well as a medium threshold of irritation is required with a good contact to the owner. Easy to train, the Dobermann enjoys working, and shall have good working ability, courage and hardness. The particular values of self confidence and intrepedness are required, and also adaptability and attention to fit the social environment.

HEAD: *Top Skull*—Strong, fits the body. Viewed from above the head resembles a blunt wedge. The line across the head when viewed from the front shall go almost straight across; it shall not fall off to the ears. The frontal bone, which is a parallel continuance of the bridge of the nose, shall fall off to the neck in a slightly rounded curve. The orbital bone should be pronounced without being prominent. The wrinkle on the forehead is still visible. The occipital bone should not be prominent. Viewed from the front and from above, the sides of the head should not appear too cheeky. The slight roundings of the sides of the upper jaw and the cheekbone should be in overall harmony to the length of the head. The muscles of the head are strongly developed. Stop is slight but well defined.

FOREFACE: *Nose*—The nose is well developed, rather wide than round with large openings, without giving the impression of being predominant. In black dogs it is black, in brown dogs corresponding lighter shades. *Muzzle*—The muzzle has to be in the proper relation to the skull and is strongly developed. The muzzle is deep, with the mouth opening reaching far back to the molars. A good muzzle width must also be present on the upper and lower incisor area. *Lips*—They should lie flat and smooth on the jaws and ensure a good closure of the mouth opening. Dark pigmentation; in brown dogs a somewhat lighter coloring is permissible. *Jaw/Dentition/Teeth*—Powerful broad upper and under jaw, scissors bite, 42 teeth correctly placed and normal size. *Eyes*—Medium-size, oval and dark in color. In browns a somewhat lighter coloring is allowed. Close-lying eyelids, covered with hair. *Ears*—The high-set ears are carried erect and are cropped to a length in proportion to the head. In a country where ear cropping is banned, the uncropped ear is equally recognized. (Medium size preferred and with the front edge lying close to the cheeks).

NECK: Good length in proportion to the body and head. Dry and muscular, carried erect and shows lot of nobility.

BODY: *Withers*—Should be pronounced in height and length especially in males, and thereby determine slope of the topline rising from the croup to the withers. *Back*—Short and firm. The back and loins are of good width and well muscled. The bitch can be slightly longer in loin because she requires space for suckling. *Croup*—It should descend slightly from the sacrum towards the set-on of the tail; appears therefore well rounded, neither straight nor falling off. Good width with strong muscles. *Chest*—The length and depth of the chest has to be in proper proportion to the length of the body. The depth should be almost half the height at the withers, the ribs with a light spring. The chest is of good width with a well-defined forechest. *Underline*—Distinct tuck-up from the end of the sternum towards the hips. *Tail*—High set and docked short, leaving two joints.

FOREQUARTERS: *General*—Viewed from all sides, the front legs stand almost perpendicular to the ground and are strongly developed. *Shoulders*—The shoulder blade lies tight to the ribcage and is well muscled on both sides of the shoulder blade ridge. The shoulder blade reaches over the top of the thoracic vertebrae, sloping and well laid back. The angle to the horizontal is approximately 50 degrees. *Upper Arm*—Good length and well muscled, angle to the shoulder blade approximately 105 to 110 degrees. *Elbows*—Lying close to the body and not bowing out. *Forearms*—Strong and straight, well muscled. Length in harmony to the body. *Wrists*—Strong. *Pasterns*—Strong bones, straight when viewed from the front, from the side only slightly tilted (maximum 10 degrees). *Forefeet*—The paws are short and tight. Toes well arched (catlike foot). Nails short and black.

HINDQUARTERS: *General*—Due to his pronounced muscle development, the Dobermann appears broad and rounded in the hips and croup when viewed from behind. The muscles that reach from the pelvis to the upper and lower thigh result in good width also in the area of the upper thigh, the knee and the lower thigh. The strong hind legs are parallel and true. *Upper Thighs*—Heavily muscled, of good length and width. Good angulation at the hip joint. Angulation to the horizontal is approximately 80 to 85 degrees. *Stifles*—The strong stifle (knee) joint is defined by the femur, the tibia (upper and lower leg bones) and the patella (kneecap). The angle at the stifle is approximately 130 degrees (lower leg bone to upper leg bone). *Lower Thighs*—Of medium length, in proportion to the total length of the hind leg. *Hocks*—Medium strong. The hock joint connects the tibia (lower legbone) with the pastern (approximately 140 degrees). *Pasterns*—Short, standing perpendicular to the ground. *Hind Feet*—Like the forefeet. Short and tight. Toes well arched. Nails short and black.

MOVEMENT: The movement is of utmost importance for performance as well as the exterior appearance. The gait is elastic, elegant, nimble, free and ground covering. The front legs reach far forward. The hindquarters have good reach and elasticity to give the necessary drive. The Dobermann moves the front leg of one side simultaneously with the hind leg of the other side. Good firmness of the back, the ligaments and joints.

SKIN: The skin is tight to the entire body and is of good pigmentation.

COAT: *Character*—The hair is short, hard and dense. It lays firm and smooth and is evenly distributed over the entire surface. Undercoat is not permissible. *Color*—The color is black or brown with rust, sharply defined markings. The markings are on the muzzle, as spots on the cheeks and above the eyelids, on the throat, two markings on the chest, on the pasterns and paws, the inside of the thigh and below the tail.

SIZE AND WEIGHT: *Height* at the highest point of withers. Males 68 to 72 centimeters (26.77 to 28.34 inches). Females 63 to 68 centimeters (24.8 to 27.77 inches). Medium size preferred. *Weight*—Males 40 to 45 kilograms (88 to 99 pounds). Females 32 to 35 kilograms (70.4 to 77 pounds).

FAULTS: Any departure from the foregoing points should be considered a fault, and the seriousness with which the fault should be regarded should be in exact proportion to its degree. *General Appearance*—Lack of gender characteristics, lack of substance, too light, too heavy, high on legs, lack of bone. *Head*—Too strong, too narrow, too short, too much or too little stop, Roman nose, lack of parallelism of the top skull, little underjaw, round or slit eye, light eye, cheeks too heavy, pendulous lip, eye globular, round or bulging too deep-set eye. Ears set too high or too low. *Neck*—Slightly short, too short, dewlap, throatiness, ewe neck, too long. *Body*—Back not firm, steep croup, roach back, swayback, too much or too little spring of ribs or not enough depth or width of chest, back too long, lack of forechest, tail set too high or too low, too little or too much tuck up. *Extremities*—Too much or too little angulation front and/or rear, loose elbows, length and placement of bones and joints not according to the standard, pigeon toed, French front, cow hocked, narrow stand, splay feet, soft feet, crooked toes, light nails. *Coat*—Markings too light, not well defined, melanism, big black spots on the feet, almost invisible or too big markings. Long, soft, dull or wavy hair as well as thin hair and bald spots, cowlicks and visible undercoat. *Temperament*—Lack of self-confidence, too high temperament, too high sharpness, too low or too high a threshold of irritation. *Size*—Deviations in height of up to 2 centimeters (0.78 inches) are to be penalized by reduction in the quality rating. *Movement*—Unsteady, restricted or stiff gait, pacing.

DISQUALIFYING FAULTS: *General*—Transposed gender characteristics. *Eye*—Hawk eye or eyes of different color. *Dentition*—Overshot or undershot, level bite and any missing teeth. *Coat*—White spots, long-haired dogs, wavy coat, pronounced thin coat or large bald spots. *Temperament*—Fearful, shy, nervous or overly aggressive dogs. *Size*—Dogs that exceed the height limits by more than 2 centimeters (0.78 inches) in either direction.

NOTE: Males should have two normal testicles fully descended into the scrotum.

THE 1899 GERMAN STANDARD

GENERAL APPEARANCE: A well-built and muscular dog, not plump and massive and not like a greyhound. His appearance must denote quickness, strength and endurance. Temperament lively and ardent. He is courageous and will not run away from anything. Devoted to master and in defending him shows the courage of a lion. He gets along with other dogs; not vicious or disloyal; faithful and watchful and a superior destroyer of animals of prey.

HEAD: Top of head must be flat or may be slightly arched, but the forehead must be broad; stretched long, the head must go over into a not too pointy muzzle. Cheeks must be flat but very muscular. A dog of about 58 centimetres (22.83 inches) height at the shoulder should measure about 41 centimetres (16.14 inches) around the forehead. The length of the head, from the occiput to the tip of the nose should be 25 to 26 centimetres (9.84 to 10.23 inches).

TEETH: Jaws of equal length. Teeth must be very powerful, well developed and tightly closed. Overbite is disapproved.

LIPS: Lying close, not drooping.

EARS: Well cropped, not too short and not too pointed.

EYES: Dark brown, medium size with intelligent good natured but energetic expression.

NECK: Powerful and straight.

CHEST: Well rounded, not flat sided, reaching to the elbow.

BACK: Straight and not too long, length from occiput to start of the tail about 75 centimetres (29.52 inches), so that the entire length, without tail, should measure about 100 centimetres (39.37 inches).

LOINS: Well developed and well filled out.

HINDQUARTERS: Powerful and muscular.

LEGS: Straight. Elbows stand perpendicular under the rump and should not turn out.

FEET: Toes well arched and closed.

TAIL: Docked not longer than 15 centimetres (5.9 inches). Bobtails much appreciated.

COAT: Hard, short and close lying.

COLOR: Primary color deep black with rust markings. Small white patch on the chest is permissible. Gray undercoat permissible on neck, behind the ears and on top of the head.

SHOULDER HEIGHT: Dogs 55 to 62 centimetres (21.65 to 24.4 inches). Bitches from 48 to 55 centimetres (18.89 to 21.65 inches).

WEIGHT: About 20 kilograms (44.09 pounds).

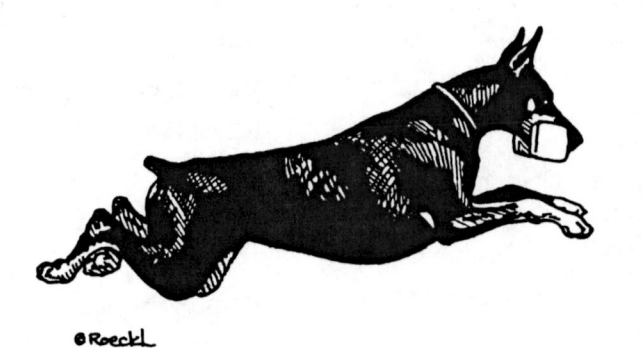

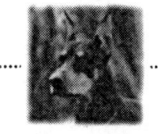

Bibliography

Books About Doberman Pinschers

Brearley, Joan McDonald. *The Book of the Doberman Pinscher*. Neptune City, New Jersey: T.F.H. Publications, 1985.

Curnow, Fred and Jean Faulks. *The Dobermann*. London: Popular Dogs Publishing Co., 1990.

Donnelly, Kerry. *Doberman Pinschers*. Neptune City, New Jersey: T.F.H. Publications, 1997.

Gruenig, Philipp. *The Dobermann Pinscher, History and Development of the Breed*. New York: Orange Judd Publishing Co., Inc., 1939.

Harmer, Hillary. *Doberman Pinschers*. New York: Arco Publishing Co., Inc., 1971.

Irven, Jan. *All About the Dobermann*. London: Pelham Books, 1986.

Ladd, Mark. *Dobermanns, An Owner's Companion*. Swindon, Wiltshire, U.K.: Crowood Press, 1989.

Migliorini, Mario. *The Doberman Book*. New York: Arco Publishing Co., 1985.

Nicholas, Anna Katherine. *The World of Doberman Pinschers.* Neptune City, New Jersey: T.F.H. Publications, 1987.

Richardson, Jimmy. *Doberman Pinschers Today.* New York: Howell Book House, 1995.

Rietveld, Simon. *History of the Dobermann.* Limited Edition 1,000 copies. Holland: Foundation Dobermann Magazine, 1982.

Schmidt, William Sidney. *The Doberman Pinscher.* Wheat Ridge, Colorado: Hoflin Publishing, 1981.

Walker, Joanna, and Other Noted Authorities. *The New Doberman Pinscher.* New York: Howell Book House, 1981.

Zwan, J.M.v.d. *In the Beginning . . . a History of the Dobermann.* Zwan, Holland: Racmo-Meppel, 1991.

———. *The Dobermann, A Pictorial History.* Zwan, Holland: Racmo-Meppel.

BOOKS ON GENERAL REFERENCE, STRUCTURE, MOVEMENT

American Kennel Club. *The Complete Dog Book,* 19th Edition revised. New York: Howell Book House, 1998.

Brown, Curtis M. *Dog Locomotion and Gait Analysis.* Wheat Ridge, Colorado: Hoflin Publishing, 1986.

Elliott, Rachel Page. *The New Dog Steps.* New York: Howell Book House, 1983.

Lyon, McDonald. *The Dog in Action.* New York: Howell Book House, 1981.

Wagner, Alice and Ab Sidewater (editors). *Visualizations of the Standards.* Philadelphia: Popular Dogs Publishing Co., 1962.

BOOKS ABOUT HEALTH

Belfield, Wendell, DVM, and Martin Zucker. *How to Have a Healthier Dog,* Second Edition. San Jose, California: Orthomolecular Specialties, 1993.

Brown, R.M., DVM. *The Doberman Owners' Medical Manual.* Jackson, Wisconsin: Breed Manual Publications, 1986.

Giffin, James, MD, and Liisa Carlson, DVM. *Dog Owner's Home Veterinary Handbook,* Third Edition. New York: Howell Book House, 1999.

Plechner DVM, Albert J., and Martin Zucker. *Pet Allergies—Remedies for an Epidemic.* Ingelwood, California: Very Healthy Enterprises, 1986.

Shute MD, Wilfrid E. *Health Preserver, Defining the Versatility of Vitamin E.* Emmaus, Pennsylvania: Rodale Press, 1977.

BOOKS ON GENETICS

Gonick, Larry and Mark Wheelis. *The Cartoon Guide to Genetics.* New York: Harper Perennial, 1991.

Hutt, Frederick B. *Genetics for Dog Breeders.* New York: W. H. Freeman and Company, 1979.

Padgett, George. *Control of Canine Genetic Diseases.* New York: Howell Book House, 1998.

Willis, Malcolm B. *Genetics of the Dog.* New York: Howell Book House, 1989.

BOOKS ON BEHAVIOR AND TRAINING

Alderton, David. *The Wolf Within.* New York: Howell Book House, 1998.

Dunbar, Ian, Ph.D., MRCVS. *Dog Behavior: An Owner's Guide to a Happy, Healthy Pet.* New York: Howell Book House, 1998.

Fogle, Bruce, DVM, MRCVS. *The Dog's Mind.* New York: Howell Book House, 1990.

Fox, Michael W. D.Sc., Ph.D., MRCVS. *Understanding Your Dog.* New York: St. Martin's Press, 1992.

McMains, Joel. *Dog Logic: Companion Obedience.* New York: Howell Book House, 1992.

BOOKS ON SHOWING AND PERFORMANCE SPORTS

Alston, George, with Connie Vanacore. *The Winning Edge: Show Ring Secrets.* New York: Howell Book House, 1992.

Barwig, Susan and Stewart Hilliard. *Schutzhund Theory and Training Methods.* New York: Howell Book House, 1991.

Brucker, Jeff and Betty (now Leininger). *Preparation and Presentation of the Show Dog.* Atlanta: Brucker Enterprises, 1978.

Johnson, Glen. *Tracking Dog, Theory and Methods.* Westmoreland, New York: Arner Publications, 1975.

Olson, Lonnie. *Flyball Racing: The Dog Sport for Everyone.* New York: Howell Book House, 1997.

O'Neil, Jacqueline. *All About Agility*, Revised Edition. New York: Howell Book House, 1999.

Simmons-Moake, Jane. *Agility Training: The Fun Sport for All Dogs.* New York: Howell Book House, 1991.

DOBERMAN PERIODICALS

Doberman Digest
8848 Beverly Hills
Lakeland, FL 33809-1604

The Doberman Quartley
1296 Gibson Road, Suite 198
Woodland, CA 95776

Doberman World Annual
Hoflin Publications
4401 Zephyr Street
Wheat Ridge, CO 80033-3299

GENERAL PERIODICALS

AKC Gazette and Events Calendar
5580 Centerview Drive
Raleigh, NC 27606-3390

Dog News
1115 Broadway
New York, NY 10010

Dog World
P.O. Box 6500
Chicago, IL 60680

Front and Finish, The Dog Trainers News
P.O. Box 333
Galesburg, IL 61402

OffLead
100 Bouck Street
Rome, NY 13440

VIDEOS

The Doberman Pinscher
American Kennel Club
5580 Centerview Drive
Raleigh, NC 27606-3390

The Doberman Pinscher—How to Select a Puppy and Develop a Champion
Sherluck MultiMedia
29001 176th Avenue, SE
Kent, WA 98042

Index

CPSIA information can be obtained at www.ICGtesting.com
Printed in the USA
BVOW03s0450030315

390061BV00027B/257/P